Boardroom Employment Law

From Recruitment to Dismissal

Boardroom Employment Law

From Recruitment to Dismissal

JULIAN YEW and ADAM GRANT

ICSA
PUBLISHING

Published by ICSA Information & Training Ltd
16 Park Crescent
London W1B 1AH

Typeset in 9.75 on 13 pt Goudy with Vectora by Hands Fotoset, Woodthorpe, Nottingham and printed in Great Britain by Hobbs the Printers Ltd, Totton, Hampshire.

British Library Cataloguing in Publication Data
A catalogue record for this book is available from the British Library

ISBN 978–1–86072–387–2

Contents

The Authors

Julian Yew is a senior employment solicitor at London law firm, Wedlake Bell. He has considerable experience advising private and public companies and senior executives in relation to corporate governance and boardroom disputes. His expertise lies in exit management and the resolution of employment disputes. Julian is the author of *Dismissals: Law & Practice* (Law Society Publishing 2004), updating editor of *Employment Law & Practice* (ICSA Publishing 2003-2005) and contributing author to *Tolley's Employment Law*. He is a regular commentator on the latest employment developments in the legal and industry media including *Chartered Secretary*, *Personnel Today*, *People Management* and *The HR Director*. He also speaks regularly at seminars, workshops and round table discussions on topical employment law issues affecting UK companies.

Adam Grant is an employment solicitor at London law firm, Wedlake Bell. He has drafted service agreements for various private and public companies (AIM listed). He has also negotiated service agreements for senior executives in the financial services industry including "sign on" bonuses and represented them in high-value bonus disputes and issues arising from post-termination competition. Adam regularly assists UK incorporated companies to keep abreast of the latest legal employment law developments which affect employment agreements. He has also written articles for the *New Law Journal* and *Employment Law Journal*.

Table of legislation

Statutes

Statutory Instruments

European Directives

Table of cases

Preface

Relationships, whether personal or business, are often entered into with the best of intentions. The unfortunate reality however is that relationships break down at some future stage for a variety of reasons and if caught unprepared, the experience can often leave a bitter aftertaste for the uninitiated.

In the complex field of employment relationships, it is vital for employers to mark the circumference of the relationship very clearly at the outset and put in place proper mechanisms to deal with a situation when the parties, for whatever reasons, have to go their separate ways. It is trite that the price for getting it wrong can be extremely costly for any business. More significantly, poor decision making can lead to loss of shareholders' confidence in the board of directors' leadership.

This book aims to assist the Company Secretary in the boardroom by providing the officer with an overview of the legal and practical issues that often arise in the hiring of senior executives and the exit management of such key individuals. The tome captures all the relevant provisions under the Companies Act 2006, which received Royal Assent on 8 November 2006; many of those provisions became effective from 1 October 2007.

Using a "cradle to the grave" approach, the book is divided into three parts.

Part 1 deals with the formation of the employment relationship and assesses the impact of the Companies Act 2006 including the codification of the role and duties of the statutory director, followed by a practical approach to drafting effective directors' service agreements. By the latter, we mean a contract which gives protection to both the director and the company and which also satisfies corporate governance principles so that a balance is struck between what the executive wants and what the shareholders want out of the contractual relationship.

Part 2 focuses on boardroom dynamics and the breakdown of the employment relationship. Handling the termination of employment of senior executives requires particular skills, experience and sensitivity. This chapter, which is the hub of the book, examines the legal framework governing the termination of executive directors, the trends in exit strategies and the practical challenges managing notice periods, garden leave enforcements and preventing competition during the notice period and post termination. We also offer guidance on the negotiation of executive severance packages in relation to their office, employment and shareholding and highlight regulatory issues arising on termination under the Listing Rules, Combined Code, Corporate Governance guidelines and the Companies Act 2006.

Recent case law includes *Commerzbank AG v Keen* [2006], *Takacs v Barclays Services Jersey Ltd* [2006], *McCarthy v McCarthy & Stone plc* [2006] and *Selective Beauty U.K. Ltd v Hayes* [2005] on bonus awards and share options on termination of employment are addressed. The picture is not complete without a consideration of shareholder issues on termination. We examine the rights of shareholders by reference to provisions in the articles of association and/or shareholders' agreements, shareholder rights under the Companies Act 2006 and the relationship between unfair dismissal claims and "unfair prejudice" petitions. We "bury the hatchet" with a discussion of some practical tips on the effective use of compromise agreements to achieve a "clean break" so that both the company and executive can effectively shake hands and move on with their respective business. Recent cases such as *Sean Mervyn Collidge v Freeport Plc* [2007] on the giving of false warranties by a director and CMC *Group Plc v Michael Zhang* [2006] on the recoupment of settlement sums under a compromise agreement are also addressed.

Part 3 consists of an appendix of specimen documents.

To aid the reader, we have adopted a system of checklists at the end of some of the chapters so that key points can quickly be assimilated by the busy company officer. We hope that this book will provide a useful source of reference tool for the company secretary who has to grapple with complex employment related issues emanating from the boardroom.

We wish to thank the following people for bringing this book to fruition:

To Isabel Gillies and her publishing team for the conception and birth of this book; to our colleagues Marlies Braun (Corporate), Jonathan Cornthwaite (IP & Commercial), Jane Wolstenholme (Pensions) for their contributions to different elements of this book. Last but not least, to our respective partner (Rob) and spouse (Emma) for putting up with all those evenings and weekends when we selfishly devoted ourselves to the completion of this book.

The law is stated as at 31 March 2008.

Julian Yew and Adam Grant
Employment Group
Wedlake Bell Solicitors

PART 1

FORMATION OF THE EXECUTIVE RELATIONSHIP

CHAPTER 1

Corporate governance

Codification of directors' duties under the Companies Act 2006 (CA 2006)

Directors occupy a fiduciary position in the company and must not abuse their position as directors, either in relation to the company or its property. Directors' duties and liabilities towards their company's shareholders and other third parties are largely governed by the general law and, in particular, since 1 October 2007, by the CA 2006. However, these duties may be overlaid by the express or implied terms of any employment contract, by the powers and obligations of the company's articles of association, and by the terms of the delegation of powers to individuals or to committees.

CA 2006 substantially rewrites company law with the aim of making it more flexible and user-friendly, especially for small businesses. One of the centrepieces of the legislation is the codification of directors' duties. The statutory statement of general directors' duties replaces the current combination of directors' statutory and common law duties. These duties took effect on 1 October 2007, except for the conflict of interest duties which come into force on 1 October 2008 (the Companies Act 2006 (Commencement No. 3, Consequential Amendments, Transitional Provisions and Savings) Order 2007).

CA 2006 explicitly states that directors' duties are based on existing common law and equitable principles that were developed through case law. Accordingly, when interpreting and applying the new duties, the corresponding common law rules and equitable principles must be taken into account.

Before going into more detail on the particular directors' duties, it is worth emphasising at the outset that the legislation makes it clear that the codified duties are owed to the company (and not to any individual shareholder or any other stakeholder), and only the company can enforce them. However, in certain limited circumstances, shareholders may be able to bring a derivative claim against directors on the company's behalf.

Further, CA 2006 does not distinguish between executive and non-executive directors, and the duties owed by a non-executive director are no different from those owed by an executive director.

Directors' general duties

The general duties also apply to shadow directors and, in the case of the duty to avoid conflicts of interest under section 175 CA 2006 and the duty not to accept benefits from third parties under section 176 CA 2006, to former directors.

Chapter 2 of Part 10 of CA 2006 sets out a catalogue of seven general duties for directors, which provides that directors must:

- act within their powers (section 171 CA 2006);
- promote the success of the company (section 172 CA 2006);
- exercise independent judgment (section 173 CA 2006);
- exercise reasonable care, skill and diligence (section 174 CA 2006);
- avoid conflicts of interest (section 175 CA 2006);
- not accept benefits from third parties (section 176 CA 2006); and
- declare any interest the director has in a proposed transaction or arrangement with the company (section 177 CA 2006).

Duty to act within powers

> "A director of a company must (a) act in accordance with the company's constitution, and (b) only exercise powers for the purposes for which they are conferred." (Section 171 CA 2006)

A company's constitution is defined to include the company's articles of association, as well as shareholder resolutions and decisions affecting the articles of association.

This duty codifies the existing principle of law under which a director should exercise their powers in accordance with the terms on which they were granted, and to do so for a proper purpose. If they use their powers for a different purpose, they exceed their authority and are liable for breach of duty irrespective of whether they believe their conduct to be in the interests of the company. CA 2006 does not define what constitutes such a "proper purpose", so this must be assessed in the context of the specific situation under consideration.

Duty to promote the success of the company

> "A director of a company must act in the way he considers, in good faith, would be most likely to promote the success of the company for the benefit of its members as a whole...". (Section 172 CA 2006)

This is probably the most contentious of the directors' duties. It replaces the fiduciary duty of loyalty to act in the company's best interests and introduces the concept of "enlightened shareholder value" into UK law.

This duty combines a subjective and an objective element: it requires a director to act in a way which he personally considers will best promote the company's success (subjective element). What constitutes such a success is not defined in the legislation. The decision as to what will promote the success of the company, and what constitutes such success is instead one for the director's good faith judgment. In the debates of the then Companies Bill, Lord Goldsmith stated that "success in the context of commercial companies will normally mean long-term increase in value".

CA 2006 then introduces a (non-exhaustive) list of factors that directors will need to "have regard to" when discharging their duty (objective element). This list of factors includes the:

- likely long-term consequences of the decision;
- interests of employees;
- need to foster business relationships with suppliers, customers and others;
- impact of the company's operations on the community and the environment;
- company's reputation for high standards of business conduct; and
- need to act fairly between members of the company.

In having regard to the factors listed above, the duty to exercise reasonable care, skill and diligence applies. Although the legislation does not define the words "have regard to", the Government made it clear that this means to "think about" and is not about simply "ticking boxes".

This new duty raises many questions, few of which have been answered by the Government. In particular, it is not entirely clear what weight directors ought to give each of these factors, and how they should resolve conflicting factors. However, it is clear that the primary duty is to act in the interest of the shareholders as a whole (and not to any other stakeholder), whilst regard must be had to the other specified interests. Uncertainties will inevitably remain, at least until relevant case law starts to emerge.

Concerns have been expressed by the business community that this new duty could have the effect of increasing bureaucracy in companies, making the decision-making process more cumbersome and potentially increasing the liability of directors (see "Companies Act (2006) – Directors' duties", Association of General Counsel and Company Secretaries of the FTSE 100 ("GC 100"), 7 February 2007). In response to these concerns, the Government has made it clear that the new duty is not intended to impose additional bureaucratic burdens on companies, but instead reflects what is already commonly regarded as good practice.

In February 2007, GC 100 issued best practice guidelines, among other things, as to how consideration of the various factors listed in section 172 CA 2006 should be recorded in board and committee decisions.

Duty to exercise independent judgment

> "A director of a company must exercise independent judgment." (Section 173 CA 2006)

This codifies the existing principle of law under which directors must exercise their powers independently, without subordinating their powers to the will of others, whether by delegation or otherwise. Under the new statutory duty, directors must not fetter the future exercise of their discretion unless they are acting in accordance with an agreement which has been duly entered into by the company, or in a way authorised by the company's constitution.

This duty does not prevent directors from taking advice where appropriate and, although not conferring a power on the directors to delegate, it does not prevent a director from exercising a power to delegate conferred by the company's constitution.

Duty to exercise reasonable care, skill and diligence

> "A director of a company must exercise reasonable care, skill and diligence." (Section 174 CA 2006)

This duty replaces the existing duty of care and skill and retains the dual objective/subjective test under common law which mirrors the test laid down in section 214 Insolvency Act 1986. Directors owe a duty to the company to exercise the same standard of care, skill and diligence that would be exercised by a reasonably diligent person with:

- the general knowledge, skill and experience that may reasonably be expected of a person carrying out the same functions as the director in relation to that company (objective test); and
- the general knowledge, skill and experience that the director actually has (subjective test).

This is particularly important for non-executive directors who must keep in mind that whatever specialist skills and knowledge they have acquired in their profession must be brought to bear on their actions and decisions as a director.

Conflict of interest duties

CA 2006 codifies the conflict of interest duties in four separate sections which can broadly be grouped as (1) interests in transactions or arrangements with the company (these must be disclosed but do not require approval), and (2) all other conflicts (which normally require approval either by the shareholders or the board). The conflict of interest duties come into force on 1 October 2008.

Duty to avoid conflicts of interest

> "A director of a company must avoid a situation in which he has or can have, a direct or indirect interest that conflicts, or possibly may conflict with the interests of the company." (Section 175 CA 2006)

This duty applies to conflicts of interests or duties in relation to transactions or arrangements to which the company is not a party, in particular, to the exploitation of property, information or opportunity by a director for personal purposes regardless of whether the company itself could have taken advantage of the property, information or opportunity.

The duty is not infringed if the director's action cannot reasonably be regarded as likely to give rise to a conflict of interest, or if the matter is authorised by the disinterested directors. Private companies can automatically make use of this new board authorisation of conflicts unless their articles of association expressly state otherwise. However, with regard to public companies, board authorisation must be expressly permitted in the company's articles of association. Otherwise, if board authorisation is not permitted, conflicts can still be authorised by the shareholders.

Duty not to accept benefits from third parties

> "A director of a company must not accept a benefit from a third party conferred by reason of (a) his being a director, or (b) his doing (or not doing) anything as a director." (Section 176 CA 2006)

Although this duty is widely phrased and does not provide for a *de minimis* threshold, there is a similar exception as under section 175 to the effect that this duty will not be infringed if the acceptance of the benefit cannot reasonably be regarded as likely to give rise to a conflict of interest.

In contrast to a conflict of interests within the scope of the general duty to avoid conflicts in section 175 above, receipt of a benefit can only be authorised by the shareholders, not the board.

Duty to declare an interest in proposed transactions or arrangements with the company

> "If a director of a company is in any way, directly or indirectly, interested in a proposed transaction or arrangement with the company, he must declare the nature and extent of that interest to the other directors." (Section 177 CA 2006)

There is no requirement in section 177 that the director be a party to the proposed transaction or arrangement as the interests that need to be declared may include those of "connected persons". This term includes the director's parents, children and step-children, any person (other than a sibling or other close family member) with whom the director lives as partner in an enduring family relationship, a civil partner, and children or step-children of the director's unmarried partner if they are under 18 and live with the director. There is no *de minimis* threshold.

The declaration must be made in writing before the company enters into the transaction or arrangement. If the declaration later turns out to be, or becomes, inaccurate or incomplete, the director must make a further declaration.

There is no need to make a declaration if the director is unaware of the interest (but he is presumed to be aware of matters of which he ought reasonably to be aware), if the interest cannot reasonably be regarded as likely to give rise to a conflict of interest, if the other directors are already aware of the interest, or if it concerns the terms of his service contract that have been or will be considered by the board or a committee.

Duty to declare an interest in existing transactions or arrangements with the company

> "Where a director of a company is in any way, directly or indirectly, interested in a transaction or arrangement that has been entered into by the company, he must declare the nature and extent of that interest to the other directors." (Section 182 CA 2006)

This duty is not a general statutory duty but is linked to the conflicts of interest duties. It is very similar to the duty to declare an interest in a proposed transaction or arrangement. The most important difference is that a breach of the duty to declare an interest in proposed transactions or arrangements with the company only triggers civil consequences (such as making the transaction potentially unenforceable and requiring the director to account for any profits), while a breach of the duty to declare an interest in existing transactions or arrangements with the company may constitute a criminal offence.

Insolvency Act 1986 (IA 1986)

The Insolvency Act 1986 makes various kinds of misconduct by officers in relation to companies which become insolvent a criminal offence, carrying potential sentences of imprisonment and/or a fine. The offences include dishonest misconduct by officers of the company during the 12 months immediately preceding the commencement of the winding-up and effecting transactions to defraud creditors within five years prior to the commencement of the winding-up. Directors and officers who are guilty of misfeasance are liable to make restitution to the company. The two most significant provisions, however, deal with fraudulent and wrongful trading.

Fraudulent trading

Section 213 IA 1986 imposes civil liability on a director who is shown to have knowingly carried on the company's business with the intention of defrauding creditors of the company or of any other person, or for any fraudulent purpose. Under section 993 CA 2006, fraudulent trading is a criminal offence punishable by imprisonment and/or a fine.

Wrongful trading

Prior knowledge

Directors may be held personally liable if the court believes that they knew, or ought to have known prior to the winding-up of the company, that there was no reasonable prospect of avoiding insolvency (section 214 IA 1986).

Taking every step to minimise potential loss

No declarations for a contribution will be made if the court is satisfied that, after he knew or ought to have concluded that there was no reasonable prospect that the company would avoid going into insolvent liquidation, the director took every step that he ought to have taken with a view to minimising the potential loss to the company's creditors.

Sanctions

Where a person is held responsible for wrongful trading, he may be disqualified from being a director of any company or in any way concerned in the promotion, formation or management of any company for up to 15 years.

Transactions at an undervalue

Once the company is or may be insolvent, the interests of its creditors become the directors' main concern. In addition to the offences already described, statutory rules under section 423 IA 1986 permit certain transactions to be overturned, where they may have the effect of disadvantaging the company's creditors.

In certain circumstances, a liquidator or administrator can apply to the court for an order to set aside transactions made by the company at the time it became insolvent. A transaction will be vulnerable if entered into as long ago as two years before the company actually went into liquidation, where the other party to the transaction was a connected person such as a director.

A transaction at an undervalue may occur when the company confers a benefit without obtaining adequate consideration, at a time when it is unable to pay its debts. If the transaction is between the company and a connected person, such as a director, the onus is on that person to prove that the company was not insolvent at the time. The court has power to set aside such a transaction if it took place within two years prior to the company going into liquidation or administration.

It is a defence to show that the transaction was made in good faith for the carrying on of the business and in the reasonable belief that the company would benefit.

Corporate manslaughter

The Corporate Manslaughter and Corporate Homicide Act 2007 (CMCHA 2007) came into force on 6 April 2008. It changes the current position at common law by abolishing the common law offence as it applies to corporations and creates a new offence of corporate manslaughter (referred to as corporate homicide in Scotland) that applies to certain types of "organisations" (with the most notable ones in this context being corporations (including companies) and partnerships). An organisation that is subject to the Act is guilty of the new offence if the way in which its activities are managed or organised (1) causes a person's death, and (2) amounts to a gross breach of a relevant duty of care owed by the organisation to the deceased.

Individuals (including company directors and managers) cannot be guilty of either the main offence under the Act or of aiding, abetting, counselling or procuring the commission of corporate manslaughter. A senior individual may, however, be liable for gross negligence manslaughter under common law (even after the Act comes into force) if it can be shown that he was the "directing mind" within the organisation and was himself responsible for the actions of the company that lead to the death, and also under health and safety legislation.

Directors' remuneration – corporate governance issues

CA 2006

Any company (other than a listed company) must produce certain information concerning directors' remuneration by way of notes to the company's accounts. Listed companies (this includes companies on the Official List but not AIM) are required to set out a large part of the information concerning directors' remuneration in a directors' remuneration report which forms part of their annual accounts and reports, and send a copy of the annual accounts and reports to every shareholder, every debenture holder and every person entitled to receive notice of general meetings. The directors' remuneration report requires listed companies to make much more detailed disclosures in relation to their directors' remuneration than is required of other companies. Although the final accounting and reporting regulations (which will, when in force, replace the relevant provisions in the Companies Act 1985 including those based on the Directors' Remuneration Report Regulations 2002) have not yet been released, we expect that, with regard to the information to be provided in directors' remuneration reports, they will require disclosure of, among other things, the amount of each directors' emoluments and compensation, and details on share options, long-term incentive schemes and pensions. The Large and Medium-sized Companies and Groups (Accounts and Reports) Regulations 2008 (SI 2008/410) contain a new requirement for listed companies to report in their directors' remuneration report on how they have taken pay and employment conditions elsewhere in the group into account when setting directors' pay. This new requirement must be included in reports for financial years beginning on or after 6 April 2009.

The remuneration report must be approved by ordinary shareholder resolution although entitlement of a person to remuneration is not made conditional on the resolution being passed. The directors must deliver a copy of the directors' remuneration report to the Registrar of Companies along with the annual accounts and reports within six months following the end of the company's financial year.

CA 2006 introduces a new statutory safe harbour provision with regard to the directors' liability for narrative reports. Section 463 CA 2006 provides that, in relation to the directors' report (which includes the business review), the directors' remuneration report and any summary financial statements derived from either of these reports, directors will only be liable to their company for any losses it suffers as a result of any untrue or misleading statement in, or omission from, such a report provided he knew (or was reckless as to whether) the statement was untrue or misleading, or knew the omission to be dishonest concealment of a material fact. Directors are not liable to anyone other than the company for losses resulting from reliance on these reports.

The Combined Code

The Combined Code on Corporate Governance (the "Combined Code") sets out a code of best practice comprising principles of good governance and provisions applicable to all companies admitted to the Official List and incorporated in the United Kingdom. The version currently in force is dated June 2006. While the provisions of the Combined Code are not strictly applicable to AIM companies, it is recommended that, as a matter of good practice, AIM companies should, where appropriate, comply with the requirements of the Combined Code. AIM companies should also have regard to the corporate governance guidelines published by the Quoted Companies Alliance. A fully listed company is required to report in its annual accounts on how it applies the principles of the Combined Code and to confirm that it complies with the Combined Code provisions and, in relation to the areas of non-compliance, provide an explanation. This requirement does not apply to an AIM traded company but, if its compliance with the Combined Code is relatively complete, it is worth including such a report in the company's accounts.

The Combined Code includes a number of detailed principles relating to the level and make-up of directors' remuneration, the procedure for determining a director's remuneration and the establishment of remuneration committees:

Principles governing directors' remuneration

Levels of remuneration should be sufficient to attract, retain and motivate directors of the quality required to run the company successfully, but the company should avoid paying more than necessary. A significant proportion of executive directors' remuneration should be structured so as to link rewards to corporate and individual performance.

There should be a formal and transparent procedure for developing policy on executive remuneration and for fixing the remuneration packages of individual directors. No director should be involved in deciding his own remuneration. The Combined Code provides that, in relation to companies listed on the Official List, a remuneration committee must be established to set the remuneration of all executive directors and of the chairman. The remuneration committee should consist exclusively of non-executive directors who are independent and comprise at least three, or in the case of smaller companies, two such directors.

Remuneration for non-executive directors should not include share options.

Investor protection

There are a number of bodies advising investment institutions in relation to investor protection, the two most influential of which are the Association of British Insurers (ABI) and the National Association of Pension Funds (NAPF). Both of these bodies advise major institutional investors about how they should act or vote in relation to various areas of corporate practice relating to directors such as corporate governance and director remuneration. Any company, whether fully listed or on AIM, which seeks to achieve long-term investment support from institutional investors will need to bear in mind any specific guidelines or recommendations issued by either the ABI or NAPF.

Both the ABI and NAPF have recently released their 2007 editions of guidelines on executive remuneration. In December 2002, the ABI and NAPF released a joint statement on executive contracts and severance.

The ABI and the NAPF guidelines have no legal force. However, non-compliance may result in adverse publicity, something companies will want to avoid. Both investor associations aim to update their remuneration guidance on an annual basis, usually towards the end of the year.

CHAPTER **2**

The role of directors in a listed company

Overview

Directors in public companies, particularly listed companies, have responsibilities in connection with the following:

- the Combined Code on Corporate Governance 2006;
- rules governing insider dealing;
- the market abuse regime of the Financial Services and Markets Act 2000;
- the Model Code for listed company directors' securities transactions;
- in the event of a takeover bid, the Takeover Code on Takeovers and Mergers; and
- the FSA's Listing Rules.

Some of these responsibilities are discussed below.

The Combined Code

The following principles of the Combined Code are particularly relevant for directors.

Principles relating to directors

Every company should be headed by an effective board which is collectively responsible for the success of the company. There should be a clear division of responsibilities between the chairman and the chief executive. There should be a balance of executive and non-executive directors (including independent non-executives).

There should be a formal, rigorous and transparent procedure for the appointment of new directors.

The board should be supplied in a timely manner with information in a form and of a quality appropriate to enable it to discharge its duties. All directors should receive induction on joining the board and should regularly update their skills and knowledge.

The board should undertake a formal and rigorous annual evaluation of its own performance and that of its committees and individual directors.

All directors should be submitted for re-election at regular intervals (of no more than three years), subject to continued satisfactory performance. The board should ensure planned and progressive replacement or reconstitution of its members.

Principles governing accountability and audit

It is the board's responsibility to present a balanced and understandable assessment of the company's position and prospects in all financial and other public reporting.

Companies listed on the Official List must establish an audit committee of at least three independent non-executive directors (at least two independent non-executive directors, in the case of smaller companies below the FTSE 350), with at least one member of the audit committee having recent and relevant financial experience. The committee should monitor the integrity of the financial statements and any significant financial reporting judgments; review the internal financial control and risk management control systems; review the scope and effectiveness of the audit, and the independence and objectivity of the external auditors; and develop a policy relating to the supply of non-audit services by external audit firms.

The audit committee must be provided with sufficient resources to undertake its duties, and information must be volunteered to the audit committee by the other directors and employees. The audit committee must be prepared to take an independent stand against the executive management, even though it retains its position as a committee in a unitary board structure and is not independent of the board.

The directors should review at least annually the effectiveness of all the company's internal controls, including financial, operational and compliance controls and risk management systems. Where possible, all the risks that the company and its business faces should be identified and assessed, and appropriate steps taken to manage them.

Principles governing nominations

All companies listed on the Official List must have a nomination committee to determine the process for all board appointments. A majority of the committee should be independent non-executive directors. The nomination committee should, amongst other things:

- be responsible for identifying and nominating for the approval of the board, candidates to fill board vacancies as and when they arise;
- before making an appointment, evaluate the balance of skills, knowledge and experience on the board and, in the light of this evaluation, prepare a description of the role and capabilities required for a particular appointment;

- review annually the time required from a non-executive director;
- regularly review the structure, size and composition (including the skills, knowledge and experience) of the board and make recommendations to the board with regard to any changes; and
- keep under review the leadership needs of the organisation, both executive and non-executive, with a view to ensuring the continued ability of the organisation to compete effectively in the marketplace.

The nomination committee should make recommendations to the board:

- concerning plans for succession for both executive and non-executive directors;
- concerning the re-appointment of any non-executive director at the conclusion of their specified term of office;
- concerning the re-election by shareholders of any director under the retirement by rotation provisions in the company's articles of association;
- concerning any matters relating to the continuation in office of any director at any time; and
- concerning the appointment of any director to executive or other office other than to the positions of chairman and chief executive, the recommendation for which would be considered at a meeting of the board.

The board should not agree to a full-time executive director taking on more than one non-executive directorship in a FTSE 100 company, nor the chairmanship of such a company.

Principles governing relations with shareholders

There should be dialogue with institutional shareholders based on the mutual understanding of objectives. The board as a whole has responsibility for ensuring that a satisfactory dialogue with shareholders takes place. The company should use the AGM to communicate with investors and to encourage their participation.

Market abuse and insider dealing

Disclosure of inside information under the FSA's Disclosure Rules

The Disclosure Rules contain disclosure obligations for companies whose shares are admitted to trading on a regulated market such as the Official List. The primary disclosure obligation under the Disclosure Rules requires a listed company to notify a Regulatory Information Services (RIS) as soon as possible of any price sensitive inside information that directly concerns the company (unless one of the exceptions applies which allows for the disclosure of inside information to be delayed).

"Inside information" is information of a precise nature which is not generally available, relates directly or indirectly to one or more issuers of qualifying investments or the qualifying investments themselves, and would, if generally available, be likely to have a significant impact on the price of the qualifying investment or on the price of related investments. Information that is likely to be considered price-sensitive and therefore relevant to a reasonable investor's investment decision includes information which affects the company's assets and liabilities; performance or expectations of performance of the company's business; the company's financial condition; and information previously disclosed to the market.

The Disclosure Rules further contain guidance for the company's directors to carefully and continuously monitor the company's performance and consider whether changes in the circumstances of the company are such that an announcement to the market is required.

Market abuse

In order to implement the Market Abuse Directive in the UK, amendments were made to the Financial Services and Markets Act 2000 (FSMA). The principal offence of market abuse is contained within sections 118 and 118A of FSMA (as amended by the Financial Services and Markets Act 2000 (Market Abuse) Regulations 2005). These market abuse provisions complement the existing insider dealing legislation. "Market abuse" is behaviour (whether by one person alone or by two or more persons acting jointly or in concert) which occurs in relation to "qualifying" investments admitted to trading on prescribed markets (that includes AIM companies and those on the Official List) or for which an admission has been made which falls within any one or more of the categories of behaviour as set out below:

- where an insider deals, or attempts to deal, in a qualifying investment or related investment on the basis of inside information relating to the investment in question;
- where an insider discloses inside information to another person otherwise than in the proper course of the exercise of his employment, profession or duties;
- where the behaviour (a) is based on information which is not generally available to those using the market but which, if available to a regular user of the market, would be, or would be likely to be, regarded by him as relevant when deciding the terms on which transactions in qualifying investments should be effected; and (b) is likely to be regarded by a regular user of the market as a failure on the part of the person concerned to observe the standard of behaviour reasonably expected of a person in his position in relation to the market;

- where the behaviour consists of effecting transactions or orders to trade (otherwise than for legitimate reasons and in conformity with accepted market practices on the relevant market) which (a) give, or are likely to give, a false or misleading impression as to the supply of, or demand for, or as to the price of, one or more qualifying investments; or (b) secure the price of one or more such investments at an abnormal or artificial level;
- where the behaviour consists of effecting transactions or orders to trade which employ fictitious devices or any other form of deception or contrivance;
- where the behaviour consists of the dissemination of information by any means which gives, or is likely to give, a false or misleading impression as to a qualifying investment by a person who knew or could reasonably be expected to have known that the information was false or misleading; and
- where the behaviour (a) is likely to give a regular user of the market a false or misleading impression as to the supply of, demand for or price or value of, qualifying investments; or (b) would be, or would be likely to be, regarded by a regular user of the market as behaviour that would distort, or would be likely to distort, the market in such an investment,

and the behaviour is likely to be regarded by a regular user of the market as a failure on the part of the person concerned to observe the standard of behaviour reasonably expected of a person in his position in relation to the market.

Market abuse does not require the person engaging in the behaviour in question to have intended to commit market abuse as the regime does not necessarily require knowledge, intent or recklessness on the part of the alleged abuser for a market abuse offence to be committed.

The FSA may impose on any person a penalty of such amount as it considers appropriate, if it is satisfied that a person is or has engaged in market abuse or, by taking or refraining from taking any action as required, has encouraged another person or persons to engage in behaviour which, if engaged in by the first person, would amount to market abuse. Alternatively, the FSA may, instead of imposing a penalty on a person who has engaged in market abuse, publish a statement to the effect that such person has engaged in market abuse. The FSA may also apply to the court for an injunction to prevent market abuse or a restitution order in relation to market abuse. The court may make an order requiring the person concerned to pay the FSA a penalty of such amount as it considers appropriate.

The FSA has issued a Code of Market Conduct giving guidance in determining as to whether or not behaviour amounts to market abuse. The Market Abuse Directive contains "safe harbours", and these are reflected in the Code of Market Conduct. Behaviour which falls within a "safe harbour" will not constitute market abuse. These safe harbours include behaviour conforming with specific FSA rules (such as, for example, the Listing Rules and Disclosure Rules, and the Combined Code) and certain activities conducted pursuant to the City Code on Takeovers and Mergers.

Criminal insider dealing regime

The Criminal Justice Act 1993 includes provisions relating to insider dealing. It covers four classes of improper conduct:

- trading on the basis of inside information;
- procuring others to trade on your behalf on the basis of inside information;
- disclosing inside information improperly knowing this will, or is likely to, lead to insider dealing; and
- encouraging others generally to trade on the basis of inside information.

The legislation applies only to "regulated securities", which encompass stocks and shares, any debt security (including debentures, debenture stock, loan stock, certificates of deposit, gilts and local authority stock), warrants to subscribe, options, futures and index contracts which are dealt in, on (or under the rules of), or which have their price quoted on, a recognised investment exchange.

Inside information is information which relates to particular securities or to a particular company of securities (and not to securities generally or companies of securities generally) which is specific or precise, has not been made public, and would, if made public, be likely to have a significant effect on the price of any securities.

An individual is an insider if he knows that he has inside information, and knows that he has it from an inside source, i.e., that he has the information:

- through being a director, employee or shareholder of a company which has issued securities;
- through having access to the information by virtue of his employment, office or profession; or

the direct or indirect source of his information is a person with such a relationship with the company.

Listed company directors' securities transactions under the Model Code

Persons discharging managerial responsibilities (PDMRs) in listed companies (this class includes (i) directors and (ii) senior executives of the company who are not directors but have regular access to inside information relating directly or indirectly to the company and the power to make managerial decisions affecting the future development and business prospects of the company) are subject to the Model Code requirements, which are set out in an annex to Listing Rule 9 of the FSA's Listing Rules. Companies whose shares are admitted to trading on AIM must comply with a similar model code under the AIM Rules.

The purpose of the Model Code is to ensure that PDMRs do not abuse (and do not place themselves under suspicion of abusing) inside information that they may be thought to have, especially in periods leading up to an announcement of the company's results. Listed companies are expected to adopt a code of dealings based on the Model Code and to take all proper and reasonable steps to secure that PDMRs comply with it.

The basic principle of the Model Code is that PDMRs must not deal in the company's securities without advance clearance from an appropriate person. Clearance must not be given (1) during a prohibited period or (2) on considerations of a short-term nature (an investment with a maturity of one year or less will always be considered to be of a short-term nature). A prohibited period is any close period of the company, i.e., 60 days before a preliminary announcement of annual results; if the company reports on a half-yearly basis, the period from the end of the relevant financial period up to and including the time of such publication; and 30 days before the announcement of quarterly results.

The Model Code further includes guidance on when dealings are permitted during a prohibited period such as dealing in exceptional circumstances, awards of securities and options, exercise of options, qualification shares, saving schemes and acting as a trustee.

PDMRs must take reasonable steps to prevent any dealings by or on behalf of any person connected to him in any securities of the company on considerations of a short-term nature, and to prohibit dealings by or on behalf of such connected persons in the company's securities during a close period. A PDMR must also advise his connected persons and investment managers acting on his behalf or on behalf of persons connected to him: (1) of the name of the listed company within which he is a person discharging managerial responsibilities; (2) of the close periods during which they cannot deal in the securities of the company; and (3) that they must advise the company immediately after they have dealt in securities of the company.

Disclosure of board changes under the FSA's Listing Rules

Listed companies must notify an RIS as soon as possible, and in any event by the end of the business day following the decision or receipt of notice about the change, of any change to the board including the appointment of a new director; the resignation, removal or retirement of a director; important changes to the role, functions or responsibilities of a director; and the effective date of the change if it is not with immediate effect. With regard to any new director appointed to the board, the Listing Rules further require listed companies to notify an RIS as soon as possible, and in any event within five business days of the decision, of, among other things, details of all directorships held by the director in any other publicly quoted company at any time in the previous five years, indicating whether or not he is still a director.

Investor protection

The ABI has published corporate governance guidance on responsible voting, the role and duties of directors (which includes guidance on the board of directors, their appointment and removal, their duty to employees, and borrowing power), the responsibilities of institutional shareholders and articles of association.

The NAPF Corporate Governance Policy and Voting Guidelines are designed to assist shareholders and others in interpreting the Combined Code when considering voting decisions at company meetings. They apply only to companies listed on the Official List. Separate NAPF guidelines have been published for investment companies and AIM companies.

Disclosure of directors' interests in shares

The Disclosure and Transparency Rules and the Listing Rules contain provisions requiring the disclosure of interests in shares by directors of companies with shares admitted to the Official List. The AIM Rules contain similar provisions with regard to companies whose shares are admitted to AIM.

Sections 323 to 329 of the Companies Act 1985 used to require directors to disclose to the company their interests and dealings in shares in, and debentures of, the company or any holding or subsidiary company within a group structure, including any interest held by the directors' children or spouse. These provisions were repealed with effect from 6 April 2007 without replacement in CA 2006. Accordingly, for companies whose shares are neither admitted to the Official List nor AIM, there is no particular requirement to disclose directors' interests in their shares.

The Disclosure and Transparency Rules (DTR)

Persons discharging managerial responsibilities (PDMRs) in listed companies and their connected persons must notify the company within four business days of certain transactions conducted on their own account in shares of the company, or of derivatives or any other financial instruments relating to those shares (DTR 3.1.2R). Notifiable transactions include acquisitions and disposals of shares; acceptance of awards; accepting or receiving an option or gifts from the company or a third party; and the exercise of options by a PDMR. The company must notify an RIS of this information as soon as possible, and no later than the end of the business day following receipt of the information by the company.

In addition, directors who are holding shares in their companies are subject to the general vote holder notification requirements of DTR 5 which apply to all shareholders of companies whose shares are admitted to trading on a regulated market (such as the Official List) or a UK prescribed market (such as AIM). DTR 5 replaces the relevant statutory provisions of the Companies Act 1985 as of 20 January 2007 and requires shareholders to notify the company if the percentage of their voting rights reaches, exceeds or falls below 3 per cent and every whole percentage figure thereafter (different thresholds apply to shares held in non-UK issuers). The company must release the details of such shareholdings to an RIS as soon as possible on receipt of a notification.

The Listing Rules

Listed companies must include in their annual financial report a statement setting out, among other things, (1) the interests of the directors (in respect of which transactions are notifiable in accordance with DTR 3 above) who are in the post at the end of the accounting period, and (2) the interests of persons connected with the directors of which the company is aware, or of which the company ought to be aware if reasonable inquiry had been made (LR 9.8.6R).

CHAPTER **3**

The role of a non-executive director

Responsibilities

The non-executive director (NED) has evolved over time. NED positions were once viewed as a reward for someone approaching the twilight of their career, but who did not yet want to retire. The NED was paid a handsome reward for seemingly limited effort. However, in an environment where corporate accountability has increased significantly, emphasised by the Higgs Report on the *Role and Effectiveness of Non-Executive Directors* (published 20 January 2003), the role of the NED in the boardroom has become much more significant.

The NED's primary objective is to provide impartiality and guidance for the executive board of directors. Usually, the NED will have experience of working in a wide variety of businesses, and can use that experience to help guide the executive board.

There are a number of considerations as to the type of person who should be appointed as the NED. Primarily, the company may look at what value they can add in terms of overall industry experience and/or contacts. However, it is becoming commonplace for the NED to be brought in to provide niche skills, such as accounting and marketing expertise. Therefore, a company should consider the relevant skills of the NED, rather than just the kudos that comes with the appointment. However, the more the NED is integrated into the day-to-day running of the business, the more it erodes their impartiality.

Letter of appointment

The NED is usually engaged under a letter of appointment. A sample letter of appointment can be found at Appendix C. We now deal with some of the key drafting considerations in the letter of appointment.

Appointment (clause 1)

The term should not be excessive, and it is recommended, that the appointment should be terminable on notice of one year or less.

The appointment of the NED should always be subject to the company's articles of association and any other relevant codes and regulations. It is important to ensure that the company does not have to make any notice payment, if for any reason the NED is not re-elected as a director. Payment can also be avoided where the NED is guilty of dishonesty or other misconduct, or is in serious or persistent breach of the appointment.

Duties (clause 2)

The law makes no distinction between the duties of a statutory director and the NED. Therefore, the NED should be fully aware of what he is agreeing to by taking on the appointment, especially as this is often a part-time role. For a summary of directors' duties, refer to Chapter 1.

In addition to their statutory duties, the NED is also expected to adhere to corporate governance rules and guidance such as the Higgs Report.

The time and responsibility envisaged in performing the NED role should also be clearly established in the letter of appointment.

Fees, expenses and insurance (clause 3)

As the NED is not an employee, he will receive a fee for his services. The level of the fee is to be determined by the company (subject to any restrictions under the articles of association), and should be commensurate with the level of seniority and value that the NED brings to the company.

As an "office holder", the NED's fees should be paid after deduction of tax and national insurance contributions at source, under the Pay As You Earn (PAYE) system.

It is usual for the company's directors and officers insurance policy to extend protection to the NED.

Independent professional advice (clause 4)

In order for the NED to fully discharge his duties, it is recommended that the company should allow the NED to obtain independent legal advice where necessary. This prevents the NED's position being compromised.

Cross-directorships; disclosure; outside interests and conflicts of interest (clauses 5 to 7)

The impartiality of the NED must be retained both within the company and in regards to any other employment and board appointments he may have. These clauses place a positive duty on the NED to disclose any potential conflicts and to seek the company's approval to avoid a conflict.

Confidentiality (clause 8)

As a statutory director, the NED owes both statutory and common law duties to the company. This clause sets out expressly, what is expected of the NED both during the appointment and after the appointment ends.

CHAPTER 4

Drafting service agreements

Overview

Executives tend to have various rights and obligations that are governed by different rules depending on their role as an employee, as an officer, and sometimes as a shareholder of the company. As an employee, the executive has employment protection rights, including those under the Employment Rights Act 1996 (ERA 1996). Where the director is a shareholder, he may also have rights under a shareholders' agreement, and minority shareholder protection under section 994, CA 2006. As an officer of the company, the director's rights and obligations are governed by the company's articles of association, CA 2006 and any other related legislation.

The executive assumes a high level of responsibility which entails an assumption of legal rights and obligations beyond that expected of a standard employee. There are also a number of contractual issues which go beyond the scope of a normal employment contract. Unlike an employment contract, which usually deals with the basic elements of the employment relationship such as pay, hours, holiday and notice period, a service agreement is a more formal document which provides more tailored and complicated provisions governing the contractual relationship. It is usual to structure the service agreement using a "carrot and stick" approach. The executive's loyalty is bought with salary, shares, bonuses and long notice periods: in return, loyalty is enforced during employment with the duty of fidelity, confidentiality, restrictive covenants and garden leave provisions, and on termination, with express restrictive covenants and confidentiality agreements.

The interests of both parties should be balanced in the service agreement, although how far the scales will tip on either side would very much depend on a number of commercial factors, such as the nature of the proposed appointment, the experience and track record and the value the executive will add to the board and the shareholders. Essentially, it will boil down to the bargaining positions of the parties.

Whatever might be the commercial drivers, an effective service agreement is one that ensures the company has flexibility in managing what will be an expensive asset to the business. The service agreement should provide clear and objective performance standards which are commensurate with the company's financial obligations during and on termination of employment. If the executive's employment is terminated, the company should have the flexibility to manage any transitional period and thus minimise any risk of damage to the business. Contractual provisions on compensation for termination of employment for directors must also satisfy CA 2006 and take into account institutional recommendations.

The service agreement should always take into account any existing company handbook or policies. It is important that these documents are as consistent as possible, especially where the handbook and/or policies have contractual effect. However, if the terms of the service agreement are to override all other documents, this should be made clear in the service agreement.

A draft service agreement can be found at Appendix B of this book. It gives an overview of the different types of provisions that are normally incorporated within a standard service agreement. It is strongly recommended that any service agreement is drafted by your legal advisor or at the very least, reviewed by them prior to it being issued to the executive as any contractual agreement needs to be specifically tailored to meet the commercial aims and expectations of the parties.

The remainder of this chapter examines the key components of a service agreement and drafting considerations for the company. The commentary below relates to provisions in the service agreement in Appendix B.

Written particulars of employment

Under section 1 ERA 1996, the company is as a minimum required, whether in full or by instalments, to give the executive a written statement of particulars of certain terms of his contract not later than two months after the employment commences. The written particulars required to be given include:

- the name of the employer and the employee;
- the date employment began;
- the date continuous employment began;
- the scale or rate of remuneration, or method of calculating remuneration;
- the intervals at which remuneration is to be paid, i.e., weekly, monthly
- hours of work;
- holiday entitlement;
- sick pay provisions;
- pension arrangements, including whether a contracting-out certificate is in place;
- notice period;

- job title;
- where the employment is not intended to be permanent, the period for which it is expected to continue, or if for a fixed term, the date when it is to end;
- place of work;
- any collective agreements which directly affect the terms and conditions of the employment;
- where the employee is required to work outside the UK for more than a month, certain further particulars concerning that period, the currency of remuneration, any additional remuneration and benefits, and any terms and conditions relating to the return;
- disciplinary and complaints rules, or referring out to an easily accessible document. If the employer fails to comply with this requirement a tribunal may award between two to fours weeks' pay (based on the statutory cap). This however, is not a free-standing right and must be brought together with a claim such as unfair dismissal or discrimination.

Identifying the "carrots"

In the case of a listed company, the executive's remuneration package must be approved by a Remuneration Committee. The Committee will typically be solely comprised of NEDs. Appointments to the Committee are usually for a period of up to three years, which may be extended for two further three-year periods, provided the director remains independent.

It is vital to ensure that the Committee members are independent of management and free from any business or other relationship which could interfere with the exercise of their independent judgement. The chairman or chief executive, group HR director and any other executive director may be invited to attend and speak at meetings of the Committee, but are not allowed to participate in any matter which impacts upon their own remuneration arrangements. Meetings are usually scheduled at least twice each year.

The usual terms of reference for the Committee include:

- agreeing the framework and/or broad policy for remuneration, terms of employment and any changes for the company's Chairman, executive directors and senior executives, including service agreements, remuneration, policy for and scope of pension arrangements, basis of bonus and bonus awards and participation in and awards under share, incentive and benefit plans; and the targets for any performance related pay schemes;

- agreeing terms for cessation of employment;
- approving any long-term share incentive and benefits plans and to administer such schemes;
- recommending to the board the form and content of the report to shareholders on directors remuneration including the work of the Committee.

The objective of the remuneration policy is to ensure that the chairman, executive directors and other senior executives of the company are provided with appropriate incentives to encourage enhanced performance and are rewarded for their individual contributions to the success of the company. In addition, it should ensure that the company's remuneration policy is competitive and at a level which will enable it to attract, retain and motivate the board and executive management of the appropriate calibre. The remuneration of non-executive directors is usually a matter for the chairman and the executive members of the board.

We now return to drafting considerations in the service agreement.

Appointment (clause 2.1)

Careful consideration must be given to the role which the executive is required to undertake. If the executive will be acting as a statutory director, this should be stated. If the executive's duties encompass multiple roles, this should also be made clear.

Apart from the original directors, the subsequent appointment of directors is typically governed by the company's articles of association and, to some extent, CA 2006. The articles of association usually provide that the directors be appointed by the shareholders or certain classes of shareholders (see, for example, article 17 of the draft model articles for private companies that are due to come into force on 1 October 2009). However, they may also provide that directors be appointed by the existing directors, and less frequently, by third parties. The most common provision in the articles of association, often based on regulation 79 of Table A to the Companies Act 1985, is that the existing directors appoint new directors. Directors appointed in this manner, typically only hold office until the next annual general meeting (AGM), where they may be reappointed by the shareholders.

Board approval of the appointment of a director by the shareholders may be required by the articles of association.

Table A permits the appointment of a director by shareholders without board approval, provided that at least 21 clear days' notice of the shareholders' resolution appointing the director is given (see regulation 38 of Table A to the Companies Act 1985). A notice period between 14 and 35 clear days applies where the proposed appointee is not recommended by the board and is not retiring by rotation. In light of the new notice provisions introduced by the 2006 Act (since 1 October 2007 a uniform 14 clear days' notice period applies to all general meetings for private and public companies (other than AGMs of public companies, where 21 clear days' notice is required), regardless of the type of resolution being proposed), the draft model articles do not contain a similar provision. Thus, in relation to companies incorporated under CA 2006 adopting the model articles as their default set of articles of association, directors may be appointed by ordinary shareholder resolution without board approval and without having to follow a particular procedure as to notice.

It is often the case that with changing business needs, roles will evolve and either augment, diminish or cease. The company must therefore consider providing for some form of flexibility to allow it to reasonably change the executive's duties. However, even with a contractual right to make changes, the company must have a legitimate business reason for making a change and consult with the executive about any fundamental changes to his role. Failure to do so could leave the company exposed to potential employment-related claims.

Term (clause 2.2)

The term of appointment and the executive's notice period are closely linked. This leaves the company with a number of considerations.

From a statutory perspective, continuity of employment will begin on the day the executive commences work. As continuity of employment is a statutory concept it cannot be modified by agreement between the employer and the employee (*Collinson v BBC* [1998] IRLR 238, EAT). Section 210(5) ERA 1996 presumes that a person's employment is continuous unless the contrary is shown. Beware of situations where the executive is promoted from a normal employee status or where the executive's employment has transferred across from another business as part of a TUPE transfer (section 218(2) ERA 1996, and regulation 4 of the Transfer of Undertakings (Protection of Employment) Regulations 2006 (SI 2006/246)).

Fixed term or rolling notice period

If the executive does not have pre-existing service, the company has greater flexibility in determining the structure of the executive's tenure. When adopting a fixed-term approach, the notice wording (clause 15,) will need to be amended to deal with the individual circumstances. The potential fixed-term options include:

(a) *Pure fixed term*. This option ties both parties in for a defined duration, with neither party able to legally provide notice to the other during the entirety of the employment relationship. Termination of the employment relationship during the currency of the fixed term, except in the event of summary termination, would constitute a breach of contract.

This option is more likely to be used when the executive has been brought in to work on a project with a limited life span or to provide cover for an absent employee. The incentive for the executive is that he will be guaranteed work for a defined period.

Section 188 CA 2006 does not allow directors' service contracts in excess of two years' duration without the approval of the shareholders in general meeting. Under section 188(6), approval is not required by the members of a company which is either a non-UK company or a wholly owned subsidiary. Under section 189 CA 2006, if the company agrees to a provision in contravention of section 188, the provision is void, to the extent of the contravention, and the contract is deemed to contain a term entitling the company to terminate it at any time by the giving of reasonable notice.

Although this option provides that the fixed term will automatically come to an end without the need for notice, it is advisable that the company comply with the statutory dismissal procedures. The executive has protection under regulation 3 of the Fixed-term Employees (Prevention of Less Favourable Treatment) Regulations 2002 (SI 2002/2034) which means that he should not be treated less favourably than a full-time employee. If the executive accrues a year's service, he will have the right to bring a claim for unfair dismissal, so the company should not assume that the expiry of the fixed term simply brings the relationship to an end. After two years' continuous service, the executive will also accrue the right to claim a statutory redundancy payment.

(b) *Initial fixed term with notice thereafter*. Where the executive is required to manage a project for a limited duration, the company may wish to tie the executive into an initial term during which time neither party can give notice to the other. To do so would constitute a breach of contract except in the event of summary termination. After the fixed term, the employment relationship will then be governed by the normal notice provisions of the agreement.

Although this option provides certainty for both parties, it can also prove disadvantageous to the company. If for whatever reason the employment relationship does not work out and the company wishes to terminate the executive's employment early, it will have to compensate the executive for the remainder of the 'initial fixed term'.

(c) *Fixed term with notice within the fixed term*. This works on the same basis as the fixed term but allows either party to end the employment relationship *during* the term without being in breach of contract. This option is likely to be useful where the company requires short-term cover but is uncertain of its precise business needs at the outset.

The company should be aware that if the executive has been employed on a fixed term for four or more years, the appointment will become permanent unless a further fixed-term contract can be objectively justified (regulation 8 of the Fixed-term Employees (Prevention of Less Favourable Treatment) Regulations 2002).

Indefinite term with notice period

The employment relationship will operate subject to the right of each party to terminate it on notice.

Notice period

It is a statutory requirement that the service agreement provide details of the length of notice that the executive is required to provide to the company or receive from the company. Notice periods for termination allow the contracting parties a period of time to make their respective arrangements on termination of the employment relationship. There is no requirement for the notice period to be given by the executive to be the same as that which the company is obliged to provide the executive. However, there are a number of statutory, contractual and regulatory issues which must be considered by the company.

Statutory position

Under section 86 ERA 1996, the executive is entitled to receive the following notice, dependent on length of service:

- one week – if the executive is employed for at least one month but less than two years;
- an additional week's notice – for each full year of continuous service up to a maximum of 12 weeks' notice for 12 years or more continuous service.

By way of illustration, if the executive had been employed for seven years, under the statutory regime, he would be entitled to *at least* seven weeks' notice. If he had been employed for 15 years, he would be entitled to *a maximum of* 12 weeks' notice.

Once the executive has been continuously employed for more than one month, he is only required to give to the company one week's notice at any time. Therefore, statutory notice periods are more generous to the executive and much more onerous on the company.

Contractual notice

There is no legal requirement to provide a notice period beyond the statutory minimum requirement, but it is usual practice for the executive to be subject to a longer notice period in view of his seniority. A longer notice period would also help to minimise disruption to the company's business, in the event of termination.

There is no golden rule as to what length of notice must be given, but it is not uncommon for the executive to have at least a three-month notice period. Corporate governance rules recommend that notice periods for executives should not last longer than 12 months and that they should not be rewarded for failure. In addition, under section 189 CA 2006, a contract which is in excess of two years (which has not been approved by shareholders) is deemed to contain a term entitling the company to terminate it at any time by the giving of reasonable notice.

When considering the duration of any contractual notice period, it may be prudent to work with weeks rather than months, due to the overlap with section 86 ERA.

No notice period

If there is no agreed contractual notice period for termination, the default statutory position under section 86 ERA will apply. However, it is possible for the parties, particularly the executive, to argue that a longer notice period should apply instead.

Case law has shown that there are a number of elements to consider when deciding what would be a reasonable duration of a notice period. These include: the employee's length of service (*Hill v CA Parsons & Co. Limited* [1972] 1 Ch 305), seniority, status (*Mulholland v Bexwell Estates Co. Limited* [1950] 66 TLR (pt. 2) 764), and what is usual in the particular trade in question.

Payments in lieu of notice (clause 15)

A clause covering payment in lieu of notice (PILON) will give the company greater flexibility when deciding how to treat the executive once notice is served.

A PILON can best be described as the right not to require the executive to work out his notice period. This can be a valuable right, especially where the executive is likely to be obstructive and damaging to the business during the notice period. A PILON clause would contractually allow the company to pay the executive in lieu of his notice without repudiating the service agreement (provided that the dismissal is fair), so that key provisions such as restrictive covenants remain enforceable.

Typically, the PILON clause will exclude payment of benefits during the PILON. The rationale for this is that the executive is no longer an employee and should therefore cease to be entitled to employment-related benefits.

The company should decide whether it wants the certainty of being able to require the executive not to work out his notice period when the employment relationship has broken down (an "absolute" PILON clause) or the flexibility of the option to do so on termination (a "discretionary" PILON clause). The former creates a contractual obligation on the company so any monies payable to the executive may be claimed as wages (or contractual debt). The latter on the other hand does not create a strict contractual entitlement to a payment in lieu of notice. Therefore, if no notice payment is made by the company, such monies may be claimed as damages and are therefore subject to mitigation (i.e. any earnings the executive has received from his new employment must be accounted for).

There are three types of scenario which merit discussion:

1. *Express PILON clause*. The service agreement may expressly allow the company to dismiss the executive on making a PILON e.g. "the company shall make a payment in lieu....". This prevents the executive claiming damages for wrongful dismissal or breach of contract. However, a contractual *right* to make a PILON will by the same token create an *obligation* on the company to make that payment. The Executive will therefore be entitled to be paid his full notice pay as wages (and subject to income tax and NIC) without the need to take into account mitigation (*Abrahams v Performing Right Society Limited* 1995 ICR 1028, CA). Whether the executive is entitled to the amount as one lump sum (accelerated receipt) depends on whether there is provision for staggered payments and "built-in mitigation".

In *SCA Packaging Ltd v HM Customs and Excise* [2006] UKSPC 541 Jul 40, SCA Packaging had made a number of employees redundant over the period 1996 to 2001. The termination payments generally included a payment in lieu of notice, from which the company did not deduct PAYE tax and NICs unless they exceeded £30,000. HMRC had assessed unpaid tax and NICs at around £70,000 and SCA Packaging appealed against that assessment. The Special Commissioners held that, where a redundant employee agrees to leave on short notice, the payment in lieu of notice, as set out in the employee's contract, is made in respect of the employment and is therefore taxable in full. The decision may be summarised as follows:

- Although the employer's provisions on how short notice in the event of redundancy would be handled were set out in a separate memorandum of agreement, those provisions were incorporated into each employee's contract of employment because they touched directly on the relationship between employer and employee.
- The redundancy terms set out in the memorandum of agreement specified that, on termination for redundancy, a payment would be made in lieu of any unexpired period of notice and defined the formula that would be used for calculating the amount of the payment.
- As these terms were an integral part of the redundancy payment provisions, they could not be viewed as a payment of damages for breach of contract. The payments were made in performance of the contract, not in breach of it.
- If the contract states that an employee "will" be entitled to a period of notice or pay in lieu of that notice, the payment is contractual, not for breach of contract. On the other hand, if the contract states that an employee is entitled to a period of notice

but the employer "may" pay in lieu of that notice, the employer may choose whether to apply the contractual terms and make a payment in lieu of notice, or ignore the contractual terms and make a payment of damages for breach of contract, subject to the employee's duty to mitigate the loss.

- The fact that a contract contains specific provisions for redundancy notice and payment does not provide a right for the employer to terminate on short notice. The employer may seek the employee's agreement to go on short notice, but the redundancy provisions only apply if the employee agrees. If the employee agrees, the existing contract must be treated as having been varied.
- If the payment in lieu is made under such a variation of the original contract, any part of the payment that derives from the agreement to go on short notice stems from the employment (as opposed to resulting from the termination) and is, as a result, taxable in full.
- Where there is no right to redundancy payments under a contract, a payment in lieu is not made for the modification of the contract but for the cancellation of it. Therefore, the payment derives from the termination, not from the employment, and is not taxable (unless it exceeds £30,000).
- The fact that a non-contractual payment in lieu of notice is made habitually does not turn it automatically into a payment deriving from the employment. It does not, in itself, make it "contractual". If an employer habitually makes payments in lieu of notice in circumstances where the payments derive from the termination, that practice does not turn them into payments deriving from the employment.

2. *Discretionary PILON clause*. Typically, such a clause would provide that "the company may make a payment in lieu" or "has the discretion to make a payment in lieu ...". A failure to make a payment in these circumstances gives rise to a claim for damages for breach of contract. In *Cerberus Software Limited v Rowley* 2001 ICR 376, CA, Mr Rowley, a sales and marketing director, was entitled to six months' notice on termination of employment. Clause 17 of his contract provided that "Notice may only be given as to expire at the end of a monthly pay period. It is agreed that the employer may make a payment in lieu of notice to the employee. The employee shall not be entitled to any other benefit other than pay or money in lieu of such benefits in respect of any period for which he has been paid in lieu of notice". The Court of Appeal held that where the company is given a choice whether or not to make a payment in lieu of notice under the employee's contract, the language is totally inconsistent with a contractual right given to the employee to insist that he be paid six months' salary in lieu of notice. As the employer chose to terminate Mr Rowley's employment summarily, this constituted a breach of contract or wrongful dismissal, which meant that Mr Rowley was required to mitigate his loss in relation to his claim for notice pay and benefits. The case of *Abrahams v Performing Right Society Limited* 1995 ICR 1028, CA was distinguished.

Where the company exercises the discretionary PILON clause in favour of the executive, the sum becomes payable as wages, rather than damages for breach of contract (*Breakspear v Colonial Financial Services (UK) Limited* 2002 EWHC 1456, QBD).

3. *Implied PILON – custom and practice*. Where there is no express contractual term relating to the making of payments in lieu of notice, but the company has a custom of giving payments in lieu of notice, tax and NIC may be payable by the company. The Inland Revenue set out their approach to customary PILON payments in HMRC Tax Bulletin 63, published in 2003. In summary, even if no PILON clause is contained in the executive's service agreement, if the nature of the payment is in reality a "payment in lieu of notice" and it is "an automatic response to a termination" it will be considered taxable in full by the Revenue. A payment in lieu of notice will not be taxable if is evidence to show that any payments made were individually negotiated, that reducing the payment to take mitigation into account was considered and that the payment is for net, rather than gross, loss.

In Morrish v NTL Group [2007] ScotCS CSIH_56 (03 July 2007), Mr Morrish was dismissed without being given the 12 months' written notice required by his employment contract. He claimed damages for breach of contract. NTL offered him a payment of salary in lieu of notice which he rejected, as this did not include bonus payments which he would have earned had he been allowed to work out his notice period. NTL argued that there was an implied term giving it the right to terminate the contract by making a payment of a proportion of his salary and emoluments corresponding to the period of notice stipulated in the contract. The Court of Session rejected such a suggestion. It held that there was no reason to imply such a term which would have the effect of depriving Mr Morrish of the normal remedy of damages for breach of contract, the purpose of which would be to put him in no worse a financial position than that in which he would have been had NTL fulfilled its contractual obligations. As a result, Mr Morrish was able to claim an award of damages to include the bonus he would have earned in the 12-month notice period. This case demonstrates the importance of having an express or discretionary PILON clause in the service agreement, without which it would not be possible for the company to make a PILON based on the employee's salary only.

Notice pay during sick leave

Where the executive's contractual notice period exceeds the statutory minimum notice period by at least one week, the executive may not be entitled to any notice pay in the event of sickness and absence during the notice period (*Scotts Company (UK) Limited v J. Budd* [2003] IRLR 145 EAT). This is because the right to payment during a notice period whilst an employee is unable to work due to illness under section 88(1) ERA 1996 is qualified by section 87(4) ERA 1996. Section 87 (4) provides that "'section 88 does not apply if the notice to be given by the employer to terminate the contract must be at least one week more than notice required under section 86(1)". Note however that section 87(4) does not have any effect where the executive's requisite notice to the company is exceeded by one week, which would very likely be the case.

Structuring notice payments (clause 15.2)

If the executive is subject to a lengthy notice period (e.g. six months or more), it is possible to reduce the company's financial exposure to notice pay. Where a payment in lieu of notice is contemplated, the company may be able to stagger the executive's receipt of notice payments as the executive is under a common law duty to mitigate his loss on termination of employment. A "built-in mitigation" clause ensures that in the event that the executive secures alternative employment during the notice period, the company may be absolved from any future periodic payments. The executive is likely to resist such a clause and its inclusion will very much depend on the commercial bargaining powers of the parties.

When notice pay is not payable (clause 15.3)

Where the executive commits an act of gross misconduct justifying summary dismissal, he has no entitlement to receive notice pay. What amounts to gross misconduct should be clearly listed either in the service agreement or company handbook. In all other cases, the executive should be given notice to avoid a wrongful dismissal claim.

Remuneration (clause 6)

The executive's remuneration is usually dictated by market forces and commercial needs. However, the company must also pay heed to any restrictions imposed by the articles of association, statute or corporate governance rules.

Clause 6.1 deals with the level of basic salary. This is defined as "base salary" for the purposes of the payment in lieu of notice clause (clause 15.2) and for pensionable salary purposes. Clause 6.1 also deals with when salary is payable and where it is to be paid.

Where the executive is employed under a service agreement, it should be made clear that remuneration payable by the company is inclusive of any fees or other remuneration arising from the executive's office as a statutory director.

- Clause 6.2 – the executive will expect his remuneration to be kept in line with market rates and therefore, the company should consider incorporating a mechanism to review his remuneration on a yearly basis and the month in which it is anticipated such a review would take place. It is recommended that the company make clear that there is no obligation to award a pay increase following a review and that any salary increments are at the absolute discretion of the company.

Where there is a discretionary clause, the company needs to ensure that it exercises it discretion in good faith otherwise it may be in breach of an implied term not to act perversely or irrationally. The executive may even be able to show that there is a historical practice of giving a set percentage pay increase (*Clark v BET plc* [1997] IRLR 348).

The company must also guard itself against potential claims for equal pay. Gender pay gaps remain a topical issue.

Under section 13(1) ERA 1996 an employer may not make a deduction from an employee's wages unless:

- it is required or authorised to be made by a statutory provision or a relevant provision in the employee's contract; or
- the employee has previously consented in writing to the deduction.

Clause 6.3 provides the company with the necessary contractual authority to make deductions from the executive's wages.

Bonuses (clause 7)

Bonuses can sometimes be the most important part of the executive's remuneration package, and can easily eclipse any normal salary payments. Therefore, this can become one of the more contentious areas between the executive and the company. There are a number of ways to structure bonus awards.

A guaranteed bonus

Where the executive is leaving his employer part-way during a financial year, he may end up losing his entitlement to a bonus which he would otherwise accrue. The Executive will often expect to be compensated for this financial loss in the form of a guaranteed bonus. Guaranteed bonuses are usually offered to incentivise the executive to leave his current employer.

A guaranteed bonus may also be sought where the executive is recruited to establish or develop an area of the business over a long term. Where such a venture involves a level of risks, the executive is likely to negotiate a guaranteed bonus as a basis of leaving his current employment.

When awarding a guaranteed bonus the company must consider a number of factors:

- the amount of the guaranteed payment;
- when the guarantee payment becomes payable;

- whether the guaranteed bonus is pensionable;
- whether to stagger any payments;
- whether there will be any claw-back provisions should the executive leave the company within a defined timeframe;
- whether to pay it in cash or through options;
- forfeiture provisions.

It is strongly recommended that there are express provisions in the service agreement withholding payment in the event that the executive is subject to disciplinary proceedings at the date of payment of any such bonus. More importantly, the guaranteed bonus should cease to be payable by the company if the executive's employment is terminated for "cause". What amounts to "cause" requires careful consideration and drafting.

Performance-related bonus

Performance-related bonuses are essentially driven by individual team targets, and/or company performance set by the company. This can work to the benefit of both parties. On the one hand, the executive is motivated in the knowledge that he has the opportunity to earn a bonus on top of his normal remuneration. On the other hand, the company can benefit from enhanced performance levels by the executive and/or his team.

The drafting considerations mentioned above apply equally to performance-related bonus payments.

Whereas operating a pro rata bonus entitlement may improve staff morale and minimise litigation in the event that the executive's bonus payment is forfeited on termination, recent case law suggests that if the scheme expressly provides that continued employment is necessary to qualify for the payment, the company will not need to pro rate the bonus (*Commerzbank AG v Keen* [2007] IRLR 132, CA, 341). Without such an express clause, any decision not to award bonus if the executive leaves part-way through the year may be opened to legal challenge.

Discretionary bonus

A discretionary bonus is by far the most common option, and a sample clause is provided at clause 7. The company should be clear what aspects of the scheme are intended to be discretionary. For example, does the discretion relate to the amount of the bonus which might be payable, or to the decision to award any bonus when certain criteria have been met by the executive? The more formulaic the discretionary bonus scheme, the less flexibility the company would have.

Although a discretionary scheme provides the company with greater flexibility when making a bonus award, such a scheme is also more vulnerable to legal challenge. The discretionary nature of the bonus scheme does not allow the company free reign to make arbitrary bonus awards because there is an implied obligation not to exercise the discretion perversely or irrationally (*Clark v Nomura International plc* [2000] IRLR 766). When awarding the bonus, the company and where appropriate, its Remuneration Committee, should ensure that the process is fair and consistent to avoid any claims for breach of contract in the High Court.

In *Commerzbank AG v Keen* [2007] IRLR 132, CA, 341, the Court of Appeal held that the courts would only intervene with discretionary bonus awards where the employer has exercised its discretion in an unfair and inequitable manner. This would occur where making of a low or nil award was a breach of the implied term of trust and respect, or the employer's exercise of its discretion was legally "perverse".

The courts will look at factors such as:

- the executive's previous and recent performance;
- whether there is a paper trail as to how and why the decision was taken; and
- the employer's pattern of recent bonus payments which have "through custom" become certain and expected.

Expenses (clause 8)

The company's policy and procedure for incurring and claiming expenses should be clearly set out for the executive's benefit. Sections 70-72 ITEPA 2003 provide that expenses are generally taxable as earnings. However section 336 ITEPA 2003 allows a deduction from earnings to be made if:

- the executive is obliged to incur and pay it as holder of the employment; and
- the amount is incurred wholly, exclusively and necessarily in the performance of the duties of the employment.

There are special rules which apply to certain types of expenses: section 337 ITEPA 2003 travel (travel in performance of duties); section 338 ITEPA 2003 (travel for necessary attendance); section 340 ITEPA 2003 (travel between group employments); section 342 ITEPA 2003 (travel between employments where duties performed abroad); section 343 ITEPA 2003 (deductions for professional memberships) and section 344 ITEPA 2003 (deductions for annual subscriptions); and sections 356-358 ITEPA 2003 (business entertainment and gift expenses).

The company's expenses policy should define the rules for corporate travel and expenses. It is recommended that a financial limit is set on the amount of an individual expense. Anything above that limit should be authorised by the company. The company should also impose a cumulative limit on expenses, as a number of expenses may fall below the authorisation level yet still be costly.

The timing of when expenses claims must be made is also critical. Executives can often forget to make expense claims in a timely manner. This could lead to expenses claims not being processed in the correct financial year or recorded in time to appear on client bills. When this happens, expenses are often written off. All expenses claims should be subject to production of relevant receipts and vouchers,without which the expenses claims may not be paid out.

Holidays (clause 8)

The statutory position on holidays is governed by the Working Time Regulations 1998 (SI 1998/1833) (WTR). The WTR implement the provisions of the Working Time Directive (Council Directive 93/104/EC). The WTR allow workers to take holiday. This includes an individual who has entered into or works under:

- a contract or employment; or
- any other contract, whether express or implied, oral or in writing, whereby the individual undertakes to do or perform personally any work or services for another party to the contract, who is not a client or customer of any profession or business undertaking carried on by the individual.

Under regulation 13(1) WTR, workers were entitled to four weeks' holiday inclusive of public and bank holidays in each holiday year. As of 1 October 2007, this entitlement increased to 4.8 weeks' holiday per year inclusive of public and bank holidays. This level is due to increase to 5.6 weeks as of 1 April 2009 (Working Time (Amendment) Regulations 2007/2079).

It is customary for the executive to receive 25 to 30 days' holiday plus statutory public and bank holidays.

- Clause 9.1 – where the executive commences employment part-way through the holiday year, his holiday entitlement is calculated on a pro rata basis. Where the executive is working part-time, his holiday entitlement should also be calculated on a pro rata basis but should be no less favourable than a full-time employee's entitlement. There is no continuous service requirement to qualify for annual holidays under the WTR.
- Clause 9.2 – it is important to specify details of the executive's leave year, failing which regulation 13(3) WTR provides that the holiday year will start on the later of 1 October 1998 or the date on which the employment began, unless modified by a "relevant agreement" (a written contract of employment could be a relevant agreement).

- Clause 9.3 – there is often confusion when calculating the payment due in respect of outstanding holiday, usually on termination of the executive's employment. Where the executive works full-time, the company should divide the executive's remuneration by the number of working days in the calendar year, roughly 260. Similarly, the payment due in relation to accrued but untaken holiday pay must be calculated on the basis of the annual salary divided by the number of working days for each day's holiday entitlement. It should be based on working days (1/260) and not calendar days (*Leisure Leagues UK Limited v Maconnachie* [2002] IRLR 600).
- Clause 9.4 – the Executive has no automatic right to carry forward untaken holiday from one holiday year to the next. Under WTR, if the holiday is not taken, it will be lost. Where work pressures have prevented the executive from taking his holiday, the company may wish to consider allowing the executive to "carry forward" to the next holiday year any accrued but unused holidays. It is recommended that there should be a limit on the number of days to be carried over and that this should first be authorised by the company. The company may also wish to specify that carried-over holiday entitlement is taken within the first few months of the new holiday year to prevent too much holiday accruing.
- Clause 9.5 – the executive has the right to be paid in lieu of statutory holiday that has accrued and not been taken at the date of termination. The company is only obliged by law to give pay in lieu of any untaken statutory holiday under the WTR and is not obliged to give pay in lieu of additional contractual leave unless this is expressly provided for in the service agreement.
- Clause 9.5.1 – this entitles the company to deduct an appropriate amount from the executive's final salary where the executive has taken holiday in excess of his accrued entitlement as at the date of termination.
- Clause 9.5.2 – this limits the executive's payment in lieu of accrued but untaken holiday to his statutory holiday only. It is not possible to forfeit the executive's leave entitlement under the WTR even in the event of gross misconduct (*Witley & District Mens' Club v Mackay* [2001] IRLR 595), although this is possible in relation to any other accrued contractual holiday entitlement.
- Clause 9.6 – this entitles the company to require the executive to take any outstanding holiday during the notice period. This provision helps to reduce the company's exposure to notice pay or may be helpful in removing the executive where there is no garden leave provision to fall back on.
- Clause 9.7 – this allows the company to withhold any accrued but untaken holiday pay where the executive fails to work out his notice period.
- Clause 9.8 – where the executive is absent through sickness during part of the holiday year, it may be possible to limit holiday accrual to the statutory entitlement only. In *Stringer & Ors v Her Majesty's Revenue and Customs* [2006] UKHL 8, the Advocate General has recently ruled that:

- entitlement to paid statutory holiday *does* accrue whilst a worker is absent on sick leave;
- however, workers may not take their holiday while they are *on* sick leave; and,
- the worker may designate some future period after the expiry of their sick leave to take their accrued holiday that they were unable to use, even if that period is the next holiday year.

This decision is still to be ratified by the European Court of Justice and the UK courts, but it is a warning that statutory holiday entitlement is likely to accrue during sick leave.

Company car (Schedule 1, paragraph 4)

The provision of a company car as an employment benefit has become increasingly unpopular in recent years, due to changes to its tax treatment since April 2002.

Where this benefit is offered to the executive, it is prudent to have detailed rules governing the use of the company car either within the service agreement or in a separate policy.

- Schedule 1, paragraph 4.1 – this deals with the need for the executive to hold a valid driving licence as a condition of being granted the use of a company car. It also sets out the type of car that the executive will receive and whether the car should be used for business purposes only or can also be used for private use. Where possible, the company should avoid setting out the exact specifications of the company car to which the executive is entitled as it will provide the company with greater flexibility when the executive becomes entitled to another vehicle.

If the executive is allowed to also use the company car for private use, it will be a taxable benefit for the executive. The taxable benefit of a company car registered on or after 1 January 1998 is calculated by reference to its carbon dioxide emissions, with cars with lower emissions qualifying for a lower tax rate. From 6 April 2008, a company car will need to have carbon dioxide emissions of less than 135g/km to qualify for the lowest 15 per cent tax rate, instead of the 140g/km currently applicable. A new lower rate of 10 per cent will be available from that date, for cars emitting less than 120g/km.

Furthermore, allowing the executive private use of the car may expose the company to a claim for a loss of that benefit if the executive's employment is wrongfully or unfairly terminated.

- Schedule 1, paragraph 4.2 – it is not uncommon for the company to bear the reasonable running costs of the car, such as insurance, MOT and maintenance. The company may also bear the fuel costs incurred in using the car for business purposes. The company will also need to decide whether it pays for fuel costs incurred by the executive for private use of the car (if private use is permitted). If so, this can constitute a taxable benefit under section 149 ITEPA 2003.

If the company wishes to avoid paying NIC and the executive wishes to avoid paying income tax on private fuel costs where the company bears the initial cost of fuel, then the company should make it very clear to the executive from the outset that it wishes to be reimbursed for these costs within the relevant tax year. From the executive's perspective, he will avoid a tax charge for expensed fuel by repaying the company for private fuel costs in the tax year in question.

- Schedule 1, paragraph 4.3 – it is usual for company cars to be replaced when they have reached a pre-determined mileage or age.
- Schedule 1, paragraph 4.4 – this clause sets out the executive's obligations in relation to his use of the car.

The executive should ensure that any relevant provisions in the company's car policy and insurance policy are observed.

If the executive is contractually required to drive a vehicle in order to perform his duties satisfactorily, then the company will need to be informed of any driving disqualification or driving offences which affect the executive performance. In these situations, the company should reserve the right to terminate the executive's employment in the event that he is disqualified from driving a vehicle.

Car allowance (Schedule 1, paragraph 5)

- Schedule 1, paragraph 5.1 – the executive may prefer to receive a car allowance because it has a more favourable tax treatment, i.e. no tax is charged for the car itself, although the executive will be taxed on the car allowance at his highest marginal rate. The same considerations apply regarding the need for the executive to have a valid driving licence to qualify for car allowance.

Although this benefit is paid together with the executive's salary, it should be made clear that the car allowance is not included in the salary for the purposes of calculating the executive's pension entitlement.

- Schedule 1, paragraph 5.2 – as with a company car benefit, the company will pay the executive's fuel costs incurred in business use, but must consider whether it wishes to reimburse the executive for private fuel costs. The same tax considerations apply as described within the company car section.
- Schedule 1, paragraph 5.3 – if the executive is disqualified from driving, the provision of car allowance will cease on the basis that this benefit is only granted if the executive is legally entitled to drive.

Life assurance (Schedule 1, paragraph 1)

A life assurance scheme generally consists of the company paying subscriptions into a life assurance policy on the executive's behalf, which pays out a lump sum to the executive's beneficiary if they die during the term of their employment. The sum is usually between two and four times the executive's annual salary.

- Schedule 1, paragraph 1.1 – before commencing the payment of premiums, the company may wish to wait until the executive has successfully completed any probationary period. This can be used as an incentive for good performance. If the life assurance scheme forms part of a pension scheme provided by the company, then entitlement to both benefits should correspond accordingly.

Participation in the life assurance scheme should always be subject to the terms and conditions of the company's insurance provider. The company should ensure that the contractual promise can be delivered upon under the terms of the insurance.

The executive should be subject to underwriting checks carried out by the insurance provider before being approved for the policy and the company should reserve the right to make participation subject to a reasonable level of premium being charged.

- Schedule 1, paragraph 1.2 – it is possible that the executive may not qualify for a payment under the life assurance scheme and therefore the company must avoid making a contractual promise to honour the scheme regardless of the insurers' decision.
- Schedule 1, paragraph 1.3 – this gives the company the flexibility to cease providing life assurance, change insurers or the level of cover provided without obtaining the executive's prior consent. The company should bear in mind the implied duty of trust and confidence when considering termination of an existing life assurance benefit. It is important that the company does not include specific details relating to the insurance policy in the service agreement as the insurer may well change at a later date.

Under regulation 34 of the Employment Equality (Age) Regulations 2006 it is lawful for the company to cease providing life assurance cover when the executive reaches the company's normal retirement age, or where there is no normal retirement age, the age of 65.

Sickness and injury (clause 10)

Statutory sick pay is only payable to employees who have been off sick for four or more consecutive days (including Sundays and holidays). Multiple absences of four days (unless separated by a period of at least eight weeks) may count as one qualifying period in respect of a week's sick pay. The maximum entitlement is 28 weeks in a three-year period, after which the employee would have to claim Disability Benefit.

Many employers provide occupational sick pay that is more generous than SSP. It is important to ensure that the executive complies with the rules of the company's occupational sick pay scheme. Typically, such schemes consist of a set period of full pay followed by a set period on half-pay. The company should ensure that any period of sick pay is calculated on a rolling 12-month basis. Where sick pay benefits are based on the calendar year, this can be very costly to the company. Where payment of contractual sick pay is discretionary, failure to exercise the discretion in a fair manner could lead to claims of potential discrimination and/or breach of contract.

- Clause 10.1 – this deals with reporting requirements. These would usually be set out in the company handbook, and the methods of reporting will vary depending upon the level of seniority of the executive. The company should make clear to whom the executive should report into in the event of absence, when the absence should be reported and by what method, telephone, email etc. Telephone reporting is the usual procedure.
- If absences are less than seven calendar days, the executive will usually be able to self-certify his absence. Anything over and above this level of absence subsequently must be supported with a doctor's certificate and a further certificate for each week of absence.
- Clause 10.2 – to qualify for SSP, the executive must meet certain statutory requirements under the Statutory Sick Pay (General) Regulations 1982, SI 1982/894.
- Clause 10.3 – this allows the company to reclaim sick pay where the executive makes a financial recovery from a third party. For example, if the executive is injured in a road accident, he may be able to claim compensation from his insurance company for any lost earnings. This clause requires the executive to account for such compensation he has received, to prevent double recovery.
- Clause 10.4 – the company may ask the executive to submit to a medical prior to joining employment, or to attend an annual medical check up. This does not mean that the company can simply reject an application or refuse to continue to employ the executive on the basis of his health because there may be a statutory obligation to make reasonable adjustments under section 6 of the Disability Discrimination Act 1995. Instead, this information will help determine what tasks the executive can undertake and would allow the company to consider whether any reasonable adjustments need to be made to the working environment to accommodate the executive's disability.

  The company should also include an express clause in the service agreement which allows it to require the executive to submit to a medical examination during his employment. This is useful if the executive goes on long-term sick leave. If the executive unreasonably refuses to do so, he would be in breach of contract, which would entitle the company to terminate his employment.

Private medical insurance (Schedule 1, paragraph 2)

Health benefits represent a competitive new front in the war for talent. Private medical insurance (PMI) is paid for and provided by employers to ensure both the welfare and productivity of the executive. This benefit allows key individuals in the company to be treated, recover and return to work from a medical complaint a lot quicker than they would have been if they went via the NHS, so minimising the disruption to the company of a medical-related absence.

- Schedule 1, paragraph 2.1 – Before commencing the payment of premiums, the company may wish to wait until the executive has successfully completed any probationary period.

In relation to PMI, the company will need to consider whether it wishes to provide this cover to the executive's family. If so, this should also extend to civil partners, to avoid discrimination (regulation 3(3) of the Employment Equality (Sexual Orientation) Regulations 2003).

- Schedule 1, paragraph 2.2 – it is possible that the executive may not qualify for a payment under the private medical insurance scheme and therefore the company must avoid making a contractual promise to honour the scheme regardless of the insurer's decision.
- Schedule 1, paragraph 2.3 – this gives the company the flexibility to cease providing private medical insurance, change insurers or the level of cover provided without obtaining the executive's prior consent. It is important that the company does not include specific details relating to the insurance policy in the service agreement, to avoid problems if the insurer is changed at a later date.

Permanent health insurance (Schedule 1, paragraph 3)

Permanent health insurance (PHI) or long-term disability cover (LTD) provides a replacement income, as a proportion of salary, to employees who are off work through long-term illness between leaving employment and normal retirement age. The award, typically between 50 per cent and 65 per cent of the executive's normal salary, is subject to a medical report and usually offsets state incapacity benefit. Critical illness insurance (CII) is similar to PHI but it provides a lump sum to the employee until he retires. From the executive's perspective, CII can be more useful than PHI if he has a terminal condition. From the company's perspective, CII provides a clear break with the executive.

The provision of PHI or CII alleviates the burden on the company to make provision for long-term occupational sick pay.

- Schedule 1, paragraph 3.1 – the same drafting considerations apply as in Life Assurance and PMI. There are a number of key considerations:
  - The executive's right to receive PHI benefits will be subject to the terms of the insurance policy. However, if the company fails to make reference to this fact in the service agreement, then it cannot rely upon the terms of the policy defeating the terms under the service agreement (*Jowitt v Pioneer Technology (UK) Ltd* [2003] ICR 1120).
  - If the insurance policy contains significant exemptions to the PHI benefits, such as forfeiture of benefits on leaving employment, the company cannot rely on these exemptions unless the executive was shown the policy or was told to read it (*Villella v MFI Furniture Centres Ltd* [1999] IRLR 468).
  - The company should always ensure that the PHI terms in the service agreement match those between the company and the insurer. Any obligations to the executive under the company's PHI scheme should not be greater than the PHI cover taken out with the insurer. Failing to observe this rule may result in the company bearing a significant uninsured loss.
- Schedule 1, paragraph 3.2 – this ensures that the company is not obliged to make payments to the executive under the PHI scheme unless it has already received payment from the insurance provider. Depending on the terms of the PHI policy, payments may be made directly to the executive or via the company, and the company will not be obliged to make payments where the insurer pays the executive directly.
- Schedule 1, paragraph 3.5 – if the executive is a director of the company, long-term absence may prevent him from carrying out his duties satisfactorily. This clause allows the company to require the executive to resign his position as director when he is receiving benefits under the PHI scheme. Further, it gives the company the flexibility to appoint a replacement for the executive to carry out the duties he used to perform.

If the executive is receiving PHI benefits, it may be difficult for the company to end the employment relationship, particularly where the insurance policy states that the executive must remain in employment to continue to receive the benefit. The courts will probably imply a term into the service agreement to prevent the company bringing the employment to an end where this is solely aimed at ending the PHI benefits (*Aspden v Webbs Poultry* [1996] IRLR 521; *Hill v General Accident Fire and Life Assurance Corporation plc* [1998] IRLR 641). However, in *Briscoe v Lubrizol Ltd* [2002] EWCA Civ 508, 2002 IRLR 607, the court held that if an employee is off work on long-term sick leave, it is lawful for his employer to dismiss him if he is guilty of gross misconduct, even though the result will be to bring to an end any right he may have as an employee to benefit from the employer's permanent health scheme.

The company should also consider negotiating a clause with the insurer that continued employment is not a requirement of continuation of PHI benefits once the payments have begun.

Pension (Schedule 1, paragraph 6)

Section 1(4)(d)(iii) ERA 1996 requires employers to provide employees with details of any pension provision (as part of the written statement of terms of employment). The written statement must specify whether a contracted-out certificate is in force for pension purposes in respect of the employment (section 3(5) ERA 1996). Under section 160 of the Pension Schemes Act 1993, an employee cannot be required to join an occupational pension scheme.

A pension scheme may be contributory (paid into by both the executive and the company) or non-contributory (entirely funded by the company). The executive may normally also make additional voluntary contributions (AVCs).

The company may provide an occupational pension scheme (i.e. a scheme established by the employer for its employees) or undertake to pay contributions to a personal pension scheme (including a group personal pension scheme, a stakeholder pension scheme or a self-invested pension scheme (SIPP)). Occupational pension schemes may provide benefits on a final salary (defined benefit) basis or a money purchase (defined contribution) basis; benefits under personal pension schemes are normally money purchase.

Most pension schemes target retirement at a specified date and are therefore potentially discriminatory on grounds of age. However the age discrimination regulations include fairly wide exemptions covering most pension scheme practices which could otherwise be held to be discriminatory.

Tax treatment

There is tax relief available in respect of pension schemes which meet the requirements of the tax legislation in force from time to time. The executive will not be subject to income tax or NIC on contributions made by the company to a tax approved or registered pension scheme, and can claim income tax relief (but not NIC relief) on contributions made by the executive. Salary or bonus sacrifice arrangements (under which the executive gives up contractual entitlement to part of the salary or bonus in exchange for higher company pension contributions) may be made to maximise the NI advantages of tax favoured pension schemes.

The legislation imposes certain limits on the contributions which can be made and the benefits provided by tax favoured pension schemes. The basis on which tax favoured pension schemes are treated was radically changed with effect from 6 April 2006.

Prior to 6 April 2006 and after June 1989, if the executive joined a pension scheme they were subject to an earnings cap, which limited the amount of their earnings which could be taken into account for approved pension schemes. As at 6 April 2006 the cap was £108,600. In practice, schemes could provide a pension of up to two-thirds of the cap (depending on length of service). Pension benefits could be provided in excess of the limits through non-approved pension schemes, commonly known as funded unapproved retirement benefit scheme (FURBS), unfunded unapproved retirement benefit schemes (UURBS) or secured unfunded unapproved retirement benefit scheme (SUURBS). This was often done in order to attract senior executives who were not subject to the earnings cap in their current employment (where service began before 1989). Under the new regime, unapproved arrangements of this type may no longer be relevant.

Form 6 April 2006 the regime applicable to pension schemes changed completely, as did the jargon. Tax favoured treatment now applies to "registered pension schemes". The statutory earnings cap no longer applies (although note that some schemes have chosen to retain it), and the old limits on contributions and benefits no longer apply. Instead there is a system of allowances calculated on an individual basis and taking into account all benefits under registered pension schemes for each individual, rather than applying limits on the value of the benefits which any given pension scheme can provide for each year of service.

The most important allowance is the "lifetime allowance", which is £1.65m for the tax year 2008/09 (rising to £1.8m by 2010/11 and to be reviewed thereafter). If the executive draws pension benefits with a value in excess of the lifetime allowance, he will incur tax penalties (although note that unlike under the previous regime, benefits in excess of the allowance are not prohibited, but merely heavily taxed).

Prior to 6 April 2006, the executive could not pay pension contributions in excess of 15 per cent of salary (subject to the earnings cap for post-1989 members), and there were problems with concurrent membership of a company pension scheme and personal pension schemes. Since April 2006, the executive has been able to claim tax relief on contributions to all registered arrangements up to 100 per cent of UK taxable salary. In theory, the executive could pay higher contributions, provided that the aggregate of the contributions paid to money purchase schemes and the value of benefits accrued under defined benefit schemes in any year does not exceed the annual allowance (£235,000 for the tax year 2008/09). Concurrent membership of different schemes is not restricted.

If the executive is highly paid, and has accrued benefits prior to 6 April 2006 with a value in excess of the new lifetime allowance, there are transitional arrangements to minimise the impact of the change in the rules. The executive may qualify for primary protection or enhanced protection of their pre-2006 benefits. It is possible to register for enhanced or primary protection until 6 April 2009 (where the conditions are met).

This is a complex area and specialist financial advice should be sought if it is likely to be applicable.

Final salary versus money purchase scheme

A final salary scheme (defined benefit scheme) promises a fixed or guaranteed pension based on a stated fraction of the executive's pensionable salary as at the date of retirement or loss of employment and their length of service (typically 1/60th or 1/30th of salary per year of service). The executive's pension entitlement is not directly related to the amounts the executive or company have contributed to the fund. Pension payments are financed from the pension fund, which consists of both the company's and the executive's contributions. If the scheme's assets are insufficient, the company will have to make increased contributions to fund the promised pensions. The company therefore bears most of the risks, including in particular price and salary inflation, investment underperformance and improving mortality (increased longevity). The executive does bear the risk that the scheme may be under-funded and the company is unable to make good the funding (e.g. on an insolvency of the company). To protect against this risk, all final salary schemes pay a levy to the Pension Protection Fund, a body set up under statute to provide a safety net in the form of a minimum level of compensation for members of under-funded pension schemes whose sponsoring employers fail.

A money purchase scheme (defined contribution scheme), does not guarantee the amount of the pension payments. Money is paid by the company and the executive, or the company alone, into a fund. The executive's pension will depend on how well the investment fund performs and the annuity rates at the time of retirement – the market risks are therefore transferred to the member.

There are other possible forms of benefit structure (e.g. CARE, or career average schemes) which aim to share risk more equally between the company and the executive, but these are outside the scope of this book.

Occupational versus personal pension scheme

Occupational pension schemes are established by employers for the benefit of some or all of their employees. They are usually run by trustees who hold assets on trust for the scheme members. The rules of the scheme will usually confer considerable discretion on the trustees on how the scheme should be run. Employers will normally bear the expenses of the running the scheme, and in the case of final salary schemes the funding risk.

The trustees of the scheme must provide employees with certain information either as of right or on request, e.g. the scheme rules, the scheme's annual report and accounts and an annual statement detailing the pension benefits to which the executive will be entitled.

Personal pension schemes are managed by the provider (often an insurance company) and the legal relationship is between the executive and the provider. Occasionally employers may set up so-called "group personal pension schemes" under their name and sponsored by them. However, the legal relationship is not affected by this. The employer may agree to make contributions to the pension arrangement of a fixed amount or a fixed percentage of salary, and in some cases to bear the initial set-up costs, but its liabilities are normally limited to that express commitment. On-going expenses will be charged against the employee's rights.

Leaving the scheme

A pension scheme must offer options to the executive when he leaves his employment. These can include:

- a refund of contributions (if the executive has been a member for less than two years);
- a transfer of benefits under the scheme (usually if the executive has worked for more than two years) into a new company pension scheme or personal pension scheme; or
- a deferred pension (i.e. a right to draw a pension from the scheme on the eventual normal retirement date).

Most schemes will also allow members to draw a pension on early retirement after age 50 (or from 2010 after age 55) or on retirement before that age by reason of ill- health. The conditions will vary from scheme to scheme – the consent of the trustees or the company may be needed, and the pension may be actuarially reduced to take account of the early payment.

Shares and share options

Share options can be a valuable motivational tool when trying to retain and attract the best employee. Share options can:

- create money for the company;
- generate wealth for employees;
- improve productivity by providing incentives for high performance;
- promote a sense of identity;
- promote long-term loyalty of employees.

Shares may be granted outright or via options. A share option is a right to buy a set number of shares in the company at a fixed price during a set period of time. The executive is usually given the right to purchase shares at a price set by reference to the market price prevailing when the options were granted, but has to wait for a period of time before the options become exercisable. The exercise may also be subject to performance conditions.

For example, the company may grant an option over 100 shares at an option price of £5 per share. In two years' time, the value of each share may be £10. The participant exercises the option by paying the company £500 and is issued 100 shares, which are then worth £1,000. There is no income tax payable on the grant of share options. However, when unapproved options are exercised, income tax is payable on any gain up to the date of exercise (i.e. the difference in the market price at the date of exercise and the option price – £500 in the example). When the shares are sold, the executive may also have to pay capital gains tax on any increase in value between the date of exercise of the option and the date of sale. Unapproved share schemes such as this are the least tax efficient type of scheme.

There are a number of tax favoured option scheme structures, which are relevant if the scheme meets certain statutory conditions and where necessary is approved by HM Revenue & Customs:

- enterprise management incentive (EMI) schemes;
- company share option plans (CSOPs);
- share incentive plans (SIPs);
- save as you earn option plans (SAYE or Sharesave plans).

Each of these plans has its own rules and notably limits on the value of the shares which may be subject to the option. If the executive acquires shares pursuant to one of these schemes in accordance with the relevant terms, he will normally avoid the charge to income tax on exercise of the options and be liable only for capital gains tax. Changes to the capital gains tax regime with effect from April 2008 (which have been announced) may make such schemes more attractive.

Some employers establish phantom share options. Such a scheme does not involve the use of actual shares: instead, cash bonuses are paid based on increases in the value of notional shares credited to employees. The bonuses are taxed as salary.

A provision for share options should ideally not be contained within the service agreement but should be set out in a side letter or collateral contract. This will reduce the risk of a claim for compensation for loss of share options in the event that the executive's contract is wrongfully terminated, although the contract should also include specific wording excluding liability to that effect (*Micklefield v SAC Technology Ltd* [1991] 1 All ER 275).

When devising a scheme, the company should consider the rules governing eligibility (e.g. open to all or key employees only), the qualifying criteria (e.g. subject to performance conditions, and if so what those conditions should be), and the rules on disposal and forfeiture of unvested options. The national insurance and the accounting treatment of the options will also be relevant. Companies listed on the Stock Exchange or on AIM should also ensure that they abide by the guidelines issued by the Association of British Insurers (or can justify not doing so).

In terms of forfeiture, a distinction is usually drawn between a 'good leaver' (termination without cause) and a 'bad leaver' (termination for cause/gross misconduct). Termination without cause will usually include cessation of employment on grounds such as death, redundancy, retirement or ill-health. Most schemes will usually provide that the options will lapse automatically should an employee resign, although some schemes confer a discretion on the compensation committee, to be exercised on a case-by-case basis. A clause providing for automatic termination of options is likely to be construed as only applying where the employment was lawfully terminated, otherwise the employer would be allowed to take advantage of its own wrong (*Levett v Biotrace International Plc* [1999] ICR 818).

Share options are often linked with a change of control clauses. Share options are commonly triggered in the following ways:

(a) on a change of control (no termination of employment is required) – single trigger;

(b) on a change of control where the executive's employment is terminated and the executive is a good-leaver – double trigger; and

(c) on a change of control provided the executive remains in employment for a specified period: however, the executive may leave within a 30-60 day period provided that the departure is on a good-leaver basis – modified single trigger.

Corporate change (clause 17)

Change of control provisions entitle senior executives to enhanced severance packages in the event of the company being taken over or merged. They are also known as "golden parachute clauses". Historically, the justification for change of control clauses was that they provided security to directors who would not otherwise join or remain in the company. Such provisions have in recent years fallen out of favour with shareholders, for the following reasons:

- directors' contracts often include long notice periods;
- the new owners of the company may only terminate a director's employment without notice only if there are grounds for summary dismissal;

- directors who are demoted after a takeover can resign, claim constructive dismissal and seek damages consistent with their loss.

Typically, the "change of control clause" will provide that in the event of the company transferring control of the business to another company and the corporate change resulting in the executive's dismissal or a material reduction in his responsibilities, the executive will be entitled to a lump sum payment, sometimes known as a "liquidated damages" payment. If the payment seems to be excessive and out of proportion to the benefit to the company, it can be challenged by shareholders on a number of grounds, including the following:

- the payment breaches sections 171 to 174 CA 2006;
- the payment is a penalty clause, not a liquidated damages payment; and
- the payment was put in place to act as a "poisoned pill" to deter a potential takeover bidder.

Rule 21 of the City Code on Takeovers and Mergers provides that companies that are the targets of bona fide offers, or that expect to be so imminently, must not enter into a contract "otherwise than in the ordinary course of business" unless they have obtained the prior approval of shareholders in general meeting. This restriction captures any variation to a service agreement which constitutes an abnormal increase in emoluments or a significant improvement in the terms of service.

Thus, if the Remuneration Committee believes that the change of control provisions are necessary for the executive, it is advisable for the Committee to minute the reasons why and to ensure that the amount of the proposed payment is a genuine pre-estimate of the executive's loss. There are two suggested drafting options:

- Option 1 – within a specified period after a change of control, this clause allows the executive to serve notice upon the company to terminate his contract.
- Option 2 – this clause allows the company to offer the executive alternative employment in the event that the formation of the company changes in any way which results in the termination of the executive's original service agreement.

Identifying the "sticks"

Conditions of employment

The company should ensure that before the executive commences employment, there are no barriers to prevent him from joining or from performing his contractual duties. The following merit discussion:

- the need for a UK work permit;
- pre-existing restrictive covenants;
- references;
- professional qualifications.

Ideally, these risks should be flushed out in the executive's conditional offer letter (see Appendix A) and within the service agreement. If the conditions are not met, the offer of employment can be withdrawn by the company. If the executive has already commenced employment, the company, should be able to either claim damages, if a false warranty has been given by the executive, or terminate the executive's employment on grounds of gross misconduct (dishonesty) or illegality (see Chapter 8).

Work permit

- Clause 2.6 – the executive should be required to warrant that he is eligible to work in the United Kingdom, and this should be supported by the company having sight of original relevant documents confirming the executive's eligibility to work lawfully in the UK. Under the Immigration, Asylum and Nationality Act 2006, a civil penalty of up to £10,000 can be imposed on companies who employ illegal workers. The company will not be liable to the fine if it can show that it complied with any "prescribed requirements" and did not know that the employee was not eligible to work in the UK. The prescribed requirements require the company to see certain documents, verify, retain, copy or record the content of such documents produced and/or take steps prior to, or at specified intervals, or on specified occasions during, employment. It is also a criminal offence to knowingly use or exploit illegal workers.

Inclusion of the warranty puts the onus on to the executive to prove that he is entitled to work in the UK.

Pre-existing covenants

- Clause 2.5 – the executive is usually required to warrant that there are no restrictions which would prevent him from joining the company. He should also be required to indemnify the company against any claims by his former employer/s against the company for the economic tort of interference and/or inducing a breach of contract.

References

References should be obtained prior to the executive commencing employment, but if this is not possible, it should be made clear that the company reserves the right to terminate the executive's employment summarily, should a reference prove unsatisfactory to the company.

Professional qualifications and regulatory authorisation

Depending on the executive's role on the board, he may be required to hold a professional qualification or be authorised to act by a regulatory body. Under section 19 FSMA 2000, any person who carries on a regulated activity in the UK must be authorised by the Financial Services Authority, or exempt. Breach of section 19 may be a criminal offence and punishable on indictment by a maximum term of two years' imprisonment and/or a fine.

- Clause 2.7 – this clause places a positive obligation on the executive to keep the company informed should he no longer continue to hold a relevant qualification or no longer be an "authorised person".

Probationary period

- Clause 2.3 – although probationary periods are not always applicable for senior executives, it is prudent for the company to have the benefit of a probationary period wherever possible.

A probationary period provides a passage of time within which both parties have the opportunity to review the working relationship. Such probationary periods are commonly between three and six months.

At the end of the probationary period, both parties should meet to review their respective positions. The company should reserve the right to extend the probationary period at its absolute discretion. However, should the probationary period come to an end without the company taking any active steps to extend it, a further period of probation cannot be implied in the service agreement (*Przbylska v Modus Telecom Limited* EAT 6.2.07 (0566/06)).

Obligations during employment

The executive owes various obligations to the company. His statutory duties are those set out in Chapter 1. His express contractual duties are those that are set out in the service agreement. In addition, the executive also owes a number of implied duties to the company. The following is a non-exhaustive list of implied duties:

- the executive should be ready, willing and able to work;
- the executive has to exercise reasonable competence in his role;
- the executive has to take reasonable care in the performance of his duties and to indemnify the company for any loss suffered as a result of his incompetence (*Lister v Romford Ice and Cold Storage Co Ltd* [1957] AC 555);
- the executive has to comply with the reasonable and lawful orders or instructions of the company in relation to duties normally falling within the scope of his job (*Haden v Cowen* [1982] IRLR 314);
- the executive owes the company a duty of good faith and fidelity during his employment (*Faccenda Chicken Limited v Fowler* [1986] 3 WLR 288). For example, the executive may not work in competition with the company during employment;
- the executive must not disclose to third parties the company's confidential information and trade secrets obtained during the course of, and as a result of, his employment (*Bents Brewery Co Ltd v Hogan* [1945] 2 All ER 570). Neither may the executive use the company's confidential information for his own purposes (*Cranleigh Precision Engineering v Bryant* [1964] 3 All ER 289);
- where the executive is a director and owes a fiduciary duty to act in the best interests of the company, he has a duty to report his own wrongdoing and also the misconduct of other employees (*Fassihi and others v Item Software* (UK) Ltd [2004] EWCA Civ 1244);
- where the executive is a senior employee but not a director, he is also under a duty to report the misconduct of other employees (*Sybron Corporation v Rochem Limited* [1983] 2 All ER 707);
- the executive may have a duty to disclose health and safety failures under regulation 14 of the Management of Health and Safety at Work Regulations 1999 (SI 1999/3242).

- Clause 3 – this contains a list of the executive's express and implied duties and obligations. The clause reminds the executive of the express duties that are owed to the company during employment; limits any outside activities which may interfere with the executive's proper performance of his duties and places a positive duty on him to act in the company's best interests.

- Clause 3.1.8 – this requires the executive to report his own wrongdoing as well as any wrongdoing of other employees. In *Tesco Stores Limited v Pook & ors* [2004] IRLR 618 the High Court found that senior employees have a positive fiduciary duty to disclose their own misconduct. However, it is unclear how senior an employee needs to be in order to come within the fiduciary duty, or the extent of the duty (for example, what constitutes the type of misconduct a senior employee needs to disclose).

- Clause 3.2.1 – this allows the company to make the executive's services available to another group company without requiring the executive's specific consent. In such circumstances, the executive would retain the same terms of employment and his continuity of employment would remain unbroken (section 218(b), ERA 1996). The company should be wary of any long-term assignment, in case it creates an intra-company TUPE transfer for the purposes of regulation 3(1)(a) of the Transfer of Undertakings (Protection of Employment) Regulations 2006 (SI 2006/246).

Place of work (Clause 3)

The company should consider carefully where it wishes the executive to be primarily based. Usually, there will be one main place of work but the company must also consider whether the executive will be required to work in any group company offices or client offices within or outside the UK.

- Clauses 3.1.9 and 3.1.10 – these give the company the flexibility to move the executive anywhere within a reasonable distance. However, the mobility clause must be exercised reasonably. The company should consult with the executive over any proposed relocation. In *United Bank v Akhtar* [1989] IRLR 507 Mr Akhtar was required to move in accordance with a mobility clause. However, he was given very little notice and the bank chose not to exercise its discretion to assist him with relocation expenses. The EAT held that this amounted to a fundamental breach of three implied terms:
  - that the employers would give reasonable notice of any transfer;
  - that the employers would not exercise the discretion to provide relocation expenses in a way which makes the performance by the employee of his obligations to move impossible;
  - that the employer would not act in a way that undermines mutual trust and confidence.

  In the absence of a specific mobility clause, there is a limited right for the company to make a temporary change to an employee's place of work.

Where there is a mobility clause, the company should also consider creating a relocation policy. A relocation policy would typically contain rules on:

- positions eligible for relocation;
- journey time and/or distance criteria for entitlement to relocation assistance;
- relocation expenses that are eligible for financial assistance (e.g. mortgage assistance, disruption compensation);
- rules for reclaiming relocation expenses;

- basis for calculating the amount payable;
- length of notice of relocation;
- length of time the employee must remain in position in order not to be liable for repaying relocation assistance.

Interests in other businesses (clause 4)

- Clause 4 – whereas clause 3 gives the company control of the executive's activities during his working hours, this clause goes a step further and looks at the executive's general interests. The company can limit the executive's interest in other businesses, especially where they are likely to be in direct competition with the company. The company may wish to provide a carve-out for non-competing interests. It is usual to allow the executive to hold for investment purposes up to between three per cent and five per cent of the shares in a listed company.

Hours of work (clause 5)

As a worker, the executive is protected by the regulation 4 of the Working Time Regulations 1998 (SI 1998/1833) (WTR 1998) which provides that he may not work in excess of 48 hours per week. This is calculated over a standard 17-week reference period, although it may be extended to 52 weeks by a collective or workforce agreement.

Workers may, however, contract out of the maximum 48-hour working week (regulation 5 WTR 1998) but they have a right to "opt-in" by giving the company notice (such notice cannot exceed three months).

The company must decide whether it requires the executive to work a set number of hours per week or to give him autonomy over how he carries out his duties. In either scenario, it is more likely than not that it would become necessary for the executive to opt out of the 48 hour working week limit. If the executive determines the whole of his working time, he may fall within the regulation 20(1) WTR 1998 exception, which means that there is no requirement for him to opt out of the 48-hour limit. This may, however, be an unattractive prospect for the company if it is concerned that the executive may be a workaholic.

Confidentiality (clause 11)

The company will need to protect its confidential information both during and after the executive's employment. Disputes often centre on what the executive is allowed to take with him after the employment has ended and what legitimately belongs to the company.

There is an implied duty of confidentiality in every contract of employment.

There are two types of information which deserve protection:

- information which the employee must treat as confidential (either because he is expressly told that it is confidential or because from its character it obviously is so) but which remains in his head and becomes part of his own skill and knowledge in the course of his employment; and
- specific trade secrets so confidential that, even though they may necessarily have been learned by heart, they cannot lawfully be used for anyone's benefit but the employer's.

In *Faccenda Chicken v Fowler* [1987] Ch 117, the Court of Appeal held that whether a particular type of information constitutes a "trade secret" depends on all the circumstances of the case including, but not limited to:

- the nature of the executive's employment;
- the nature of the information;
- whether the company impressed on the executive the confidentiality of the information; and
- whether such information may be easily isolated from other information which the executive is free to use or disclose.

Generally, "objective knowledge" belongs to the company and may be protected, but "subjective knowledge" belongs to the executive. When applying the "objective" and "subjective" test, the courts may look at the honesty of the employee (*Printers & Finishers Ltd v Holloway* [1965] 1 WLR 1) In *FSS Travel & Leisure Systems Ltd v Johnson* [1998] IRLR 382, such a test was approved by the Court of Appeal. However, in *SBJ Stephenson Ltd v Mandy* [2000] IRLR 233, the High Court held that the proper distinction to make is not a mechanistic one between information in the employee's head and information deliberately learned in order to be used later. The Court relied on the House of Lord's distinction in the case of *Herbert Morris Ltd v Saxelby* [1916] 1 AC 688, HL between 'objective knowledge' which is the employer's property (even when residing in the employee's own memory), and 'subjective knowledge' such as the employee's own abilities, skill, aptitudes, etc., which remain his. In the *Mandy* case, the client list which SBJ was seeking to protect constituted "objective knowledge", which was a legitimate interest capable of protection.

The implied duty not to misuse confidential information endures after the executive's employment has ended only if the information amounts to a 'trade secret' (*Wallace Bogan & Co. v Cove & Ors* [1997] IRLR 453). There is no guarantee that the executive's knowledge will always amount to a "trade secret" and thus be protected by the common law (*AT Poeton (Gloucester Plating) Ltd v Horton* [2000] ICR 1208, CA).

To avoid this uncertainty, the company should always ensure that the service agreement contains an express confidentiality covenant. An express clause is more likely to act as a deterrent to the executive and his future employer if they know that there is a risk of being sued. Confidential information should be carefully defined in the service agreement (see Schedule 2) and reviewed regularly to ensure that the information defined reflects the reality of the business and is wide enough to encapsulate any new confidential information which has come about since employment commenced.

Where the company is unable to prove misuse of confidential information by the executive, the Copyright and Rights in Database Regulations 1997 (SI 1997/3032) (the Database Regulations) may be helpful. The Database Regulations implement the EC Database Directive 96/9/EC ("Database Directive"). The Regulations are useful where the executive has taken parts of a computer database, typically customer or supplier lists belonging to the company.

A database is "a collection of independent works, data or other materials" which:

- are "arranged in a systematic or methodical way", and
- are "individually accessible by electronic or other means".

This is a broad definition, and is likely to cover most computer systems which contain lists of contacts and the like.

Not every "database" qualifies for protection under the Database Regulations. Such a right subsists only if "there has been substantial investment in obtaining, verifying or presenting the contents of the database". "Investment" is also given an expanded meaning and "includes any investment, whether of financial, human or technical resources".

The "maker" of the database is the first owner of the right. The "maker" is usually "the person who takes the initiative in obtaining, verifying or presenting the contents of a database and assumes the risk of investing in that obtaining, verification or presentation shall be regarded as the maker of, and as having made, the database". In a typical employer/employee relationship, this person would nearly always be the company. However, the point is put beyond doubt by regulation 14(2) of the Database Regulations, which provides that where a database is made by an employee in the course of his employment, "his employer shall be regarded as the maker of the database", unless there is an agreement to the contrary.

A person infringes the right if, without the consent of the owner, he "extracts or re-utilises all or a substantial part of the contents of a database". "Extraction" means "the permanent or temporary transfer of" any of the contents of a database "to another medium by any means or in any form". This would very probably cover most means by which an employee might take parts of a database: downloading it, copying it to disc, sending it by email, or printing it out.

"Re-utilisation" means making the contents of a database "available to the public by any means". This is unlikely to be relevant to the type of case where a former employee wants to use the information for a new employer or a competing business of his own, but may be important where the employee is threatening to disclose the information to others.

"Substantial", in relation to any investment, extraction or re-utilisation, means "substantial in terms of quantity or quality or a combination of both". This is a concept derived from copyright, and likely to be interpreted in a similar way. It is well established that the question of whether there has been "substantial" copying is not determined simply by mechanically comparing the proportion of the work copied to the total of the work – the question is whether, having regard to both the nature and quantity of the copying, an important or significant part of the work has been used.

Even if the individual extraction is insubstantial, the Database Regulations also provide that repeated and systematic extraction or re-utilisation of insubstantial parts of the contents of a database may amount to the extraction or re-utilisation of a substantial part of those contents. The combined effect of these provisions is that in many employment cases, such as where the executive has downloaded a customer list, or details of pricing or tendering information, from the company's computer system, the employer may well be entitled to sue for infringement of its database right.

The database right can be a more attractive way of protecting proprietary information belonging to the company. A claim can be made irrespective of considerations of confidentiality and duration of confidence and the originality of the information. The legal claim focuses on the existence or not of "a substantial investment in obtaining, verifying or presenting the contents of the database". Because infringement in this context is demonstrated by extraction or reutilisation of all or a substantial part of the company's database, proof of such a right should be comparatively easy. In terms of remedy, the company has the potential of seeking damages as a final remedy or delivery up of its database and springboard injunctions as an interim remedy. In *Fixtures Marketing Ltd v Svenska Spel AB*, Case C-203/02, 9 November 2004, the ECJ adopted a narrow interpretation of the Database Directive. It held that to acquire database right protection, the employer's investment in the database has to be of the right sort. "Investment" must refer to investment in the creation of the database itself. Resources used to seek out existing independent materials and collect them in a database were relevant, but not resources used to create materials or data. Further, "infringement" has to involve wholesale or substantial copying from the database.

- Clause 11.1 – when drafting, the company should ensure that the wording covers all types of proprietary information which it considers confidential and to which the executive would have access.
- Clause 11.2 – this clause widens the definition of what is classified as confidential information.

- Clause 11.3 – if information is in the public domain, the company can no longer claim that it is confidential. However, the executive can be penalised if it is his wrongful actions which have allowed this confidential information to become publicised.
- Clause 11.4 – this clause places a positive obligation on the executive during and after employment to assist the company in ensuring information remains con fidential.

Records (clause 11)

This clause places a limit on information which the executive may take and what must be returned at the end of the employment relationship. This will assist the company in protecting its confidential information.

Intellectual property (clause 13)

An intellectual property clause is relevant where the executive will be involved in creating some form of process or invention which could prove invaluable to the company and which the company would want to retain even after the executive's employment has terminated. If this is unlikely, it may be possible for the company to insert a shortened clause.

"Intellectual property" and "executive intellectual property"

The definition of "intellectual property" has been broadly drafted with a view to capturing all existing, vested and contingent intellectual property rights throughout the world. It includes on a non-exhaustive basis specific references to the main types of intellectual property recognised under English law, but if the executive is intended to carry out any work for any group company in any jurisdiction other than the United Kingdom, it would be prudent to supplement this list by reference to any other type of intellectual property that is recognised by the laws of that jurisdiction but not recognised by English law.

The definition of "executive intellectual property" has been also very broadly drafted in order to capture intellectual property rights in work created by the executive, whether or not during his normal working hours and whether or not using company facilities.

- Clause 13.1 – this clause places an obligation on the executive to immediately notify the company of the general nature of any Invention (as defined) made wholly or partially by him during their employment. With a view to being as favourable to the company as possible it is not limited to Inventions that are made during normal working hours or using the facilities of the company or any Group Company.

With regard to the reference to section 39 of the Patents Act 1977 (PA 1977), see the commentary on clause 13.2 below.

- Clause 13.2 – under the Patents Act 1977, any invention made by an employee shall (as between him and his employer) be taken to belong to the employee (section 39(2)), other than in two specified situations, in which case the invention shall be taken to belong to the employer (section 39(1) PA 1977). These two specified situations are if the invention:
  - was made in the course of the normal duties of the employee or in the course of duties falling outside his normal duties, but specifically assigned to him, and the circumstances in either case were such that an invention might reasonably be expected to result from the carrying out of his duties (section 39(1)(a) PA 1977); or
  - was made in the course of the duties of the employee and, at the time of making the invention, because of the nature of his duties and the particular responsibilities arising from the nature of his duties, he had a special obligation to further the interests of the employer's undertaking (section 39(1)(b) PA 1977).

  These provisions cannot be overridden by contract, and these clauses have therefore been drafted with a view to giving maximum rights to the company within the constraints referred to above.
- Clause 13.3 – this clause obliges the executive to make full written disclosure of any Invention if required to do so by the company or any Group Company, and (if so requested) to assist them in applying for patent protection for such Invention.

Under section 40 of the Patents Act 1977, an employee who has made a patented invention is entitled to apply for statutory compensation to be paid by the employer where it is "just" that he should receive that compensation. The two situations stipulated by the section are:

(a) where the invention belongs to the employer, and the invention and/or the patent are of "outstanding benefit" to the employer (section 40(1) PA 1977); and

(b) where the invention belongs to the employee, and the employee's rights in it have been assigned or exclusively licensed by him to the employer, and the employee's benefit from that assignment or licence is "inadequate in relation to the benefit derived by the employer from … it" (section 40(2) PA 1977).

- Clause 13.4 – although UK legislation provides that certain intellectual property rights in work created by employees will *prima facie* vest in their employers, subject to agreement to the contrary (for example, the copyright in literary, dramatic, musical, artistic and film works created by employees), clause 13.4 is intended to provide an express contractual stipulation that, with the exception of entitlement to employee patents as discussed above, all intellectual property rights in work created by the executive will be the entitlement of the company or the group company.

- Clauses 13.5 and 13.6 – these are standard-form and widely drafted covenants for further assurance on the part of the executive designed to ensure that the rights referred to in clause 13.4 will be assigned to the company or group company, and also that the executive will be obliged at the company's expense to assist in maintaining or protecting those rights.
- Clause 13.7 – moral rights are statutory rights that arise in favour of the creators of most types of work protected by copyright. Since they cannot be assigned, this clause provides for the executive to waive them in favour of the company or any group company.
- Clause 13.8 – the purpose of this clause is to oblige the executive during employment, to assist the company or any group company with protecting and enforcing its intellectual property, and also in defending itself against claims made for infringement of third party intellectual property.
- Clause 13.9 – this clause is intended to contain an acknowledgement by the executive that, other than to the extent provided by law (see above), the executive is entitled to no further compensation in respect of his compliance with clause 12.
- Clause 13.10 – this is a standard-form appointment by the executive of the company to be his attorney to execute the documents and do things necessary to give the company the benefit of clause 13 in the event that he is unwilling or unable to execute those documents or do those things himself.
- Clause 13.12 – this clause brings the executive within the parameters of section 39(1)(b) of the Patents Act 1977, as discussed above.

Termination of directorship and employment (clause 15)

It is important for the company to decide whether the executive's "office" as director should drive the contractual relationship, or whether his "employment" as an executive should drive the relationship instead. By making it clear what happens to the remaining contractual relationship should the executive cease to wear one of the two hats, this will avoid potential claims for unfair dismissal if the executive is required to step down from the board or if his employment terminates (see *Mountain Spring Water Co Ltd v Colesby* [2005] UKEAT/0855/04) and *Cobley v Forward Industries Technology Ltd* [2003] IRLR 706.

Two options are available under clause 15.1:

- Option 1: the executive's "office" as a director dominates the contractual relationship and the company has a choice as to whether it wishes the executive to remain in employment as an "employee" on cessation of his office.

- Option 2: the executive's "employment" dominates the contractual relationship. The clause establishes the period of notice required to be given by either party to terminate the employment relationship. It also allows the company an absolute discretion as to whether or not to make a payment in lieu of notice.

Under clauses 15.5 and 15.5.4, the executive is required to resign from his office if his employment is terminated by the company.

- Clause 15.2 – this allows the company to terminate the executive's employment summarily or with statutory minimum notice only. Save for circumstances where the executive has committed an act of gross misconduct, the executive should, in all other cases, be given his statutory minimum notice to avoid a wrongful dismissal claim.
- Clause 15.3 – see Chapter 6 for further discussion on retirement.
- Clause 15.4 – this clause allows the company to terminate the executive's employment following long-term sickness absence on a reduced notice period However, if the executive has been absent for in excess of a year or his absence is likely to last a year or more, it is likely that he would be deemed "disabled" for the purposes of section 1 of the Disability Discrimination Act 1995. Therefore, care should be taken to minimise the risks of claims for disability discrimination and breach of contract where the executive is entitled to permanent health insurance.
- Clause 15.5 – this clause deals with the practicalities of the executive's departure. Clause 15.5.1 requires the executive to deliver up to the company all records and confidential information. Clause 15.5.3 allows the company to recoup any debts owed to it by the executive, and clause 15.5.4 requires the executive to resign any appointments upon the company's request.
- Clause 15.6 – this is an express reminder to the executive that he has ongoing obligations to the company even though his employment has come to an end.

Garden leave (clause 16)

Garden leave is an effective tool in protecting the company's legitimate business interests when notice for termination has been given. Sometimes it can be more beneficial than a post-termination restrictive covenant, as the company is able to immediately isolate the executive from the business to reduce the risk of competition with the company. The downside for the company is the financial cost of placing the executive on garden leave.

Where the service agreement does not provide for garden leave, the company will be unable to put the executive on garden leave absence without the executive's express consent, particularly in cases where there is a right to work (e.g. where the employee's skills require frequent exercise) (*William Hill v Tucker* [1998] IRLR 313). Clause 16.1

provides for an express contractual right to place the executive on garden leave once notice to end the employment relationship has been given by either party. It is also possible to have a form of garden leave clause applying at any time during the employment, although this is less common.

- Clauses 16.2 and 16.4 – during garden leave, the terms of the service agreement remain in place and therefore the executive continues to owe contractual and common law duties to the company. This will also mean that the executive is entitled to receive his remuneration and benefits during the notice period.
- Clause 16.5 – garden leave allows the company to require the executive not to undertake any work or contact existing or prospective clients during the period of notice. This allows the company to take the executive out of the market for a set period and enables the company to put in place its succession plan with its clients.

Retirement age (clause 15.4)

Under regulation 30(2) of the Employment Equality (Age) Regulations 2006 (EEAR 2006), retirement is a fair reason for dismissal. The Age Regulations allow employers to adopt a default retirement age of 65 where there is no normal retirement age. Compulsory retirement at a younger age will be unlawful unless it can be objectively justified, for example, on health and safety grounds. Therefore, without a good reason, the earliest time that the company is likely to be able to retire the executive is 65. That does not mean that the executive's employment cannot be terminated before 65, just not on grounds of retirement.

Directors can no longer be required to retire when they reach 70 years of age. The 70-year age limit for directors in sections 293 and 294 of the Companies Act 1985 has been repealed since 6 April 2007, and such limits should be removed from companies' articles of association. Consideration should also be given to removing directors' ages from annual reports. Although the mere disclosure of age would not, in itself, be discrimination, it could be used in evidence should the individual subsequently suffer a detriment (e.g. not being re-elected to the board) and claim age discrimination.

Provided that the statutory retirement procedure in Schedule 6 EEAR 2006 is followed by the company, it will not be discriminatory to retire the executive at or above the age of 65, provided that it is a genuine retirement.

Dismissal, disciplinary and grievance procedures (clause 17)

Since 1 October 2004 all employers, irrespective of size, have been required to have dismissal, disciplinary and grievance procedures which comply with the minimum statutory procedures set out in the Employment Act 2002. These apply to all employees (see Chapter 6). There is no legal requirement for the statutory procedures to form part of the executive's service agreement. Therefore, it should be made clear that the statutory procedures do not form part of the service agreement, otherwise failure to follow the procedure could give rise to a claim for breach of contract.

When drafting a dismissal, disciplinary and grievance policy in the company handbook, careful consideration must be given as to who would be charged with dealing with these procedures, to ensure impartiality, especially where the executive is a member of the board. NEDs and the members of the board of an associated company of the company can assist with the internal dispute resolution process.

Electronic communications (clause 19)

The executive is likely to have access to a number of forms of communication, such as e-mail, the internet, telephone systems, and fax systems. Any misuse or unauthorised access and/or use of the company's electronic communication can lead to breaches of confidentiality, corruption of data, fraud and criminal liability. Such breaches should be the subject of disciplinary action.

- Clause 19.2 – the company should ensure that it reserves an express right to monitor the executive's electronic communications. This is a useful tool especially where the company has a genuine belief that the executive is acting in breach of his contractual obligations. However, even with an express right, the company must still ensure that it complies with its duties under the Data Protection Act 1998 and its associated codes.

In particular, the company must also ensure that it complies with the Telecommunications (Lawful Business Practice) (Interception of Communications) Regulations 2000 (SI 2000/1337) (the Telecommunications Regulations), the Regulation of Investigatory Powers Act 2000 and the Human Rights Act 1998, when monitoring electronic communications of the executive.

Restrictive covenants (clause 14)

During employment, the executive will have access to the company's trade secrets, confidential information, key customer/client relationships and business strategies. Apart from the executive's contractual duty of confidentiality, the company should seek to protect these economic interests by requiring the executive to enter into non-competition covenants. The key areas that the company will need to protect are:

- trade secrets and confidential information;
- trade connections, customers, clients and suppliers; and
- the workforce.

Restrictive covenants are generally void as a matter of public policy as they are regarded as being in restraint of trade. In order for such covenants to be enforceable, they must not go beyond what is necessary to protect the company's legitimate business interests. The courts will examine the nature, scope and duration of the covenants when assessing if they are reasonable or enforceable.

Reasonableness

Reasonableness is judged at the time the contract is made (*Thomas v Farr plc* [2007] ICR 932), not on the facts applying at the time of enforcement (*NIS Fertilisers v Neville* [1986] 2 NIJB 70). However, in order for the covenant to remain enforceable, it must remain reasonable at all times. "For a restraint to be reasonable in the interests of the parties it must afford no more than adequate protection of the party in whose favour it is imposed" (*Herbert Morris Ltd v Saxelby* [1916] AC 688). This is to be judged by looking at the nature of the company's business and then at the position the executive held in the company.

Nature of the covenants

The reasonableness of the covenants depends on the nature of the restriction in question.

(a) Non-compete/area covenant (clause 14.5): the aim of such a covenant is to prevent the executive from competing with the company after the employment relationship has ended. Such a restriction is the most draconian and should be viewed with caution. Non-compete covenants will generally only be enforced so far as they seek to protect trade secrets and other sufficiently highly confidential information when confidentiality clauses would not offer adequate protection. The geographical limit should bear some relation to the geographical extent of the business. It is also important to consider how long the information remains confidential.

A non-compete clause must be specific in its scope and must not be too wide. In *Office Angels Ltd v Rainer-Thomas* [1991] IRLR 214, CA, an area restriction of 1,000 metres from the branch was held to be invalid, as the prohibition would have excluded most of Central London.

The company should also consider if the covenant can be limited to named key competitors. In *J A Mont (UK) Ltd v Mills* [1993] IRLR 172, a non-compete covenant was held unenforceable as it restricted the employee from working anywhere in the 'tissue industry', when his employment had only been in the paper tissue manufacturing industry. In *Thomas v Farr plc* [2007] EWCA Civ 118, the Court of Appeal held that in order to show that a non-compete clause was reasonably necessary to protect confidential information, the employer needed to show that at the time of the contract the nature of the proposed employment was such as would expose the employee to information of the kind capable of protection beyond the term of the contract. The company's interests were not adequately protected by a non-solicitation clause and a confidentiality clause, both of which would be difficult to police, and the judge had been entitled to conclude that the non-competition clause was a reasonable limitation. The employee's position as managing director exposed him to sensitive information that the employer had a legitimate interest in protecting after the employment relationship had ended.

Area covenants are popular for sales staff who have worked in regions where they have built up a good reputation with the company's customers, clients and/or suppliers. The covenant must be a reasonable way of protecting the legitimate business interest. For example, if the company's main business is drawn from a three-mile radius, it would be unreasonable to insist on a six-mile radius restraint. Further, if the catchment area is disproportionate to the number of customers the company has in that area, the area covenant may be hard to justify (*Spencer v Marchington* [1988] IRLR 392). In *Allan Janes LLP v Johal* [2006] EWHC 286 (Ch), [2006] IRLR 599, a six-mile radius restriction was held unenforceable as the radial restriction would serve mainly to protect the firm from competition for a vast amount of commercial entities which were not, or had well and truly ceased to be, clients of the firm.

(b) Non-poaching of employees (clause 14.4): the maintenance of a stable workforce has been held to be a legitimate and protectable interest (*Alliance Paper Group plc v Prestwich* [1996] IRLR 25). In *Dawnay Day & Co Ltd v de Braconier d'Alphen* [1997] IRLR 442, CA, the Court of Appeal held that "An employer's interest in maintaining a stable, trained workforce is one which he can properly protect within the limits of reasonableness by an undertaking of this sort when referring to the covenant in the contract under consideration."

However, the clause should be limited to those employees whose departure from the company could damage the company's business. In the case of *TSC Europe (UK) Ltd v Massey* [1999] IRLR 22, Ch D, the covenant was held unenforceable because it restricted the solicitation of all employees including those recruited after Massey's employment had terminated. It is also advisable to limit the covenant to those employees with whom the executive had direct dealings in the year prior to his departure from the company.

(c) Non-solicitation (clause 14.2): a non-solicitation clause is intended to prevent the executive from actively making contact with the company's customers, clients and/or suppliers. A non-solicitation covenant will be unenforceable if the executive has had no significant contact with the company's customers/clients. If the executive has been involved in negotiations with potential clients, it may be possible to prevent non-solicitation of prospective customers or clients, if those negotiations are more than likely to lead to business with the company (*International Consulting Services (UK) v*

Hart [2000] IRLR 227). Clause 14.2 extends the non-solicitation covenant to encompass prospective customers or clients of the company.

(d) Non-dealing (clause 14.3): a non-dealing clause is intended to prevent the executive from dealing with the company's customers, clients and/or suppliers if or when he is approached by them. This covenant is more difficult to enforce because it can often be argued that a non-solicitation covenant is all that is needed, unless it can be said that a non-solicitation covenant would be difficult to police. A non-dealing covenant may be appropriate where there is a strong relationship between the executive and the customer, client and/or supplier of the company. The mere fact that the customer no longer wishes to trade with the company does not act to defeat an enforceable covenant (*John Michael Design plc v Cooke* [1987] 2 All ER 332).

In *Beckett Investment Management Group Limited v Hall* [2007] IRLR 293, a 12-month non-dealing covenant was enforceable because of the employees' "enormous importance" to the success of the business and the difficulty in replacing them. The Court of Appeal rejected the contention that the client's choice was restricted, as they had the option to move to another service provider.

To improve the reasonableness of the covenant, the covenant should be restricted to customers, clients and/or suppliers of the company with whom the executive had material or personal dealings.

Duration of covenant

There is no set formula as to what is a reasonable duration for a covenant. The covenant should only be as long as it adequately needed to protect the company's legitimate business interests not simply to ward off fair competition. As a rule of thumb, non-compete covenants of up to 12 months' duration are potentially enforceable (*Beckett Investment Management Group Limited v Hall* [2007] IRLR 293, *Thomas v Farr Plc* [2007] EWCA Civ 118). That is not to say that the covenant cannot be longer than 12 months, but the company will need to establish a very good business reason for a longer period to apply instead. Where the executive is also a shareholder, lengthier covenants (up to five years) are usually incorporated in the shareholders' agreement.

Interpreting the covenants

The courts will try to interpret the words used in a reasonable fashion so as to give effect to the intentions of the parties. The covenant must be clear and certain. Words used are to be given their ordinary meaning (*Mallan v May* (1844) 13 M&W). In *Spafax (1965) Limited v Dommett* [1972] 116 Sol Jo 711 the term "customer" was held to be too uncertain, but in *Dawnay Day & Co Ltd v de Braconier d'Alphen & Others* [1997] IRLR, CA, the phrase "senior employee" in a non-poaching covenant was found sufficiently certain.

The courts are not allowed to rewrite covenants, although they can delete an unenforceable provision from a contract, leaving a valid and enforceable provision (the "blue pencil test"). In *Sadler v Imperial Life Assurance Co of Canada Ltd* [1988] IRLR 388, the court established conditions for the application of blue pencilling:

- the unenforceable provision is capable of being removed without the necessity of adding to or modifying the wording of what remains;
- the remaining terms continue to be supported by adequate consideration; and
- the removal of the unenforceable provision does not so change the character of the contract that it becomes "not the sort of contract that the parties entered into at all".

This formulation was approved by the Court of Appeal in *Beckett Investment Management Group Limited & Others v Hall* [2007] IRLR 293. Clause 14.12 makes express provision for "blue pencilling".

Definitions (clause 14.1)

It is essential to ensure that the definitions of key terms within the covenants accurately reflect the business interests which require protection. The tighter the drafting, the greater the likelihood that the covenants will be enforceable.

When considering the scope of the definitions that will apply to the covenants, the company should consider, amongst other things:

- The nature of the business in which the executive will be involved.
- Who are the relevant customers, clients and/or suppliers and what exposure will the executive have to them. Will the executive have power or authority to influence these entities after their employment with the company has terminated?
- Will the executive be bringing customers, clients and/or suppliers with them?
- Which geographical area does the business and the executive operate within?
- Is there likely to be any material change in the type of business, relevant customers, clients and/or suppliers, or in the area where the business in which the executive is involved?
- Will the executive be required to perform duties for any group company?
- What is the scope of the executive's duties?
- Will the executive have employees reporting to them, and would those employees' departures from the company cause any major disruption or damage to the business?
- What trade secrets or confidential information will the executive have access to, and how long must this information remain protected?

Extension of the covenant to group companies (clause 14.9)

If it is the intention of the company to extend the protection of the covenants to group companies, this should be made clear in the service agreement. However in *Beckett Investment Management Group Limited v Hall* [2007] IRLR 293, the fact that the covenants only expressly referred to the employer holding company, and not the subsidiaries through whom the relevant business was transacted, was not fatal. Citing *Littlewoods Organisation Limited v Harris* [1977] 1 WLR 1472, the Court of Appeal ruled that the "law had to have regard to the realities of big business". Adopting a purist approach would lead to the result that the parties understood that they were entering into a "pointless provision". The Court of Appeal held in *Beckett* that absence of a reference to the subsidiary companies did not affect the enforceability of the non-dealing covenant. The Court of Appeal reached this conclusion notwithstanding that express reference was made to the subsidiary companies in other provisions of the contract.

The company should ensure that it extends or reserves an express right to extend the protection afforded in the covenants to any group company by obliging the executive to enter into further obligations if necessary.

Disclosure of covenants to competitor (clause 14.10)

Requiring the executive to provide a copy of the covenants in the service agreement to his prospective employer brings a number of advantages. Firstly, as the executive is under a contractual duty of disclosure, this minimises unlawful competition by him. Secondly, the disclosure puts the new employer (poacher) on notice that employing the executive in breach of his post-termination covenants would be unlawful and might result in the immediate withdrawal of the executive's job offer. Thirdly, flagrant disregard of the notice can strengthen any potential action by the company against the new employer.

Offsetting garden leave against restrictive covenants (clause 14.11)

It is advisable to consider reducing the length of the covenants by the length of time the executive has spent on garden leave, especially where the covenant is of a substantial duration. As there is no automatic right of set-off between the period covered by a restrictive covenant and a period of garden leave, clause 14.11 captures this potential mischief.

Legal advice

The fact that the executive had an opportunity to take legal advice will not be determinative of the reasonableness of the covenant, but it is still a factor that may be taken into account by the courts.

Standard clauses

Parties

The contracting parties in the service agreement must be clearly identified. Where there is a complicated corporate structure, consideration should be given as to which company will employ and pay the executive. It may be that the holding company is the employer, in which case there must be scope in the service agreement for the executive's services to be provided to the employer's group companies.

Interpretation

Clause 1 sets out the key definitions in a service agreement. These include the following.

AIM/FSA/UK listing authority

In a listed company, the executive will be regulated not only by contractual provisions in the service agreement but also by regulatory authorities. This needs to be made clear so the executive is aware of the full extent of his contractual and statutory obligations.

Board

Who has decision making powers over the operation of the service agreement should be clearly defined. The proposed definition extends to the board of directors of the company or any group company including any duly appointed committee or sub-committee.

Confidential information

This definition covers the standard types of confidential information but should be reviewed from time to time to capture any changes in or to the company's proprietary information.

Group company

This definition is captures the scope of the obligations that are owed by the executive to the company and its associated companies, for example, in relation to his contractual duties, intellectual property rights, confidentiality and restrictive covenants.

Data protection (clause 20)

During employment, the company will collect personal data about the executive. The Data Protection Act 1998 (DPA 1998) restricts employers from processing "sensitive personal data" without the explicit consent of the employee. This includes information on racial origin, political opinions, membership of trade unions, physical or mental health, sexual life and criminal history. The company is however, allowed to process personal sensitive data in order to perform a legal obligation. This may include, amongst other things, recording details of the executive's sickness record for sick pay purposes; holding bank details to pay salary, or asking the executive to indicate their racial or ethnic background in order to monitor equal opportunities in the workplace.

In holding and processing the executive's personal data, the company should ensure that the personal data is:

- fairly and lawfully processed;
- processed for lawful purposes;
- adequate, relevant and not excessive in relation to the purpose for which the data is being held or processed;
- accurate and up-to-date;
- not kept longer than necessary to achieve its lawful purpose;
- processed in accordance with the executive's rights;
- secure, so that it cannot be unlawfully processed or easily lost or destroyed; and
- where possible, not transferred to a country outside the European Union without adequate protection. If data transfer is likely to occur outside the European Union, the wording must be widened to allow for this.

If the executive suffers a loss as a result of the company's breach of the DPA 1998, damages may be awarded. The executive may suffer a loss if inaccurate data held leads to a dismissal, if false information has been included in a reference or if inaccurate information causes the executive loss.

Notices (clause 21)

This clause stipulates the method of communication between the parties during and on termination of termination.

Former service agreements (clause 22)

This is an entire agreement clause. It significantly reduces the risk of arguable claims being brought outside the service agreement. Drafted properly, such clauses will prevent allegations of oral or written agreements that have not been incorporated in the service agreement. An entire agreement clause is not effective in itself to exclude a claim for misrepresentation, although a statement by the executive that no representations have been relied on other than those contained in the contract will usually present a formidable obstacle. Clause 22 is likely to be relevant where following oral negotiations, the executive is promoted to a new position or where new benefits are agreed leading to a revised service agreement.

Power of attorney (clause 23)

A power of attorney allows the executive to assign his authority for the company to act in his name. Such a clause is usually for the company's benefit and is aimed at preventing the executive unduly holding up the company's affairs. However, such a power cannot simply be used to override an objection from the executive. Clause 23.2 places a positive obligation on the company to seek the executive's consent prior to exercising the power of attorney.

The service agreement should be executed as a deed if it contains power of attorney provisions. Power of attorney provisions are likely to be included if the executive is a director or if an intellectual property assignment clause is included.

Governing law and jurisdiction (clause 25)

The service agreement should be governed by English law. In addition, the company should decide where disputes on the service agreement should be heard.

A "jurisdiction clause" enables the parties to agree which country's or countries' courts are to have jurisdiction to hear disputes arising from the service agreement. The parties may decide to confer either exclusive or non-exclusive jurisdiction on the chosen courts.

- A choice of exclusive jurisdiction will prevent one party from bringing proceedings against the other in the courts of any country other than the country set out in the agreement (in this case, England and Wales). Were that party to do so, the other party would be entitled to have the proceedings stayed.
- A choice of non-exclusive jurisdiction will enable either party to bring proceedings against the other either in the courts of the chosen country, or in the courts of any other country which have jurisdiction over the dispute under their own jurisdictional rules. The suing party need not first bring proceedings in the country designated as having non-exclusive jurisdiction.

Execution

It is common for the service agreement to be executed as a deed, especially where it contains a power of attorney.

Section 44, CA 2006, which comes into force on 6 April 2008, will provide that a document will be validly executed if:

- the company affixes its common seal; or
- the service agreement is signed on behalf of the company by either two authorised signatories or a single director in the presence of a witness. Authorised signatories are the company's directors and, if there is one, the company secretary.

If the service agreement is executed by deed and there is no company secretary, the service agreement will need to be witnessed.

PART 2

TERMINATION OF THE EXECUTIVE RELATIONSHIP

CHAPTER **5**

Risk management of claims

Boardroom dynamics

There is nothing that the media love more than a juicy boardroom wrangle. Stories of corporate espionage, power struggles, empire-building, change management and succession battles are often reported in the press. A breakdown of relationship "at the top" of companies can damage shareholders' and investors' confidence in the organisation, if left unresolved.

Whilst a culture of open communication, organisation and an experienced chairman can help to create a happy and effective board, no company is immune from boardroom fall-outs. The two main reasons boards fall out are lack of clarity about their respective roles, and a lack of candour and openness. The relationship between executives and non-executives is one particular source of division where there is a mismatch in expectations between the two sides. Non-executives see their role primarily as getting the executive directors to account to the shareholders, whereas the executive directors believe they should behave as more collegiate members of the board. Boardroom disputes also arise because of ego, which is inevitable when powerful people are brought together to lead a company. Other causes of disputes include disagreements over the company's strategy, poor personal relationships, leaking information outside the boardroom or to the press, conflicts of interest between departmental needs – the so-called "empire-building", and any dealings between the company and a private business owned by one of the directors. Concern as to whether the board is meeting its legal responsibilities is another risk area, as are disputes over terms of employment and remuneration packages.

If there is a fundamental and irreconcilable disagreement on the board, the commercial reality for many companies is that the company and the disaffected executive would have to part ways.

Exit management

The exit management of senior executives is one that requires particular care, as such individuals are in a unique position. The executive has rights as a director and as an employee and, every so often, as a shareholder also. In any exit strategy, a careful analysis of the company's desire to terminate the relationship on the one hand must be measured against the executive's legal rights and any associated liabilities which may flow from the termination. It is vital to risk-manage the proposed exit to ensure that the process is smooth and to have in place damage limitation measures, should the exit become litigious.

The process can be divided into three parts: structuring the basis for the executive's termination, managing the notice period, and dealing with sensitive issues such as misuse of confidential information and competition post termination of employment. This chapter will explore each of these processes in detail.

A useful starting point is to consider the legal rights of the executive in the context of a proposed termination as this will assist the company to work with or "around" the legal framework. The executive's rights in relation to his office and employment will primarily be governed by employment legislation, CA 2006 and the service agreement itself. His rights as a shareholder will however be regulated by the articles of association and/or shareholders' agreement.

The following risks are discussed: wrongful dismissal, breach of contract, unfair dismissal and discrimination.

Wrongful dismissal

This occurs where the executive has been dismissed without any notice period and in the absence of gross misconduct. The company may be liable to a claim of wrongful dismissal where it:

- mistakenly believed that there were grounds to dismiss the executive summarily;
- does not wish the executive to work the notice period and pays the executive notice pay in the absence of a contractual right to do so;
- deliberately dismisses the executive summarily and without any notice pay even though there was no gross misconduct.

The failure to provide the executive with notice as required in the service agreement in the circumstances set out above would amount to a wrongful dismissal.

If the executive works under a fixed-term contract without a "break clause" (i.e. the right to terminate the fixed term on notice being given) and the contract is prematurely terminated, damages for wrongful dismissal will be assessed on the balance of the fixed-term period. Compensation is confined to the loss of earnings and benefits which the executive would have received had he worked out the notice period (*Focsa Services (UK) Ltd v Birkett* [1996] IRLR 325; *Morrish v NTL Group* [2007] ScotCS CSIH_56 (03 July 2007)).

As the maximum compensation the Employment Tribunal can award for wrongful dismissal claims is £25,000, and such claims can only be made when the contract has terminated, most claims by senior executives are brought in the County Court or High Court. The procedure for civil court claims is however more formal and there is the risks of costs for parties in those proceedings. Where the executive's notice period is long, disputes will often centre on the executive's duty to mitigate his losses during the notice period.

If the executive is wrongfully dismissed and the company has not complied with the statutory dismissal procedures, compensation may be increased by the Employment Tribunal by at least 10 per cent and by up to 50 per cent, subject to the £25,000 limit (section 31 and Schedule 3, Employment Act 2002).

Breach of contract

Such liability arises from a breach of any other term of the service agreement apart from the executive's notice provisions. If the executive is still employed at the time of the breach, such claims can only be brought in the civil courts, not the Employment Tribunal.

Such losses can, for example, include:

- loss of earnings as a result of the company's failure to go through a contractual disciplinary procedure;
- loss of earnings (e.g. for sick pay) and damages for personal injury due to wrongful suspension from work which breached the implied term of trust and confidence;
- loss of prospective earnings caused by the company running a corrupt business which breached the implied terms of trust and confidence and which damaged the executive's employment prospects;
- loss of an enhanced redundancy payment due to the executive;
- loss of permanent health insurance benefits under the policy or failure to make payments equivalent to benefits payable under the policy;
- loss of a bonus payment;
- loss of share options.

For many senior executives, share options represent a significant part of their remuneration package. The calculation of the loss of this benefit can be tricky, as it relies on a number of uncertain future events. In the case of *Selective Beauty U.K. Ltd v Hayes* [2005] IDS Brief 788/8, which concerns an unfair dismissal claim, the EAT gave helpful guidance as to the correct approach for assessing compensation in such circumstances. In *Hayes*, part of the executive's claim for compensation was the loss of the right to exercise options on up to 5,000 shares in the company's parent company, Selective Beauty SA (SBSA). Had he remained employed, he would have been entitled to exercise the options at a price of €17 per share. The executive claimed that it was reasonable to assume that SBSA would float during 2005 at a price of €170 per share, giving a net profit to him of €765,000, or £546,428.57. The Tribunal found that on the balance of probabilities SBSA would be floated with a share price of €170. It also decided that there was only a 20 per cent chance that he would have been in employment at the time when he could first exercise his options, and therefore it made a reduction in his award of 80 per cent. The EAT allowed the appeal and held that the Tribunal ought to have assessed the extent of each future uncertainty in percentage terms and applied that percentage to the loss claimed. The Tribunal ought therefore to have considered the following uncertainties:

- the likely value of the shares on flotation/takeover;
- the question of whether SBSA would float at all and, if so, when;
- whether the executive would have remained in employment; and
- whether he would, in fact, have decided to purchase all or any of the shares.

Whatever might be the damages for breach of contract, the executive must take reasonable steps to seek alternative employment by way of mitigation. Where the executive has found alternative employment, but it is not as well paid as the current previous job, the executive's financial loss would be the difference in pay between the two jobs.

The concept of contributory fault is irrelevant in breach of contract claims. However, the court may reduce the executive's damages for wrongful dismissal and breach of contract by taking into account the following:

- Actual earnings from new employment or hypothetical earnings by way of mitigation (*Yetton v Eastwoods Froy Ltd* [1967] 1 WLR 104; *Hardy v Polk (Leeds) Ltd* [2004] IRLR 420).
- Receipt of social security benefits, e.g. jobseeker's allowance (*Secretary of State for Employment v Stewart* [1996] IRLR 334, EAT) including any failure to apply for it (*Westwood v Secretary of State for Employment* [1985] ICR 209, HL).
- A redundancy payment, but only where the employee would not have received it but for a failure by the employer to provide notice (*Baldwin v British Coal Corporation*

[1995] IRLR 139, distinguished from *Wilson v National Coal Board* [1980] 130 NLJ 146, HL).

- Compensation for unfair dismissal if damages for wrongful dismissal have been allocated in the unfair dismissal compensation (*O'Laoire v Jackel International Ltd (No.2)* [1991] ICR 718).
- Rebates of income tax (*Hartley v Sandholme Iron Co Ltd* [1974] 3 All ER 475).
- Liability for damages counterclaimed by the employer which is independent of the repudiated contract (*Pearce v Roy T Ward (Consultants)Ltd* [1996] IDS Brief 585 where a separate loan agreement was enforceable against the employee).

Monies paid under a disability pension and pension are not deductible (*Parry v Cleaver* [1970] AC 1, HL) because they are fruits of money set aside in the past in respect of past work; the failure to deduct such sums does not result in any double recovery (*Smoker v London Fire and Civil Defence Authority* [1991] 2 AC 502). In *Hopkins v Norcros Plc* [1993] 1 All ER 565, the Court of Appeal held that an employee's receipt of his pension at age 57 when he was summarily dismissed by his employer flowed from work which the employee had done, and belonged to a category of collateral benefit which was exempt from credit/deductions at common law. Equally it is unlikely that any compensation derived from the employee's private insurance policy (e.g. insurance against loss of employment to meet mortgage payments) should be deducted.

A reduction will be applied to reflect the executive's accelerated receipt covering the damages period. In *Shove v Downs Surgical plc* [1984] ICR 532, the court applied a reduction of 7 per cent. It has however been suggested that anything between 2 per cent and 6 per cent would be more consistent with modern practice.

In relation to breach of contract claims, the executive is not required to raise a statutory grievance before making a claim in the Employment Tribunal. However if he does, the executive will benefit from an extension of time (from three months to six months) to present his claim (*J Mowells v Vox Display Limited* [2007] UKEAT/0122/07/RN).

Unfair dismissal

An executive who has accrued one year of continuous service has the statutory right not to be unfairly dismissed. If the company does not have a statutory fair reason to dismiss the executive, or if it did have a fair reason but it did not comply with the statutory dismissal procedures and did not act fairly prior to the executive's dismissal, the executive can sue for unfair dismissal.

As the value of such claims is relatively small, due to a statutory cap on compensation when compared to wrongful dismissal or breach of contract claims, some companies are willing to take the financial risks of terminating the executive's employment without going through legal procedures which can be time-consuming. Even so, such claims should be carefully managed for other commercial reasons. The declaration of an unfair dismissal by the Employment Tribunal, media interest in and costs of defending such claims, for example, can be potentially damaging for any company, particularly a listed company. If the executive is unfairly dismissed by the company, this can also impact on his rights under any share option or shareholders' agreement which increases the incentive for the executive to contest the dismissal.

Only executive directors have a right to claim unfair dismissal. Non-executive directors who are engaged as officers under a letter of appointment rather than employment contracts are unlikely to be able to claim unfair dismissal. Where the non-executive is also providing consultancy services to the company, it is important to ensure that such arrangements do not inadvertently give rise to an employment relationship.

To claim unfair dismissal, the executive must show that his employment is in Great Britain (*Serco v Lawson; Botham v Ministry of Defence; Croft & ors v Veta Ltd & ors* [2006] IDS 799). The Tribunal will look at whether the executive was actually working in Great Britain at the time of his dismissal, as opposed to what his contract says is his place of work. In the case of peripatetic or mobile employees, the Tribunal will consider the conduct of the parties and the way they have been operating the contract to decide where the base actually is, as opposed to just looking at the terms of the contract. Employees who are wholly based outside Great Britain are unlikely to have unfair dismissal protection. An exception may apply to say, a foreign correspondent for a British newspaper, who has been posted abroad and lived there for many years, but remained a permanent employee of the newspaper, or an expatriate employee of a British employer operating within an extra-territorial British enclave in a foreign country (e.g. employees working abroad in embassies or RAF bases).

No qualifying period applies where the executive's dismissal is 'automatically' unfair. (section 108 ERA 1996) An automatically unfair dismissal means that the Tribunal will not be required to consider if the company has acted fairly prior to the executive's dismissal. In other words, procedural fairness is irrelevant in automatically unfair dismissals.

A dismissal is automatically unfair if, for example, the dismissal is due to:

- the executive taking leave for a family reason (i.e. pregnancy, childbirth, maternity, maternity leave, adoption leave, parental leave, paternity leave or time off for dependants under section 57A ERA) (section 99 ERA 1996);
- a health and safety reason (*Masiak v City Restaurants (UK) Ltd* [1999] IRLR 780, EAT; *Harvest Press Ltd v McCaffrey* [1999] IRLR 778, EAT; *Balfour Kilpatrick Ltd v Acheson* [2003] IRLR 683) (section 100 ERA 1996);

- a working time reason under the Working Time Regulations 1998 (section 101A ERA 1996);
- the executive performing the functions of a trustee of a pension scheme (section 102 ERA 1996);
- the executive performing the functions of an employee representative (section 103 ERA 1996);
- the executive making a protected disclosure under the Public Interest Disclosure Act 1998 (section 103A ERA 1996);
- the assertion of a statutory right (e.g. these include the right to receive an itemised payslip and a section 1 statement, not to suffer unlawful deduction of wages or unfair dismissal, to be given statutory minimum notice) and rights under WTR 1998, Employment Relations Act 1999 and sections 68, 86, 146, 168, 168A, 169 and 170 TULRCA 1992 (see *Armstrong v Walter Scott Motors (London) Ltd* [2003] IDS Brief 740 on holiday pay under the WTR 1998) (section 104 ERA 1996);
- the executive's application for flexible working (section 104C ERA 1996) after six months' continuous employment (section 108(3)(gi) ERA 1996);
- the executive exercising the right to accompany or be accompanied to a disciplinary or grievance hearing (section 12(3) Employment Relations Act 1999);
- the assertion of rights under regulation 28(3) of the Transnational Information and Consultation of Employees Regulations 1999 (SI 1999/3323);
- the assertion of rights as part-time worker under regulation 7(3) of the Part-time Workers (Prevention of Less Favourable Treatment) Regulations 1999 (SI 1999/1551);
- the assertion of rights as a fixed-term employee under regulation 6(1) of the Fixed-term Executives (Prevention of Less Favourable Treatment) Regulations 2002 (SI 2002/2034).

It should be noted that an executive must still possess the requisite one year of service in order to sue for unfair dismissal in the following special cases:

- a dismissal in connection with a transfer of undertaking under regulation 7(1) TUPE 2006;
- a dismissal due to failure to disclose or because of a spent conviction (section 4(3)(b) Rehabilitation of Offenders Act 1974);
- a dismissal due to a breach of the statutory disciplinary, dismissal and grievance procedures (section 98A ERA 1996).

Remedies for unfair dismissal

An executive who has been unfairly dismissed may ask the Employment Tribunal for an order requiring the company to:

- reinstate him (i.e. give him back his old job);
- re-engage him (i.e. give him another job within the company);
- award him compensation for unfair dismissal;
- award him an additional award of between 26 and 52 weeks' pay where the company has failed to comply with an order of re-instatement or re-engagement (section 117(3)(b) ERA 1996);
- award him a protective award where there has been a failure to consult in connection with a collective redundancy or transfer of undertaking (section 188 TULRCA 1992 and regulation 15 TUPE 2006).
- reinstate or re-engage him pending determination of the dismissal by the Tribunal (i.e. interim relief) under section 128 ERA 1996 and section 161(1) TULRCA 1992.

Orders for reinstatement and re-engagement are subject to whether it is practical for the company to do so and whether the executive has contributed to the dismissal (section 116 ERA 1996). Where the relationship of trust and confidence has broken down, such remedies may not be possible (*Gentle and Ors v Perkins Group Ltd* (unreported) EAT, 2000, EAT/671/99 and *IPC Magazines Ltd v Clement* (unreported) EAT, 1999, EAT/456/99).

The usual remedy is compensation for unfair dismissal which consists of a basic award and a compensatory award (section 118 ERA 1996).

When calculating the basic award, account is taken of the executive's age and length of service, from which a multiplier is derived. This is then multiplied by the statutory value of a week's pay, which increases on 1 February annually (section 227 ERA 1996; s.119 ERA 1996) (see Appendix H).

A minimum basic award is payable by the employer where the executive:

- was unfairly selected for redundancy or dismissed for a reason connected with trade union membership or activities (sections 152(1) and 153 TULRCA 1992), carrying out duties as a health and safety representative (section 100(1)(a)–(b) ERA 1996), carrying out duties as a trustee of an occupational pension scheme (section 102(1) ERA 1996) and performing functions or activities as an executive representative (sections 101A(d) and 103 ERA 1996);
- was unfairly dismissed due to a breach of the statutory disciplinary, dismissal and grievance procedures (section 120(1A) ERA 1996): an award of four weeks' pay (capped); or

- was dismissed for redundancy but was later re-engaged (section 121 ERA 1996): an award of two weeks' pay (capped).
- Where the executive's selection for the redundancy dismissal was due to their activities as a safety representative, trustee of an occupational pension fund, employee representative for consultation purposes or trade union activities (section 120 ERA 1996).
- Where the executive has unreasonably refused suitable alternative employment, or accepts re-engagement but leaves during the statutory trial period, the minimum basic award is the statutory two weeks' pay (section 121 ERA 1996).

The basic award may be reduced in the following circumstances under ERA 1996.

- conduct of the executive before dismissal (section 122(2) ERA 1996);
- redundancy dismissal and statutory redundancy pay (section 122(4) ERA 1996);
- unreasonable refusal of reinstatement (section 122(1) ERA 1996);
- ex-gratia redundancy payment by employer (section 144(4)(b) ERA 1996);
- damages for breach of designated dismissal procedures agreement (section 22(3A) ERA 1996).

The maximum compensatory award for unfair dismissal is announced by the government on 1 February each year (see Appendix H). There is however no limit to the compensatory award where the reason for the employee's dismissal is due to:

- a health and safety reason (section 100 ERA 1996);
- whistleblowing (section 103A ERA 1996);
- his selection for redundancy because of health and safety activities under section 100 ERA 1996 (section 105(3));
- his selection for redundancy because of activities as an employee representative under section 103 ERA 1996 (section 105(6A) ERA 1996).

The amount of the compensatory award is based on such amount as the tribunal considers just and equitable in all the circumstances, having regard to the loss sustained by the complainant as a result of the dismissal (section 123(1) ERA 1996).

This will include financial losses, which flow from the date of dismissal to the date of hearing ('the prescribed element') and beyond the date of hearing (i.e. future losses). The Employment Tribunal will consider if the executive's loss is: open-ended (i.e. employment would have continued); limited or non-existent (i.e. employment would have ceased anyway under the *Polkey* principle); or speculative (i.e. that a dismissal might have occurred at some later stage), so that damages should be reduced to reflect that contingency (see *Hough & APEX v Leyland DAF Ltd* [1991] IRLR 194 and

Campbell v Dunoon & Cowal Housing Association [1993] IRLR 496 where compensation was reduced to 50 per cent and 75 per cent respectively). In *Scope v Thornett* [2007] ICR 236, the Court of Appeal held that the Employment Tribunal was wrong to have awarded the employee six months' compensation for constructive unfair dismissal, as she would have been dismissed by the employer in any event within that timeframe.

Where the company has caused the executive's illness, the employee will be entitled to compensation for future loss of earnings even though he was on sick leave prior to his dismissal. In *GAB Robins (UK) Ltd vTriggs* [2007] ICR 1424, the EAT held that the employee's ill health would be treated as a consequence of the dismissal, meaning that loss of earnings would form part of her compensatory award. However, the executive cannot claim compensation in excess of his actual loss. In *Burlo v Langley and anor* [2007] IRLR 145, the Court of Appeal held that the employee was not entitled to full notice pay had she been given proper notice by her employer as she would only have received statutory sick pay owing to her absence for that period.

Where the employee obtains new and permanent employment but loses it quickly, the original employer may still be liable if the loss in question was caused by the originally unfair dismissal. In *Dench v Flynn & Partners* [1998] IRLR 653, CA, the employee left her second employment after a three-month probationary period due to an inability to work amicably with her supervisor. This was held not to have broken the chain of causation.

The compensatory award will typically include the following heads of loss:

- Net loss of salary – this includes any anticipated increases at the time of hearing, not at the date of dismissal (*Gilham v Kent CC (No.3)* [1986] ICR 52).
- Net future loss of earning – a 5 per cent discount is usually applied for accelerated receipt of capital (*York Trailer Co Ltd v Sparkes* [1973] IRLR 348) although in *Brentwood Bros (Manchester) Ltd v Shepherd* [2003] IRLR 365, the Court of Appeal held that such a rate is too high given that in personal injury cases, the conventional rate of 4.5 per cent has been reduced to 2.5 per cent by statute. Pension money which an employee received on dismissal, whether the scheme was contributory or non-contributory or occupational or private, should not be deducted from compensation for unfair dismissal (*Knapton v ECC Card Clothing Ltd* [2006] I.C.R. 1084).
- Loss of pension rights – A Tribunal must consider if an employee has sustained any pension loss on dismissal (*Lambe v 186K Ltd* [2004] EWCA Civ 1045). An employee's loss of pension rights can exceed his claim for loss of earnings e.g. 10 years and 2.5 years respectively (*Brentwood Bros (Manchester) Ltd v Shepherd* [2003] IRLR 365).
- Expenses (section 123 ERA 1996) – this includes those incurred looking for new employment (*Leech v Berger, Jensen & Nicholas Ltd* [1972] IRLR 58) and removal costs (*Nihar v Granistone (Galloway) Ltd* [1974] ICR 273).

- Loss of benefits (section 123 ERA 1996) – this can include contractual and non-contractual benefits such as private use of company car, free or subsidised accommodation, mortgage allowances, school fees allowances and medical insurance cover. The loss is calculated by assessing the cost of replacing the benefits. Where the employee is deprived of life assurance benefit following their dismissal but he has suffered no financial loss because he remains alive at the date of the hearing, the loss of benefit is not recoverable (*Knapton v ECC Card Clothing Ltd* [2006] I.C.R. 1084).
- Loss of share options – In *Selective Beauty Ltd v Hayes* [2005] IDS Brief 788/8, the Managing Director was unfairly dismissed for poor performance and he claimed that as a consequence of his dismissal he had lost the right to exercise his share options in the parent company which, had it floated, would have resulted in a net gain of £546,428. The EAT held that the correct approach, where the calculation of loss involves future uncertain events is for the Employment Tribunal to make an assessment of the likelihood of such an event occurring in percentage terms and apply this percentage to the loss claimed. It was incorrect to adopt a "balance of probability" approach.
- Loss of statutory rights – this relates to the loss of continuity of employment that would be required to claim unfair dismissal, enhanced redundancy payments (*Lee v IPC Business Press Ltd* [1984] ICR 306, EAT) and longer notice periods (*Daley v AE Dorsett (Almar Dolls) Ltd* [1981] IRLR 385). It is usually assessed at about £250 (*Dugdale Plc v Cartlidge* [2007] IDS Brief 836).
- Failure to provide written particulars of employment (section 38 Employment Act 2002) – The Tribunal may make an order of two to four weeks' pay (capped) where an employee has successfully brought a claim under Sched.5 Employment Act 2002.

The compensatory award may be reduced by the Tribunal under section 123 ERA 1996 as follows.

- Sums paid by the employer (section 123(7) ERA 1996) – this includes damages for wrongful dismissal (*Babcock FATA Ltd v Addison* [1987] 2 All ER 784).
- Excess of statutory redundancy payment/redundancy compensation (section 123(7) ERA 1996)
- Failure to mitigate losses or earnings from mitigation (section 123(4) ERA 1996) – the duty to mitigate only arises after a dismissal (*Bessenden Properties Ltd v Corness* [1974] IRLR 338). An unreasonable refusal of reinstatement or re-engagement may amount to a failure to mitigate (section 123(4) ERA 1996). Where the employee has obtained an equivalent or better paid job, there is no loss to claim (save for a basic award) even if the dismissal is unfair. Where the employee's new employment is less well paid, damages will be assessed on the difference in earnings. Where the

employee is unemployed for an initial period but later secures a better paid job, the earnings gained through mitigation should not be retrospectively applied to the initial period of loss when the employee was unemployed (*Fentiman v Fluid Engineering Products Ltd* [1991] IRLR 150, EAT and *Whelan v Richardson* [1998] IRLR 114, EAT). An earlier EAT in *Ging v Edward (Lane) Ltd* (unreported) EAT, 1978 took the opposite view.

- Social security benefits – income support and jobseeker's allowance received will be deducted. The approach with invalidity benefit is to deduct the entire sum (*Puglia v James & Sons* [1996] IRLR 70) or 50 per cent of it (*Rubenstein v McGloughlin (No. 2)* [1996] IRLR 557). Housing benefit is not deductible (*Savage v Saxena* [1998] IRLR 182).
- Breach of statutory dismissal disciplinary and grievance procedures (section 31(2) Employment Act 2002) – the compensatory award may be reduced by between 10 and 50 per cent if the executive has failed to initiate or exhaust the statutory procedures.
- Contributory fault (section 123(6) ERA 1996) – only blameworthy conduct of the employee, which caused or contributed to the dismissal is relevant (*Nelson v BBC (No. 2)* [1979] IRLR 346, CA). There must be a connection or relevance between the employee's conduct and the principal reasons for dismissal (*Robert Whiting Designs Ltd v Lamb* [1978] ICR 89). In *Mullinger v Department for Work and Pensions* [2007] IDS Brief 830, the EAT confirmed that only *pre-dismissal* conduct can be considered for a reduction under sections 122(2) and 123(6) ERA 1996. Contributory fault can result in a 100 per cent reduction in the compensatory award (*W Devis & Sons Ltd v Atkins* [1977] IRLR 314), although it is rare. Where contributory fault is established, a percentage reduction in the basic and compensatory award should be the same in a majority of cases (*RSPCA v Cruden* [1986] IRLR 83) but a Tribunal can apply a different reduction where appropriate. In *Charles Robertson (Developments) Ltd v White* [1995] ICR 349, the basic award was reduced to 50 per cent but the compensatory award was reduced to nil.

No deduction should be made in relation to pension payments (*Hopkins v Nocros Plc* [1994] ICR 11), nor for an educational grant received during employment for a course to commence after the employee's dismissal (*Justfern Ltd v Skaife D'Ingerthorpe* [1994] ICR 286).

Where the executive is in receipt of unemployment benefit or income support after their dismissal, the Department for Work and Pensions may recover social security benefits paid out to the employee by way of deduction from their compensation. It is therefore often more advantageous for employees to settle their dispute, as in these circumstances no deduction will be made from their Employment Tribunal compensation.

Discrimination

The executive is also protected against discrimination on grounds of sex (includes gender, marital status and gender reassignment), race, disability, sexual orientation, religion or belief and age. The types of discrimination prohibited include direct discrimination, indirect discrimination, harassment and victimisation. It is unlawful to discriminate against a person in relation to their recruitment, the terms of their employment (including training, transfers and promotion) and in relation to the termination of their employment. Key areas to watch out for include appointments to the Board, remuneration packages and working patterns, particularly potential discrimination on grounds of sex and age. "Glass ceiling" issues for women in the boardroom remain topical.

To bring a discrimination claim, the executive must first raise a grievance and allow the company 28 days to resolve the grievance. Recent case law suggests that almost any written complaint to the employer, whether it is a resignation letter from the executive (*Thorpe and Soleil Investments v Poat and Lake* [2005] UKEAT/0503/05; *Galaxy Showers Ltd v Wilson* [2005] UKEAT/(0525/05); *Shergold v Fieldway Medical Centre* [2005] UKEAT/0487/05; *Holc-Gale v Makers UK Ltd* [2006] IRLR 178), or a letter before action from a lawyer (*Stewart v Barnetts Motor Group* [2005] UKEATS/0052/05/RN; *Aspland v Mark Warner* [2005] UKEAT/0531/05) or a letter from any other person on the executive's behalf is likely to be treated as a statutory grievance. The executive need not intend to raise the matter as a grievance or use the word "grievance" or refer to the statutory procedures or indicate that the complaint may go further. Nor is the executive required to comply with the company's own grievance procedure. If such a communication is received, the company should clarify with the sender whether or not it is intended to act as a step 1 grievance letter. More recent cases are however less generous towards employees. In *Muhammed v Royal Mail* [2007] All ER (D) 342 December, the EAT held that it is not sufficient for the employee to set out a factual complaint which could theoretically form the basis of a claim. In *Canary Wharf Management Ltd v Edebi* [2006] IRLR 416, the EAT held that references to the employee's health problems in a resignation letter which the employee claimed was a statutory grievance concerning disability discrimination, did not raise, even in a non-technical and unsophisticated way, an issue which the employer could reasonably understand to have arisen under the Disability Discrimination Act 1995. Where the executive's employment has terminated and the modified grievance procedure applies, the executive is required not only to put his grievance in writing but also the basis for it. In *City of Bradford Metropolitan District Council v Pratt* [2007] IDS Brief 823, the EAT held that the former employee's letter indicating an equal pay grievance without providing details of the comparators or the payments she was claiming did not comply with step 1 of the modified grievance procedure.

Compensation for discrimination is unlimited in relation to loss of earnings, injury to feelings, personal injury and aggravated damages.

The Court of Appeal, in the case of *Vento v Chief Constable of West Yorkshire Police* [2003] IRLR 202, gave guidance on the assessment of damages in discrimination cases. Injury to feelings can be divided into three bands:

- Top band (between £15,000 and £25,000) – sums in this range should be awarded in the most serious cases, such as where there has been a lengthy campaign of discriminatory harassment.
- Middle band (between £5,000 and £15,000) – sums in this range should be used for serious cases which do not merit an award in the highest band.
- Low band (between £500 and £5,000) – sums in this range are appropriate for less serious cases, such as where the act of discrimination is an isolated or one-off occurrence.

To minimise the risks of discrimination claims, the company should promote a culture of respect, dignity and inclusiveness of all board members through effective implementation of policies and procedures. In terms of board appointments, it is important to ensure a fair, transparent and consistent recruitment process, and that decisions are made based on merit.

CHAPTER **6**

Terminating the employment

Overview

The company may lawfully dismiss the executive if the reason for dismissal is one of the six substantive reasons permitted by law. These include conduct, capability, retirement, redundancy, illegality (contravention of a duty or restriction imposed by law) and "some other substantial reason" (section 98(2) ERA 1996, as amended).

The company can only rely on facts known to it at the time of the dismissal (*W Devis & Sons Ltd v Atkins* [1977] ICR 662). Where there are multiple reasons for the executive's dismissal, the company must show what was the principal reason for dismissal. It is for the Tribunal to investigate what is the real reason for the executive's dismissal. The Tribunal must consider the company's reason for dismissal at the time when notice was given and when the dismissal actually occurred (*Parkinson v March Consulting Ltd* [1998] ICR 276; *Stacey v Babcock Power Ltd* [1986] ICR 221). Where there is a dispute over the reason for the employee's dismissal, the burden of proving which of the competing reasons was the principal reason for dismissal lies on the employer (*Maund v Penwith District Council* [1984] ICR 143).
Different practical considerations apply in respect of each of the six reasons when deciding whether the company has acted with procedural fairness.

Statutory disciplinary, dismissal and grievance procedures

With effect from 1 October 2004, the company has to comply with the statutory disciplinary, dismissal procedure (DDP) and statutory grievance procedures (SGP). If the company fails to comply with the DDP, the executive's dismissal is "automatically unfair" (section 98A ERA 1996) and any compensation awarded to the executive shall be increased by at least 10 per cent and up to 50 per cent, subject to the statutory cap for unfair dismissals in the Employment Tribunal.

In summary, if the company is proposing "relevant disciplinary action" (i.e. suspension without pay or demotion) on grounds of conduct or capability or contemplating the dismissal of the executive, it must, unless an exception applies, follow a three-step procedure under the DDP ((1) the company must set out the allegations in writing, (2) the company must meet the employee to discuss, (3) the company must allow the employee the right of an appeal). A two-step procedure, otherwise known as the modified procedure, which avoids a meeting, applies in exceptional circumstances e.g. where there is incontrovertible evidence that the executive is guilty of misconduct. The executive does not have a free standing right to complain about a breach of the DDP (*Scott-Davies v Redgate Medical Services* [2007] ICR 348).

Equally, if the executive is claiming constructive dismissal or a breach of his statutory rights other than a dismissal, he must comply with a three-step SGP ((1) the employee must set out his complaint in writing, (2) the employee must meet with the company to discuss his grievance, (3) the company must allow the employee the right of an appeal). A modified procedure is available where the employment has ended and both parties agree to resolve the grievance without a face-to-face meeting or appeal meeting.

If the executive's dismissal is automatically unfair under section 98A ERA 1996 in terms of liability, compensation for unfair dismissal may still be reduced if the company is able to show that the executive would still have been dismissed notwithstanding non-compliance with the DPP or SGP.

As the statutory procedures have generated a wealth of litigation since its introduction, a radical review of its effectiveness at promoting internal dispute resolution was undertaken by the Government in 2006. At the time of writing, it is anticipated that when the Employment Bill 2007-2008 becomes law in 2009, the DDP and SGP will be abolished. It will also repeal section 98A of the ERA 1996 concerning procedural unfairness. A revised ACAS disciplinary and dismissal code and any other codes introduced by the Government would apply instead. If these codes are breached by the employer or employee, Employment Tribunals can increase or decrease any compensation payable by up to 25 per cent. The result of these changes is that the "*Polkey* principle" (*Polkey v AE Dayton Services Ltd* [1998] ICR 142) will once again become the basis for deciding whether a dismissal is unfair on procedural grounds.

Statutory reason(s) for dismissal

Under section 98 ERA 1996, there are six statutory fair reasons for dismissing the executive. These are discussed below.

Performance issues (capability)

It can sometimes be difficult to distinguish cases of conduct and capability, which often overlap as reasons for dismissal. "Capability" involves an inherent cause (*Sutton and Gates (Luton) Ltd v Boxall* [1979] ICR 67). Underperformance (*Fletcher v St Leonards* (unreported) EAT, 1987, EAT 25/87), inflexiblility or inadaptability (*Abernethy v Mott, Hay and Anderson* [1974] ICR 323, CA) are generally "incapability" issues. Where an employee fails to perform up to an acceptable standard due to his own carelessness, negligence or idleness, such behaviour constitutes "misconduct". Malingerers and those who go on unauthorised absence from work should be dealt with as cases of "misconduct" rather than "incapability" issues.

Where capability is the reason for dismissal, it is important to draw a distinction between incapability of performing the contract by reason of sickness absence and incapability due to lack of competence, qualification or skill. The procedure that employers need to follow in each case is different. In either case, it is sufficient if the company honestly believes on reasonable grounds that the executive is incapable or incompetent. It is not necessary for the company to prove that the executive is in fact incapable or incompetent. A single act of incompetence may justify dismissal where the safety of the public or other workers is compromised (*Taylor v Alidair* [1978] IRLR 82).

Where the executive's inability to work is due to illness, the company should deal with the situation differently depending on whether the absenteeism is intermittent or long term. The issue in such cases is how long the company can be expected to wait for the executive to return to work (*Spencer v Paragon Wallpapers Ltd* [1976] IRLR 373). The company only needs to show that the ill health relates to the executive's capability and that will be a sufficient reason to dismiss.

The company is expected to carry out a careful appraisal of the executive's performance, discuss any concerns with the executive, and give the executive a chance to improve. When deciding on the fairness of the executive's dismissal, the Employment Tribunal will take into account his length of service, past performance and failings and, where appropriate, whether training and supervision should have been provided by the company. There is arguably less need to give a warning to a very senior employee that he may be dismissed if he does not improve (*Littlewoods Organisation Ltd v Egenti* [1976] ICR).

A distinction between long-term absences caused by an underlying medical condition and repeated or intermittent absences caused by transient complaints should be drawn by the company. In long-term sickness cases, warnings may not be appropriate. The usual practice will involve the company consulting with the employee and carrying out a medical investigation (*East Lindsey District Council v Daubney* [1977] ICR 566).

Under the Access to Medical Reports Act 1988 and the Access to Health Records Act 1990, the executive must consent to his medical records being released. The executive has a legal right to examine any medical report produced by his GP/consultant before it is released to the company, provided that he does so within 21 days from the date when an application for a report is made by the company. If the executive wishes to amend the report but the GP refuses to accept these amendments, the executive can ask the GP to attach a statement stating his objection to the GP's findings. Where there is doubt on the GP's findings, the employer should request that the executive undergo a separate examination by its company doctor. If the executive refuses to undertake a medical examination, he should be warned that a decision will be taken on the basis of the information available and that it could result in a dismissal.

Depending on the medical diagnosis and prognosis, consider, the company is expected to explore whether the executive can be offered alternative employment. Dismissal should be the last resort and if taken by the company should be consistent with the treatment of other members of staff in similar situations. Further, it has been held that a reasonable employer should give proper consideration to its ill-health retirement scheme before dismissing an employee on long-term sickness absence (*First West Yorkshire t/a First Leeds v Haigh* [2007] UKEAT/0246/07).

Executives with chronic illnesses or injury should be treated with special care and sensitivity. Where their illness amounts to a "disability" under the DDA 1995, the company is required to make reasonable adjustments. A "disability" is defined as "a physical or mental impairment which has a substantial and long term adverse effect on a person's ability to carry out normal day to day activities". An impairment has a long-term effect if it has lasted for 12 months, or if it is likely to last for at least 12 months or is likely to last for the rest of the life of the employee. Cancer, multiple sclerosis and HIV infection are recognised disabilities; sickness on its own is not a legal disability (*Chacon Navas v Eurest Colectividades* SA [2006] Case C-13/05, ECJ).

Where the executive's illness is caused by the employer e.g. stress-related illness, this may be a relevant factor when considering the fairness of any dismissal, particularly at the compensation stage when assessing what is "just and equitable" (*Edwards v Governors of Hanson School* [2001] IRLR 733, EAT). In *McAdie v Royal Bank of Scotland* [2007] EWCA Civ 806, the Court of Appeal held that an employer could fairly dismiss an employee for ill-health incapability despite the fact that the employee's stress-related illness was attributed to the conduct of the employer. Although the cause of the employee's incapability is a relevant factor for the Tribunal to consider when determining whether or not a dismissal is fair, the key issue is whether the employer acted reasonably in all the circumstances. The test in an unfair dismissal case is the reasonableness of the employer's decision based on what it knew at the time. In such cases, there should be no need to look at what caused the illness and who was responsible for but it might be necessary for the employer to "go the extra mile" in finding alternative employment for the employee, or put up with a longer period of absence than might otherwise be reasonable.

In long-term sickness absence cases, issues relating to permanent health insurance (PHI), early retirement and redundancy often surface in the exit negotiations.

Where the executive is entitled to contractual sickness benefits or a PHI scheme, the company cannot terminate the executive's employment if that effectively removes the benefit of the sickness benefits or PHI scheme. There is an implied term that an employer will not do anything that is primarily aimed at defeating the employee's entitlement to a contractual benefit (*Aspden v Webbs Poultry & Meat Group (Holdings) Ltd* [1996] IRLR 521; *Brompton v AOC International Ltd* [1997] IRLR 639, CA; and *Adin v Sedco Forex International Resources Ltd* [1997] IRLR 280). Nothing however prevents the company from summarily dismissing the executive where there is "good cause", e.g. gross misconduct or repudiatory breach by the employee (*Briscoe v Lubrizol* [2002] IRLR 607) or for redundancy (*Hill v General Accident Fire and Life Assurance Corp plc* [1998] IRLR 641) even where this has the indirect effect of depriving the employee from his entitlement to PHI benefits. In these circumstances, the aim of the employer's dismissal was not to frustrate the employee's entitlement to outstanding contractual sick pay (*Smiths Industries Aerospace and Defence Systems Ltd v Brookes* [1986] IRLR 434).

Early retirement on grounds of ill health can either amount to a "capability dismissal" or dismissal for "some other substantial reason". This should be distinguished from retirement on grounds of the executive having reached the company's retirement age, where the statutory retirement dismissal procedure must be followed by the company (see below). The impact of the executive taking early retirement under the company's pension scheme should be carefully considered before early retirement is considered. If early retirement is agreed, this should not be confused with voluntary redundancy.

Disciplinary issues (conduct)

The company's disciplinary code on conduct should contain a non-exhaustive list of what types of behaviour will be deemed as misconduct and gross misconduct. Typically, examples of gross misconduct for senior executives include breaches of their fiduciary duties, corporate governance rules, dishonesty, criminal offences, and serious breaches of company policies. Conduct outside the workplace (for example, drug taking, alcoholism, violent behaviour and criminal offences) should only be taken into account if they bear some relation to the executive's position in the company (*Post Office v Liddiard* [2001] Emp LR 784).

The executive should be told what standard of behaviour is expected of him in the service agreement (*John Lewis Plc v Coyne* [2001] IRLR 139; *Goudie v Royal Bank of Scotland plc* (unreported) EAT, 2004, UKEAT/693/03). In *Bartholomew v LK Group Ltd* [2003] IDS Brief 733, the High Court held that Bartholomew, a managing director, was not guilty of misconduct when he carried out much of his work in London clubs, cafes and while walking in the park, because his employer had acquiesced to Bartholomew's flexible work pattern over a long period of time.

To avoid an unfair dismissal claim, the company is required to hold an honest belief that the executive is guilty of misconduct, possess reasonable grounds for that belief and to have carried out reasonable investigations to hold that belief (*British Homes Stores Ltd v Burchell* [1978] IRLR 379; *Midland Bank plc v Madden* [2000] 2 All ER 741, CA). In *Panama v Hackney LBC* [2003] IRLR 278, the employer's failure to obtain evidence to support its allegation of fraudulent misconduct meant that it did not have reasonable grounds for that belief. The Tribunal is required to concentrate on facts that were before the employer, rather than facts it had found when assessing whether the employer had reasonable grounds for its belief (*Post Office v Burkett* [2003] EWCA Civ 748). The test is not whether further investigation should have been carried out, but whether the investigation that had been carried out could be regarded by a reasonable employer as adequate. Further, it does not matter if the company's honest belief subsequently turns out to be wrong.

The Employment Tribunal will decide whether a reasonable employer would have done what the employer has done to the employee ("the band of reasonable responses") (*Iceland Frozen Foods Ltd v Jones* [1982] IRLR 439, EAT; *Higgins v C R Reynolds* (unreported) ET, 2000, ET 1801429/00; *Asda Stores Ltd v Malyn* [2001] IRLR 676). Thus, if a reasonable employer would have dismissed the employee in the same circumstances, it is not open to the Tribunal to substitute the employer's decision with its own decision simply because the Tribunal would not have dismissed the employee. In *Thomas v Hillingdon LBC* (2002) *The Times*, 4 October, the EAT held that it was perverse for a Tribunal to substitute the employer's decision to dismiss an employee for gross misconduct, arising from accessing hard core pornography during office hours, with misconduct.

The "band of reasonable responses" for determining the fairness of a dismissal will apply to a sanction applied by the employer as well as the process by which the employer arrived at the decision to dismiss (*Whitbread plc (t/a Whitbread Medway Inns) v Hall* [2001] EWCA Civ 268; *Sainsbury's Supermarkets v Hitt* [2003] IRLR 23; *Grattan plc v Hussain* (unreported) EAT, 2003, EAT/802/02). This means that "the band of reasonable responses" test also forms part of the "*Burchell* test".

The company is required to follow a fair procedure prior to any conduct dismissal (*Whitbread Plc (t/a Whitbread Medway Inns) v Hall* [2001] EWCA Civ 268). The basic elements of a fair procedure for misconduct dismissal involve:

- complying with the DDP where the company is taking or contemplating "relevant disciplinary action" (i.e. action short of dismissal on grounds of the employee's conduct or capability) or a dismissal in relation to the executive's conduct;
- carrying out a thorough and fair investigation;
- giving the executive notice of the disciplinary hearing and outlining the allegations against him and evidence to be relied upon by the company;

- allowing the executive to be accompanied by a fellow employee or trade union official - In *London Underground Ltd v Ference-Batchelor* [2003] ICR 656 and *Harding v London Underground Ltd* [2003] ICR 656, the EAT held that an order that did not contain some element of penalty or punishment is not a disciplinary hearing. An informal oral warning, which becomes part of an employee's disciplinary record, is in reality a formal oral warning and constitutes a "disciplinary hearing". In *Heathmill Multimedia ASP Ltd v Jones and Anor* [2003] IRLR 856, the EAT held that a meeting convened to advise two employees that their employment had to be terminated by reason of redundancy was not a "disciplinary hearing";
- allowing the executive to state his case;
- reaching a decision to dismiss only after due consideration of issues raised at the disciplinary hearing;

If the company is proposing to rely on the evidence of anonymous employees, certain guidelines should be followed (*Linfood Cash & Carry Ltd v Thomson* [1989] IRLR 235). When taking witness statements, an employer should bear in mind:

- the date, time and place of each or any observation or incident;
- the opportunity and ability to observe clearly and with accuracy;
- circumstantial evidence such as knowledge of a system, or the reason for the presence of the informer and why certain small details are memorable;
- whether the informant has suffered at the hands of the accused or has any other reason to fabricate, whether from personal grudge or any other reason or principle.

These guidelines are not law, and tribunals may depart from them in appropriate circumstances (e.g. if employees are unwilling to sign a statement or give further evidence for fear of reprisals) (*Ramsey v Walkers Snack Food Ltd* (unreported) EAT, UKEAT/0601/03/MAA and UKEAT/0602/03/MAA).

There is no legal obligation on the company to give the executive the opportunity to cross-examine the person making the complaint (*Santamera v Express Cargo Forwarding* [2003] IRLR 273). Only in rare and exceptional circumstances would a lack of cross-examination render a dismissal procedurally unfair (*Ulsterbus Ltd v Henderson* [1989] IRLR 251; *Voluntary Hostels Group v Horn* (unreported) EAT, 3 July 2002, EAT/603/01 and EAT/865/01).

Where the employer's disciplinary code allows the employer discretion to dismiss, other penalties apart from dismissal should also be considered in the exercise of the discretion. Previous warnings which have been excised from the employee's record should generally not be taken into account when a decision has to be taken on dismissal (*White v Newsquest (Stourbridge) Ltd* (unreported) EAT, 2001, EAT/565/00, EAT/1325/99). In the case of *Airbus Industries Ltd v Webb* [2008] EWCA Civ 49, the Court of Appeal held that it is not the case that a spent warning can never be taken into account. However, relying on an expired warning is an exception rather than the rule, and employers must remain satisfied that the current misconduct still amounts on its own right as gross misconduct. A final written warning should be given for conduct which stops short of justifying dismissal and where there is a risk that should the employee commit any other offence within a period of year, however minor, it will result in dismissal (*Stanley Cole (Wainfleet) Ltd v Sheridan* [2003] IRLR 52). An employer should dismiss only in exceptional cases where, for example, the "offence is so heinous and the facts so manifestly clear, that a reasonable employer could take the view that whatever the explanation the employee advanced it would make no difference" (*Polkey v A E Dayton Services Ltd* [1987] AC 344, HL).

If there has been serious misconduct and after reasonable investigation the company is unable to pinpoint the culprit, it may be appropriate to dismiss all parties who are involved rather than singling out one employee to be the scapegoat (*Monie v Coral Racing Ltd* [1980] ICR 109, CA; *Parr v Whitbread (t/a Thresher Wine Merchants)* [1990] ICR 427, EAT).

Redundancy

Redundancy is a legal concept and is defined under section 139 ERA 1996. A redundancy situation arises if:

- the company has ceased or intends to cease to carry out work for which the executive was employed; or
- the company has ceased or intends to cease to carry on that business where the executive was employed; or
- the requirements of that business for employees to carry out work of a particular kind have ceased or are expected to cease or diminish.

A redundancy situation might, for example, arise where the company is closing the business as a whole, or if the branch of its business where the executive ordinarily worked is to close. It can also arise where there is a reduction in the size of the workforce for work of a particular kind to be carried out. Whether a job is redundant is a question of fact, not law.

Mobility clauses and redundancy

If the executive has a mobility clause in his service agreement, the question is whether the company is entitled to exercise that clause to avoid a redundancy situation upon a workplace closure or whether section 139 applies instead. The courts have held that where there is a mobility clause but the employer has never exercised it before, then it is not open to the employer to deliberately exercise the mobility clause in order to avoid redundancy liability – this is sometimes called the "no dodging" principle (*Curling v Securicor Ltd* [1992] IRLR 549; *Bass Leisure v Thomas* [1994] IRLR 104; *High Table Ltd v Horst* [1998] ICR 409). If the employee is a mobile worker (having regard to the nature of their job and any previous relocations), then section 139 is unlikely to apply even though there is a workplace closure (*Evans and another v Home Office* [2007] EWCA Civ 1089). A refusal to relocate in those circumstances could be treated by the employer as a disciplinary matter (*Nelson v British Broadcasting Corporation* [1977] IRLR 148).

Redundancies and reorganisation

The fact that a new post (encompassing more job responsibilities) following a business reorganisation is different from an old post does not necessarily mean that there is a redundancy situation. The issue is whether work of a particular kind done by the employer has ceased or diminished (*Shawkat v Nottingham City Hospital NHS Trust (No.2)* [2001] IRLR 555). Not all restructurings will lead to redundancies particularly where there was no diminution in the need for employees to carry out work of a particular kind because the same number of employees are still needed albeit for fewer weeks in the working year (*Aylward v Glamorgan Holiday Hotel* (unreported) EAT, 2003, EAT1670252200). Sometimes, business restructurings lead to changes to the executive's terms and conditions of employment. If the executive refuses to accept the contractual changes and his employment is terminated, such a dismissal could be for "some other substantial reason".

Fair redundancy

Where there is a genuine redundancy, the company is still required to act fairly in bringing about the executive's dismissal (*William v Compair Maxam Ltd* [1982] ICR 156). In terms of procedural fairness, the company must put the executive at risk of redundancy, carry out a fair and objective method of selection, consult with the executive, offer alternative employment to the executive (if this is available), and pay a redundancy payment to the executive if he qualifies for such a payment.

Pre-selection of candidates

It is normal practice for employers to carry out a preliminary selection of candidates, rather than put all employees at risk and then select. This has the advantage of ring-fencing the process and avoiding unrest amongst the wider workforce. If there are other executives holding similar positions to the executive at risk of redundancy or carrying out work which involves similar skills to him, a redundancy selection pool should be created.

The company should use a fair method of selection. Factors to be taken into account in the selection matrix include productivity, punctuality, disciplinary record, adaptability and the company's future needs. The scoring system should provide clear guidelines as to how a point is ascribed. Employment Tribunals rarely interfere with the employer's selection process if what the employer did was within the "band of reasonable responses" test (*Chronos Richardson Ltd v Watson* [2001] IRLR 674). It is important to ensure that any criterion used is not indirectly discriminatory on grounds of sex, for example, where it is related to pregnancy or part-time working (*Whiffen v Milham Ford Girls School* [2001] EWCA Civ 385) or the executive's age (e.g. using "last in first out" (LIFO) as a method of selection).

It is automatically unfair to select the executive for redundancy because:

- he was, or proposed to become, a member of an independent trade union; or had taken part or proposed to take part in the activities of an independent trade union at an appropriate time; or was not a member of a trade union, or had refused or proposed to refuse to become or remain a member of a trade union; or had made use, or proposed to make use, of trade union services; or had filed to accept a bribe from their employer (sections 152(1) and 153 TULRCA 1992, as amended by section 32 Employment Relations Act 2004);
- of maternity-related grounds (regulation 20 Maternity and Parental Leave etc. Regulations 1999 (SI 1999/3312)) (*Amoah v Morgan Elliot Ltd* (unreported) ET, 2003, ET 2306156/2002);
- he took or was seeking to take paternity leave (regulation 29(2) Paternity and Adoption Leave Regulations 2002 (SI 2002/2788));
- he took or was seeking to take adoption leave (regulation 29(2) Paternity and Adoption Leave Regulations 2002);
- he requested flexible working arrangements (section 104C ERA 1996);
- he sought, in good faith, to assert a statutory employment protection right (section 105(7) ERA 1996);
- he took or was proposing to take certain specified types of action on health and safety grounds (section 105(3) ERA 1996);
- he was a shop worker or a betting worker and gave, or proposed to give, a notice "opting out" of Sunday working (section 105(4) ERA 1996);
- he was performing, or proposing to perform, any duties relevant to his role as an employee representative, or as a candidate or a participant in the election of an employee representative (section 105(6) ERA 1996);
- he was performing, or proposing to perform, any duties relevant to his role as an employee occupational pension scheme trustee (section 105(5) ERA 1996);

- of reasons relating to the national minimum wage (section 107(7A) ERA 1996);
- of reasons relating to the WTR 1998 (section 105(4A) ERA 1996);
- he made a protected disclosure within the meaning of the Public Interest Disclosure Act 1998 (section 105(6A) ERA 1996);
- of reasons relating to the Tax Credits Act 2002 (section 105(7B)ERA 1996);
- he took, or was seeking to take, parental leave (regulation 20 Maternity and Parental Leave etc. Regulations 1999);
- he took, or was seeking to take, time off to care for dependants (regulation 20 Maternity and Parental Leave etc. Regulations 1999);
- he took part in lawfully organised official industrial action lasting eight weeks or less (or more than eight weeks, in certain circumstances) (section 105(7C) ERA 1996);
- he exercised, or was seeking to exercise, rights relating to trade union recognition procedures (see Part VIII, Schedule A1 of the Trade Union and Labour Relations (Consolidation) Act 1992 (as inserted by Schedule 1 ERA 1999);
- he exercised or was seeking to exercise the right to be accompanied at a disciplinary or grievance hearing, or to accompany a fellow worker (section 12(3) ERA 1999);
- he performed or was proposing to perform any duties relating to an employee's role as a workforce representative or as a candidate to be such a representative for the purposes of the Transnational Information and Consultation of Employees Regulations 1999, or for taking certain actions in connection with these regulations, or for proposing to take or failing to take such actions (section 105(7D) ERA 1996);
- of grounds related to the Part-time Workers (Prevention of Less Favourable Treatment) Regulations 2000 (SI 2000/1551) (section 105(7E) ERA 1996);
- of grounds relating to the Fixed-term Employees (Prevention of Less Favourable Treatment) Regulations 2002 (SI 2002/2034) (section 105(7E) ERA 1996).

Note that to invoke protection under section 153 TULRCA 1992, section 105 ERA 1996, regulation 20(2) Maternity and Parental Leave etc. Regulations 1999 and regulation 29(2) Paternity and Adoption Leave Regulations 2002, the executive must show that:

- there is one or more employee in the undertaking who holds a similar position to him; and
- those employees have not been dismissed for a redundancy reason; and
- he was selected for an inadmissible reason.

At risk meetings

Once the executive has been provisionally selected for redundancy, an "at risk" letter should be issued. The letter should set out the reasons for the proposed redundancy, when redundancy consultation will take place and the terms of any redundancy payment if termination takes place. This should be a face-to-face meeting with the executive. There is no statutory right of accompaniment at this stage.

There is no need for the "at risk" meeting and redundancy consultation meeting to be two separate processes. The usual practice is for employers to offer affected employees paid leave so that they are not physically at work whilst the redundancy process is underway. It is important to keep the gap between the "at risk" meeting and redundancy consultation meetings as minimal as possible. If the company fails to start consultation meetings early when it could have done so, the executive may be entitled to compensation for loss of job-seeking opportunities (*Ekouil v Coney Island Ltd* [2002] IRLR 174, EAT). There is no general duty to consult with other employees who are not targeted for redundancy at the time of the employee's dismissal (*Bryne v Arvin Meritor LVS (UK) Ltd* (unreported) EAT, 2003, EAT 239/02).

Redundancy consultation

An "at risk" letter from the company will not constitute either consultation or an invitation to consult (*Rowell v Hubbard Group Services Ltd* [1995] IRLR 195, EAT). For individual redundancies, a consultation period of between one to four weeks is recommended, with at least two meetings with the employee. Consultation is required in all cases unless exceptional circumstances apply or where the employer can establish that consultation would have made no difference to the decision to terminate the employment (the "*Polkey* principle") (*Polkey v AE Dayton Services Ltd* [1988] ICR 142, HL). A redundancy dismissal is normally unfair where there has been no consultation at all (*Mugford v Midland Bank* [1997] IRLR 208, EAT).

If there are to be collective redundancies, there is a statutory duty to consult in good time (section 188(1A) TULRCA 1992). It is obligatory to consult recognised trade unions (Collective Redundancies and Transfer of Undertakings (Protection of Employment) (Amendments) Regulations 1999). If there is more than one recognised trade union, all of them have the right to be consulted (*Governing Body of NI Hotel and Catering College v National Association of Teachers in Further and Higher Education* [1995] IRLR 83). If there is no recognised trade union, consultation should take place with employee representatives.

If the company is "proposing" to make 20–99 employees redundant within 90 days it must consult with the employees 30 days before the proposed date of the first dismissal (*E Green & Son (Castings) Ltd v ASTMS* [1984] IRLR 135). In the case of 100 or more employees being made redundant within 90 days, there is a duty to consult 90 days in advance of any proposed dismissals (section 188(1A) TULRCA 1992). "Proposing to dismiss" in section 188(AA) does not necessarily require the contemplation of any particular number of redundancy dismissals, merely that some dismissals for redundancy would follow (*GMB v Amicus* [2003] ICR 1396, EAT). There is no duty to start consultation immediately, as long as it starts within the prescribed statutory periods.

The duty to consult is not triggered by a contemplation of collective redundancies, as "proposing" relates to a state of mind which is more certain than "having a view" as to some future redundancies (*MSF v Refuge Assurance plc* [2002] IRLR 324). However, in *Dewhirst Group v GMB Trade Union* [2003] IDS Brief 747, the EAT held that section 188 was triggered when the board of directors approved a decision to close down a manufacturing plant (resulting in redundancies) notwithstanding that shareholder consent had yet to be obtained to ratify the company's decision.

The purpose of consultation is for the company to disclose to the employee or employee representative the reason for dismissal, the number of employees affected and the proposed method of selection for redundancy (section 188(4) TULRCA 1992). Previously, it has been held that there is no need for the company to consult about the business reasons which made the dismissals inevitable; consultation is only required in relation to the consequences that flow from the employer's decision (*Securicor Omega Express Ltd v GMB* [2004] IRLR 9). As a result of the EU Collective Redundancies Directive (No. 98/59), the company is now required to consult on the business reasons behind the redundancies where the closure and redundancies are inextricably linked unless redundancies could be avoided notwithstanding the closure (*UK Coal Mining Ltd v National Union of Mineworkers* [2007] UKEAT/0397/06/RN). This means that any board decisions to close any business should be expressed as provisional only, and subject to redundancy consultation with the workforce.

The company and employee representatives must then try to:

- agree on ways in which dismissals may be avoided (e.g. providing alternative employment, withdrawing contracted-out work, introducing early retirement, relocating production, stopping recruitment and overtime);
- reduce the number of employees to be dismissed; and
- mitigate the effects of dismissal (e.g. offering training or outplacement assistance) (section 188(2) TULRCA 1992).

The company is required to comply with all of the three requirements failing which the consultation process may be deemed to have been a sham (*Middlesbrough Borough Council v TGWU and Anor* [2002] IRLR 332, EAT).

Only in certain exceptional circumstances may collective consultation be dispensed with (section 188(7) TULRCA 1992). This would apply to "special circumstances which render it not reasonably practicable" to engage in consultation. Insolvency is not in itself a special circumstance (*Clarks of Hove Ltd v Baker's Union* [1978] IRLR 366), whereas an unexpected financial crisis will be (e.g. the withdrawal of a takeover bid which led to a bank immediately placing the employer into receivership (*GMB v Rankin & Harrison* [1992] IRLR 514)). Where the employer's failure to consult is due to the default of the parent company, the special circumstances defence cannot be relied on. The mischief in section 188(7) is to remove from consideration the "[consultation] time lost as result of that delay" caused by the parent company (*GMB v Amicus* [2003] ICR 1396, EAT).

A protective award of *up to* 90 days' pay is payable if the company fails to carry out collective redundancy consultation. This applies regardless of whether 20 to 99 or 100 or more employees are at risk of redundancy, even though the statutory periods for consultation are 30 days and 90 days respectively (*D Evans v Permacell Finesse Ltd (In Administration)* [2007] UKEAT/0350/07).

Serving notice for termination

It is not possible to effect statutory consultation and serve notices for termination at the same time, in order to save time and running costs. Once notice of termination of employment is given, the company is effectively stating that the consultation process has finished (*National Union of Teachers v Avon County Council* [1978] IRLR 55). The danger for employers in issuing notices of termination *during* the collective consultation period is that meaningful collective consultation may be deemed to be lacking (*Junk v Wolfgang Kühnel*, case C-188/03, ECJ).

Redundancy notices should only be issued only when the consultation has been completed i.e. the consultation has either resulted in agreement with employee representatives, or has otherwise reached its conclusion. If consultation has been completed *within* the 30- or 90-day period, the employer may issue the notices at that point. Failure to carry out collective redundancy consultation may render the company liable to pay out a protective award of up to 90 days' pay.

"Suitable" and "reasonable" alternative employment

If, following consultation, the executive's redundancy is unavoidable, the company is required to consider whether there may be suitable alternative employment for the executive in its parent and associated companies (*Williams v Compair Maxim Ltd* [1982] IRLR 83, EAT). To avoid a claim of unfair redundancy or unfair dismissal, all that the company is required to do is to offer, where possible, *reasonable* alternative employment in the company or in any of its associated companies. "Reasonable" means any employment available during the consultation period, even if it means demotion. The company should ensure that opportunities are limited, at least in the first instance, to potentially redundant employees (*Ralph Martindale & Co Ltd v Harris* [2008] UKEAT 0166/07). Where the executive is offered *suitable* alternative employment (i.e. a different job but which carries the same status and same pay), an unreasonable refusal of the job offer may result in the forfeiture of a redundancy payment. An employee who unreasonably refuses to accept reinstatement or re-engagement (section 141(2) ERA 1996) or unreasonably leaves during the trial period (section 141(4) ERA 1996) is not entitled to claim SRP. Further, unreasonable refusal of reinstatement (not re-engagement) can lead to a reduction of any basic award provided that this is not less than two weeks' pay (capped).

Whether a job is "suitable" alternative employment is a question of fact. What constitutes "reasonable" alternative employment is a matter which should be put to the executive in any event. The company should not automatically assume that a lower position would be of no interest to the executive.

If the executive accepts "reasonable" alternative employment, he has the right to a statutory trial period of four weeks (although this trial period is extendable for retraining purposes) (section 138(3)(b) ERA 1996). The executive is still entitled to a redundancy payment if the re-engagement is terminated *within* the trial period (section 138(4)(b) ERA 1996) (*Reality (White Arrow Express) Ltd v O'Hara* (unreported) EAT, 18 November 2003, UKEAT/0447/03/TM) but not afterwards (*Optical Express Limited v Williams* [2007] IRLR 936). The reason for termination will remain as redundancy and the effective date of termination is when the original contract is lawfully ended (i.e. with notice or pay in lieu of notice) (section 138(4) ERA 1996).

Redundancy payments

If the executive has continuity of service of two years at the date of termination, he will qualify for either a statutory redundancy payment (SRP) or, if one exists, a contractual redundancy scheme (section 135 ERA 1996). SRP is calculated based on the prevailing statutory week's pay and which currently takes into account the employee's age and length of service. The company is required to set out the basis of how the SRP is calculated.

The company can operate an enhanced redundancy schemes provided that the scheme is not age discriminatory and mirrors the SRP scheme (reg. 33 EE(AD)R 2006). There are two ways of running an enhanced redundancy payment scheme:

- option 1: assess the employee's SRP and multiply the overall payment by a factor;
- option 2: assess the employee's "multiplier" and multiply it by a factor and/or assess the week's pay and multiply by a factor – the aggregate may then be multiplied again by a further factor.

By mirroring the SRP scheme, the Government has allowed older employees to receive a more generous redundancy payment.

The company may still offer "age-related" redundancy benefits, e.g. different levels of outplacement assistance, insurance benefits, care use, loans, etc. if such a practice is objectively justified. It should be noted that benefits awarded to a worker as a result of their cessation of employment also fall outside the scope of regulation 32 EE(AD)R 2006, which deals with service related benefits to employees whilst they are employed.

Executives resigning or leaving before their termination date

If the executive leaves his employment following a warning of future redundancies and before formal notice for termination has been served by the company, he is treated as having resigned and does not have the right to claim a redundancy payment (*Morton Sundour Fabrics Ltd v Shaw* [1967] ITR 84, Div Ct; *Kinmond v Rushton Connections Ltd* [1997] EAT/799/97). A warning of redundancy, which directly or indirectly, stipulates a precise date of termination may, in certain circumstances, be treated as a notice of dismissal (*Wadham Kenning Motor Group v Avery & Ors* (unreported) EAT, 1991, EAT405/91). Where the executive leaves following an announcement of a proposed closure at a specified date, which date is subject to constant review and the employer states that notices for dismissal would follow at some future time, there is no dismissal (*Doble v Firestone Tyre and Rubber Co Ltd* [1981] IRLR 300).

Where notice for termination has been served by the company, the executive may leave his employment before his employer's notice of dismissal expires in order to start a new job. The executive will not lose his right to a redundancy payment if he complies with section 136(3) ERA 1996 in terms of serving a counter-notice or if the employer agrees to his early departure.

Illegality

To dismiss the executive on this ground, the company has to show that the continued employment of the executive *actually* contravenes a statutory enactment. Where the employee has been dismissed, the burden of proof is on the employer to establish illegality, not on the employee to establish he is entitled to bring a claim. This means that employers have to very careful that they have sufficient evidence to show that continuing to employ the executive would be illegal, not that it might be.

An executive who works under an illegal contract cannot generally claim unfair dismissal when the contract is terminated. The Tribunal makes a distinction between a contract that is unlawful from the outset (e.g. to perform an illegal act or to carry out an immoral purpose), so that it is unenforceable by the parties, and one that is tainted by illegality as a result of the employer's conduct but this is unknown to the employee (e.g. where the employer fails to deduct tax from the employee's remuneration). Thus, an employee who knowingly defrauds HMRC by purporting to be self-employed

(*Beauvale Furnishings Ltd v Chapman* [2001] IRLR 670; *Napier v National Business Agency* [1951] 2 All ER 264) or who works without a work permit (*Sharma v Trustees and Executive Committee Members for the Time Being of the Hindu Cultural Society Slough* (unreported) EAT, 1990, EAT/253/90) cannot enforce the contract or pursue his employment protection rights.

Recent cases demonstrate that the courts will consider to what extent the contract is tainted by any alleged illegality (if at all) before deciding if the employee's complaint should be dismissed for want of jurisdiction. A contract which was lawful when it was made would not necessarily become unlawful by any incidental act of illegality in its performance, if the person seeking to enforce the contract did not have to rely on any conduct of illegality. In *Colen v Cebrian (UK) Ltd* [2003] EWCA Civ 1676, on the facts, the employee's conduct did not amount to fraud on HMRC and thus they were not precluded from claiming any unpaid commission and unfair dismissal against their employer. The employee's knowledge of and participation in the illegality is essential (*McEwing v Somoa Ltd* (unreported) EAT, 2004, UKEAT/0813/ 03/TM; *Wheeler v Qualitydeep Ltd (t/a Thai Royale Restaurant)* (unreported) EAT, 2003, EAT/0998/03/ TM; and *Kaid v Gruppo Ltd* (unreported) 2004, UKEAT/0546/03).

It should be noted that an executive may still sue the employer for discrimination if such a claim is not dependent on the enforceability of the contract (*Leighton v Michael; Leighton v Charalambous* [1996] IRLR 67). Where the employee is not entitled to be in employment and her contract could and should have been terminated during every day that it operated, then all the ordinary events of the contract are likely to be inextricably linked up with the employee's illegal conduct (*Vakante v Addey & Stanhope School* [2003] All ER (D) 352 (Dec)).

Where illegality is the reason for dismissal, an employer is required to act fairly prior to any dismissal. This will involve an assessment of the likely duration of any statutory prohibition (e.g. a driving ban or revocation of a driver's licence), whether the ban affects the whole or part of the employee's work and whether the employee can be redeployed taking into account the employee's views. Where a work permit has expired or the executive's right to work in the UK without a work permit has expired, enquiries should be made with the executive and also with the Borders and Immigration Agency as to whether it is lawful to continue to employ the executive whilst any applications to remain in and work in the UK are pending. In *Kelly v University of Southampton* [2007] UKEAT/0295/07, the employer unfairly dismissed a senior lecturer from the USA when her visa expired in January 2005, even though she had a work permit to work in the UK until January 2006. The EAT drew a distinction between the employer's obligation to verify the employee's right to work and her right to remain in the UK. If the company is not completely certain that the continued employment of the executive would in fact contravene the law, it should instead consider terminating the employment for "some other substantial reason" (see below) and follow the statutory procedures prior to any dismissal. In *Klusova v London Borough of Hounslow* [2007] EWCA Civ 1127, the Court of Appeal held that dismissing an employee where there has been a genuine but mistaken belief as to her immigration status which would render her continued employment unlawful can amount to "some other substantial reason".

"Some other substantial reason" (SOSR)

A dismissal for "some other substantial reason" is often relied upon by employers as an alternative reason for dismissal or where all other statutory reasons do not apply. As with all unfair dismissal claims, the Tribunal will consider if the employee was consulted and whether the dismissal was within the band of reasonable responses.

Where there is an express provision authorising the company to terminate the executive's employment if he ceases to be a director, the company must still establish a "sufficient reason" to effect a dismissal for some other substantial reason. This will involve looking at the set of facts, or beliefs held by the employer, which form the reason for the employee's dismissal. In *Mountain Spring Water Co Ltd v Colesby* [2005] UKEAT/0855/04), the Executive's Service Agreement and Table A of the Companies (Tables A to F) Regulations 1985 (SI 1985/805) provide that a director's employment will terminate immediately in the event he ceases to be a director. The Tribunal held that the executive director was fairly dismissed for SOSR because of the long history of shareholder disputes with the directors, the action of the company secretary, and that trust and confidence between the company and director had irredeemably broken down. Also, due to the above provisions, there was no breach of contract claim either.

In *Cobley v Forward Technology Industries Ltd* [2003] IRLR 706, the dismissal of a chief executive and managing director following a hostile takeover after he had led a competing bid for control of the company, was held to amount to dismissal for "some other substantial reason" and the dismissal was fair. The executive director had been lawfully removed from the board in accordance with an express term of his contract which permitted his removal by a board resolution. The court held that when effecting such a dismissal, there is no express or implied legal requirement that an employer must show the employee's continued employment would be actually harmful, or potentially harmful, to the interest of the company.

Where the reason relates to reorganisation, the Tribunal will expect the employer to have a sound business reason for the changes and to provide evidence demonstrating what these business reasons were and that the reasons were substantial (*Hollister v NFU* [1979] ICR 542). A SOSR dismissal may be made out if a business reorganisation to improve business efficiency leads to a change in employees' terms and conditions of employment and the employee unreasonably refuses to co-operate with changes that are beneficial to the employer (*Genower v Ealing, Hammersmith & Hounslow Area*

Health Authority [1980] IRLR 297; *Bramhall v Williams Cook Sheffield Ltd* [2004] (unreported)). Employers will also have to show that they have consulted with employees and given them a chance to adapt to any proposed changes.

In restrictive covenant cases, the Court of Appeal has held that an employer's desire to introduce restrictive covenants to protect its business can form a fair ground for dismissal under section 98(2) ERA 1996 (i.e. SOSR). The reasonableness of the employer's covenants is however a matter for Tribunals to consider under section 98(4) ERA 1996 when deciding if the employer has acted fairly prior to the employees' dismissal. If the executive refuses to agree to restrictive covenants when other employees have accepted the obligations, the company may be able to dismiss the executive for SOSR (*St John of God (Care Services) Ltd v Brooks* [1992] ICR 715). However, in *Willow Oak Developments Ltd t/a Windsor Recruitment v Silverwood & Ors* [2006] IRLR 607, the Court of Appeal held that, as the employees were only given 30 minutes to sign up to new covenants or risk losing their commission, and their manager had acted aggressively and intimidatingly towards them, their dismissal was unfair even if the covenants themselves had been wholly reasonable.

Other circumstances where dismissal has been for "some other substantial reason" (SOSR) include the following.

- Personality clashes with other employees where it is not possible to transfer the employee elsewhere. In *Perkin v St Georges Healthcare NHS Trust* [2005] EWCA Civ 1174, the director of finance within the Trust was dismissed because he was found to be difficult to work with, stubborn, rude to many who came across him, and generally intimidating in character. The Court of Appeal decided an employee's difficult personality could not, in itself, amount to SOSR for dismissal. Reasons related to personality, however, could, and in this case there had been a breakdown in confidence between the employer and a senior executive. The executive was held to be responsible for potentially damaging the operations of the employer's organisation, and making it impossible for the senior executive to work as part of a team.
- Dismissal for an ETO reason under regulation 4(5) TUPE 2006 (*Thompson v SCS Consulting Ltd* [2001] IRLR 801, EAT).
- Repudiatory breach of contract (e.g. absence without authorised leave) (*White v Bristol Rugby Ltd* [2002] IRLR 205).
- Expiry of a fixed-term contract and on the return of an employee from maternity leave or adoption leave (section 106(2) ERA 1996) or from suspension on medical grounds (section 106(3) ERA 1996).
- Pressure from third parties. In *Greenwood v Whiteghyll Plastics Limited* [2007] UKEAT/0219/07, the EAT held that if the employer is put under pressure by a third party (e.g. a client) to dismiss an employee who has been placed with them due to the standard of his work, the employer must consider any injustice to the employee

in dismissing him. In such a situation, the employer may have to consider job-swapping the employee with another employee at a different client site.

- Loss of confidence from customers. In *Wadley v Eager Electrical Ltd* [1986] IRLR 93, the employee was summarily dismissed following the arrest of his wife, who was also employed by the company, on charges of theft from the company. She was convicted and sentenced. The Tribunal held his dismissal was for SOSR (namely the discovery of his wife's dishonesty and consequent suspicions about his involvement in the thefts) because mutual trust and confidence and broken down. The EAT however held that to amount to a substantial reason for dismissal, a party to the employment relationship must be in breach of the duty of mutual trust and confidence and that being a member of the same household as a person who had been dishonest was not a sufficient reason for dismissal. They held that loss of confidence in the employee by the company's customers could have amounted to SOSR.
- Bringing the business into disrepute. In *Pay v Lancashire Probation Service* [2004] IRLR 129, a probation officer whose work involved rehabilitation of sex offenders was dismissed because he was found to be the director of a company selling items designed for sadomasochistic activities, whilst additionally having a stage show demonstrating sadomasochistic acts. It was held that his dismissal was for SOSR and fell within the range of reasonable responses open to the employer because of the nature of the work he was employed to do.
- Risk of disclosure of confidential information. In *Skyrail Oceanic Ltd t/a Goodmos Tours v Coleman* [1980] IRLR 226, the EAT held that such risks could amount to SOSR provided that the employer acted fairly prior to the employees' dismissal. Factors that will be relevant when assessing this could include: the position held by the employee; the employee's past conduct; whether the employee has access to confidential information; the importance of that confidential information; the position held by the other employee involved (both at the employer and at the competitor); the possibility of moving the employee or changing their job in order to remove the access to confidential information; and whether the employee had given (or was prepared to give) undertakings not to disclose confidential information. In *Chandlers (Farm Equipment) Ltd v Rainthorpe* [2005] UKEAT/0753/04/RN, the employee was summarily dismissed because of the employer's concern that she would disclose confidential information to her husband (a former employee who had joined a competitor). The Employment Tribunal stated that "the fear of passing confidential commercially sensitive information by an employee ... is a substantial reason of a kind such as potentially to justify dismissal". However it found that while the employee had access to important confidential information, there was nothing in her (or her husband's) past conduct which indicated that a disclosure (intentional or unintentional) would occur. The employer's dismissal was outside the range of reasonable responses and procedurally unfair because the employer

never put its concerns in writing, had made up its mind before talking to the employee, and did not give her an opportunity to appeal.

Retirement

The executive's employment may be terminated by the company when or after he has reached the company's normal retirement age (section 98(2(ba) ERA 1996, regulation 30(1) EEAR 2006). Where the employee's normal retirement age ("NRA") is below 65, it must be objectively justified by the company. No justification is however necessary where the NRA is on or above 65 (regulation 30(2) EEAR 2006). Where there is no normal retirement age, the statutory default retirement age of 65 applies.

Whether the executive's dismissal is on the ground of retirement (or for some other fair or unfair reason) will depend on whether the company has a normal retirement age; whether the executive was dismissed before or after the normal retirement age or, in the absence of that, the default retirement age; and whether the company has complied with the statutory retirement procedure.

The company must follow a six-step procedure. This can be summarised as follows:

1) The company must notify the executive at least six months and less than 12 months before the proposed date of retirement (para. 2 Schedule 6 EEAR 2006). If the company employer has breached its duty to notify, it has a continuing duty to notify the executive until the 14th day before their date of retirement (para. 4 Schedule 6 EEAR 2006).
2) The executive may make a request to work beyond their date of retirement either indefinitely, for a stated period, or until a stated date.
3) If the company has complied with its duty to notify, the request must be made between three to six months of the retirement date and, at least six months before the retirement date if the company has not complied with its duty to notify (para. 5 Schedule 6 EEAR 2006).
4) The company must then hold a meeting to consider the executive's request (para. 7 Schedule 6 EEAR 2006). A meeting need not be held if (a) the parties agree that the executive's employment will continue indefinitely and the company gives notice to the executive to that effect; or (b) the parties agree that the executive's employment will continue for an agreed period and the company gives notice to the executive of the length of that period or of the date on which it will end; or (c) it is not practicable to hold a meeting within the period that is reasonable, and the company considers any representations made by the executive.
5) The company must give the executive notice of its decision on the request "as soon as is reasonably practicable" (para 7(6) Schedule 6 EEAR 2006). There is no legal requirement for the company to give any reasons for its decision.

6) The company must give the executive the right of an appeal against its decision (para. 8 Schedule 6 EEAR 2006). The executive may appeal against the company's decision either to refuse their request or in relation to the period of extended employment but this must be done "as soon as is reasonably practicable" after the date of the employer's notice

The statutory retirement procedures are extremely prescriptive. If the procedures are not adhered to, there is a risk that the Employment Tribunal would find that retirement was not the genuine reason for the executive's termination of employment. If such cases, there would also be the risks of an age discrimination claim if the executive is held to be unfairly dismissed.

There is no longer a mandatory retirement age for directors under CA 2006. To avoid age discrimination claims, any requirement on officers of the company to step down on reaching a certain age must be objectively justified by the company.

TUPE related dismissals

If the business of the company is acquired by or sold to another entity (or there is a service provision change involving the executive), the executive's employment will automatically transfer to the buyer (or to incoming contractor in the case of service provision change) under the Transfer of Undertakings (Protection of Employment) Regulations 2006 (TUPE 2006). TUPE can potentially apply to a transfer of part of a business in the UK to a non-European Union country (*Holis Metal Industries Limited v GMB & Newell* [2007] EAT/0171/07). TUPE will not operate to transfer the executive's employment if the executive objects to the transfer. In that event, his employment will come to an end on the date of the transfer by operation of law (regulation 4(7) TUPE 2006). A literal interpretation of regulation 4(7) is that the objection needs to be made before the date of the transfer. However, if the executive is not aware of the identity of the transferee until the transfer has taken place, the objection is valid after the transfer date (*New ISG Ltd v Vernon and ors* [2007] EWHC 2665).

In the absence of a TUPE objection, the executive's existing terms and conditions of employment shall have effect after the transfer as if originally made between him and the buyer or transferee (regulation 4(1) TUPE 2006). In *Regent Security Services Ltd v Power* [2007] EWCA Civ 1188, the Court of Appeal held that although the employee never lost his pre-transfer right to retire at 60, he had also acquired the additional right to retire at 65 after the transfer and was free to choose between the additional right or his existing right. It remains unclear whether the executive can validly agree to a detrimental variation to some of his terms and conditions of employment in exchange for an improvement to other contractual terms. TUPE cannot however create rights that did not exist prior to the transfer. Thus in *Jackson v Computershare Investor Services Plc*

[2007] EWCA Civ 1065, the employee was not entitled to the transferee's contractual redundancy scheme as that scheme only applied to employees employed by the company before the date of the transfer.

Regulation 4(5) of TUPE 2006 provides very limited grounds upon which the company can validly change the executive's existing contractual terms. The variation must be for a reason connected with the transfer that is an economic, technical or organisational (ETO) reason entailing changes in the workforce; or a reason unconnected with the transfer. The company therefore needs to be wary of the risks of constructive dismissal claims if there is a proposal to vary the executive's existing contractual terms outside of regulation 4(5).

Regulation 4(9) of TUPE 2006 provides that "where a relevant transfer involves or would involve a substantial change in working conditions to the material detriment of a person whose contract of employment is or would be transferred under paragraph (1), such an employee may treat the contract of employment as having been terminated, and the employee shall be treated for any purpose as having been dismissed by the employer". Where this applies, regulation 4(10) of TUPE 2006 says that "no damages shall be payable by an employer as a result of a dismissal falling within paragraph 4(9) in respect of any failure by the employer to pay wages to an employee in respect of a notice period which the employee has failed to work." This means that the executive can resign with or without notice when claiming constructive dismissal against the company. If he gives notice and is willing to continue to work during the notice period, he must continue to be paid by the company in the usual way. Otherwise he may still be able to recover non-wage-related benefits for the notice period in any event.

It is automatically unfair to terminate the executive's employment if the sole or principal reason for the dismissal was a transfer or a reason connected with the transfer (regulation 7(1) TUPE 2006). The executive's employment may however be terminated before or after the transfer for an ETO reason entailing changes in the workforce (regulation 7(2) TUPE 2006) or for a reason which is unconnected to the transfer, e.g. misconduct, capability or retirement. Redundancies in connection with the transfer may fall within the ETO reason although this is generally invoked by the transferee after the transfer. Furthermore, a transferor is only able to rely on an ETO reason which relates to its *own* future conduct of the business, not one which solely relates to the transferee (*Hynd v Armstrong and ors* [2007] IRLR 338). It is therefore not open to the transferee to dictate that the purchase of the seller's business is subject to the transferor dismissing certain employees *before* the transfer. In *Whitehouse v Blatchford & Sons* [1999] IRLR 492, the transferor, a hospital, made it a condition of awarding a contract that the transferee (the incoming contractor) would reduce the number of employees by one to reduce the price of the contract. When the employee was subsequently dismissed by the contractor, the EAT interestingly held that the dismissal was for an ETO reason entailing changes in the workforce.

Only executives with one or more years of continuous service with the company can clam unfair dismissal if the sole or principal reason for their dismissal is the transfer itself or a reason connected with the transfer that is not an economic, technical or organisational reason entailing changes in the workforce (regulation 7(1) TUPE 2006).

The company must inform and consult with its employees before a TUPE transfer. It must provide union officials or employee representatives with the following information long enough before the transfer takes place in order to leave adequate time for genuine consultations:

- details of approximately when and why the transfer is going to happen;
- the legal, economic and social implications of the transfer for the affected employees;
- whether the company envisages taking any "measures" (e.g. business re-organisation) in connection with the transfer which will affect the employees, and if so, what measures are envisaged;
- and whether the prospective new employer envisages carrying out any "measures" which will affect the employees, and if so, what these measures are (e.g. post transfer redundancies, changes to contractual terms etc).

The company is only under an obligation to "inform" employees in relation to points 1 and 2. The duty to "consult" only arises where "measures" are being envisaged by the company or new employer. Where there is a failure to carry out TUPE consultation in the absence of any "special circumstances", the company and transferee are jointly and severally liable for a protective award in a sum not exceeding 13 weeks' pay per employee (regulation 15 TUPE 2006). Such awards are punitive in nature and not compensatory (*Sweetin v Coral Racing* [2006] IRLR 252).

CHAPTER 7

Terminating the directorship

Position under Companies Act 2006

With effect from 1 October 2007, section 168 CA 2006 provides that the company may by ordinary resolution at a meeting remove a director before the expiration of his period of office, notwithstanding anything in the service agreement, contract or letter of appointment. Special notice is required of a resolution to remove a director or to appoint somebody instead of a director. Under section 169 CA 2006, the director on receipt of notice of an intended resolution to remove him, is entitled to be heard on the resolution at the meeting. Where notice is given of an intended resolution to remove a director and the director concerned makes representations in writing to the company and requests his notification to members of the company, the company must, unless the representations are received by it too late for it to do so, notify the shareholders.

Position under articles of association

The company's articles of association also regulate the appointment, retirement and removal of directors from the board. Typically, the articles will provide that the executive should cease to be a director when one of the following applies:

- the executive ceases to be a director by virtue of any provision of the Companies Acts, or is prohibited by law from being a director;
- the executive becomes subject to a receiving order or compounds with his creditors generally;
- in the opinion of all the other directors, mental disorder makes the executive incapable of discharging the duties of a director;
- the executive fails, without the directors' permission, to participate in directors' meetings for more than three months, and is not prevented from doing so by illness, accident, or some other cause which the directors consider sufficient;

- a notification to the company that the executive is resigning or retiring from office as director;
- the directors decide to accept the executive's offer to resign from the office of director;
- an ordinary resolution is passed removing the executive from office.

In relation to retirement, the articles will usually provide for directors to retire by rotation. The usual procedure is as follows:

- At the first annual general meeting all the directors shall retire from office.
- At every subsequent annual general meeting half of the directors shall retire from office and offer themselves for reappointment by the members.
- The directors to retire by rotation shall be those who have been longest in office since their last appointment or reappointment by a general meeting, but as between persons who were last appointed or reappointed on the same day, those to retire shall be decided by lot.

Effect of cessation of office on employment

Terminating the executive's directorship does not automatically bring his employment to an end unless this eventuality is expressly provided for in the service agreement. Indeed, the company may not necessarily wish to bring the entire contractual relationship to an end simply because the executive is no longer a board member, as he may still be able to make a valuable contribution to the company as an employee. Unless there are provisions in the articles of association or service agreement governing the position, the company is at risks of claims for breach of contract and unfair dismissal (see *Mountain Spring Water Co Ltd v Colesby* [2005] UKEAT/0855/04 and *Cobley v Forward Industries Technology Ltd* [2003] IRLR 706).

CHAPTER **8**

Shareholder issues on termination

Articles of association and shareholders' agreement

The company's articles or the shareholders' agreements will usually prescribe what should happen in the event of a shareholder's dispute. Unlike Scotland, the Unfair Contract Terms Act 1977 (UCTA 1977) does not apply to share option schemes in England and Wales (paragraph 1(d) Schedule 1 UCTA 1977). Typically, the parties will have agreed to resort to mediation and, if that fails, for the aggrieved shareholder to have the right to require the other shareholders to buy him out at a fair price. In the case of small companies with only a few shareholders, the usual provision is for each side to offer to buy the other out and the one offering the highest price wins.

In relation to private limited companies which are not listed, the articles of association may provide that shares already awarded to the executive must be offered for sale when the executive leaves the company. To comply with the requirements of paragraph 33, Schedule 2 to the Income Tax (Earnings and Pensions) Act 2003, HMRC expects the following requirements to be met:

- The requirement to offer shares for sale must apply to *all* employees of the company (or of any participating company in a group plan) but may be restricted to certain specified reasons for cessation.
- The requirement to offer shares for sale must be mandatory. It cannot be left to the discretion of any person or persons to decide whether shares are to be offered for sale.
- The transfer notice must take effect at the time the relevant individual ceases to be an employee of the company, or of any company under the control of the company whose shares are used within the plan.
- The requirement to give a transfer notice can extend to persons to whom shares have been transferred (e.g. family members or family trusts).
- The articles must provide that anyone wishing to dispose of shares of the same class as the plan shares must offer them for sale (a 'general pre-emption' provision). The terms of sale for a voluntary sale must be no better than those which apply to employees.

- Once shares have been offered for sale there must be no facility allowing an employee or director to withdraw the irrevocable transfer notice. A total transfer condition or similar will not be acceptable. Where buyers are found for part of the shareholding, that part must be sold.
- If 100 per cent of the shareholders have consented to waive their pre-emptive rights to acquire the shares being transferred, the general pre-emption procedures would become unnecessary. Consent of less than 100 per cent is unacceptable. It is not acceptable for such a 100 per cent consent provision to apply to *employee* pre-emption.

Alternatively, the articles may provide that a transfer notice shall be given following cessation of employment. If such a provision is to apply to shares of the class used in the scheme, it must comply with the requirements of paragraphs 21(2) and (3), Schedule 3, or paragraphs 19(2) and (3), Schedule 4 to ITEPA 2003. HMRC expects the following requirements to be met:

- The requirement to offer shares for sale must be imposed by the articles of association. Such arrangements cannot be imposed by means of a shareholders' agreement or in scheme rules.
- The requirement to offer shares for sale must apply to *all* employees *and all* directors upon cessation for *any* reason and to *all* shares of the class used in the scheme held at the date of cessation.
- The requirement to offer shares for sale must be mandatory. It cannot be left to the discretion of any person or persons to decide whether shares are to be offered for sale.
- The transfer notice must take effect at the time the relevant individual ceases to be an employee or director of the company, and any company under the control of the company whose shares are used within the scheme.
- If a director or employee is given a right to acquire shares (for example, a share option) but does not exercise that right until after he has ceased to be an employee or director, then he, or any other person (for example, personal representatives), must be required to offer his shares for sale immediately he acquires them.
- The requirement to give a transfer notice can only apply to shares held by the employee or director. The requirement cannot extend to persons to whom shares have been transferred (e.g. family members or family trusts) because these shares were not acquired "in pursuance of rights or interests obtained by such directors or employees".
- The terms of sale must be the same as apply for a voluntary sale.
- Once shares have been offered for sale, there must be no facility allowing an employee or director to withdraw the irrevocable transfer notice. A total transfer

condition or similar will not be acceptable. Where buyers are found for part of the shareholding, that part must be sold.

- If 100 per cent of the shareholders waive their pre-emptive rights to acquire the shares being transferred, the general pre-emption procedures would become unnecessary. Consent of less than 100 per cent is unacceptable. It is not acceptable for such a 100 per cent consent provision to apply to employee pre-emption.

In relation to share options, "good leaver" and "bad leaver" provisions would determine whether the Executive's shares which have vested remain exercisable if they have not yet been exercised on termination of his employment. Typical "good leaver" grounds would be redundancy, disability, or retirement at or after the normal retirement age. "Bad leaver" grounds would typically include poor performance, misconduct and retirement before the normal retirement age. Typically, the scheme might provide that an executive who voluntarily ceases employment prior to the expiration of a three-year period, will generally lose all entitlement to the shares. However, if the executive ceases employment before the third anniversary of the date of grant on the grounds of retirement at a specified retirement age, he will usually be able to retain some or all of his entitlement. Such provisions might easily be challenged as discriminatory on the grounds of age and, if successful, would have to be treated as a "good leaver" by the company. It should be noted that the SAYE (save as you earn) and share incentive plan (SIP) legislation requires retiring employees to be treated favourably by being able to receive shares. The regulations provide that "no act done in order to comply with a requirement of any statutory provision" is unlawful. Therefore positive discrimination under SAYE and SIPs would seem to be lawful if the age specified in the plan is also legally compliant.

Removing retirement provisions altogether avoids age discrimination but this might prove unpopular, especially where favourable treatment on retirement is long-established, as it could lead to an employee retiring at age 65 being treated as a "bad leaver". If the company's main purpose in having a share scheme is to use it as a retention tool, and providing deferred remuneration to employees is only a secondary consideration, then the company may be comfortable justifying any direct discrimination. An alternative is to replace "normal retirement age" with a "length of service" provision. This is easier to defend legally, but many employers will not want even very long-serving employees to be able to go to a competitor with their option rights intact.

Some share option schemes contain a discretion for the board or a committee to decide that an otherwise bad leaver should be treated as good. Care will need to be taken to ensure the exercise of the discretion is consistent and not discriminatory or in breach of the implied obligation of trust and confidence. (*Mallone v BPB Industries* [2002] IRLR 452; *McCarthy v McCarthy & Stone PLC* [2007] EWCA Civ 664).

One option is to delay the favourable treatment until the end of any restrictive covenant or vesting period, rather than accelerate it to the time of retirement. There is however a risk that this approach is still indirectly discriminatory because older employees are more likely to "retire" than younger employees.

Changes to the company's existing scheme rules may require consent from HMRC, shareholders and participants of the scheme. Specialist "employee benefits scheme" advice should always be sought prior.

Unfair prejudice petition

With effect from 1 October 2007, the executive can make an application to the court under section 994 CA 2006 if the executive is a registered shareholder; and the company's affairs are being conducted or have been conducted in a manner (or there is an actual or proposed act or omission) which is unfairly prejudicial to the interests of its shareholders generally or some of its shareholders including the executive.

Such petitions are likely to be made where the executive has been or is about to be excluded from the management of the company. The executive can only bring a claim if he remains a member of the company. If, for example, the articles permit the directors to divest the aggrieved shareholder of his shares, the effect of the removal of his shareholding will also be to remove his standing either to present or continue with the unfair prejudice petition. In such a situation, the executive can apply to the court for an injunction restraining the transfer of his shares which would deprive him of a remedy under section 994 (*Re a Company No. 00330 of 1991, ex parte Holden* [1991] BCLC 597).

The court has very wide powers to deal with a section 994 petition. It may:

- regulate the conduct of the company's affairs in the future;
- require the company to refrain from doing or continuing an act complained of, or to do an act that the petitioner has complained it has omitted to do;
- authorise civil proceedings to be brought in the name and on behalf of the company by such person or persons and on such terms as the court may direct;
- require the company not to make any, or any specified, alterations in its articles without the leave of the court;
- provide for the purchase of the shares of any members of the company by other members or by the company itself and, in the case of a purchase by the company itself, the reduction of the company's capital accordingly.

The most common remedy claimed under such action is for the shares of the petitioning shareholder to be bought at a fair value to be determined by the court, if not agreed, unless there is conclusive evidence that the scheme would not be in the best interests of the company. The court would be more likely to intervene in the affairs of a company if one or more of the following could be shown:

- creditors of the company would be prejudiced by the scheme;
- the other minority shareholders shared the petitioner's opinion;
- the directors were acting in breach of their fiduciary duties and not in the best interests of the company;
- the scheme was unlawful or had an unlawful purpose.

Generally, the courts tend to take a very pragmatic approach, as the chances are that the relationships within the company have broken down due to the dispute, and are more likely to order a buyout of the executive's shares. Such petitions involve very lengthy and prohibitively costly hearings. To reduce the risks of an adverse costs order, mediation should be considered by the company and the shareholder at a very early stage.

Derivative actions

With effect from 1 October 2007, a "derivative action" may be brought by a shareholder where an actual or proposed act or omission involving negligence, default, breach of duty or breach of trust by a director of the company may give rise to a cause of action. A "derivative action" will be available for breach of duty of directors, even if the director has not benefited personally from the breach. It is immaterial whether the cause of action arose before or after the executive became a member of the company. It will not be necessary for the shareholder to show that those directors who carried out the wrongdoing control the majority of the company's shares.

Although the claim may be brought by a member of the company, the cause of action must be vested in the company and the relief must be sought on behalf of the company (as opposed to the member).

Section 261 CA 2006 introduced a two-stage procedure for an applicant who is seeking permission to continue a derivative claim:

- Stage 1: the shareholder will be required to make a prima facie case for permission to continue a derivative claim and the court will be required to consider the issue on the basis of the evidence filed by the shareholder, without requiring evidence from the defendant. The court must dismiss the application if the applicant cannot establish a prima facie case.
- Stage 2: the court may require evidence to be provided by the company (prior to the start of the substantive action).

Recent changes to the derivative action regime may lead to increased tactical litigation against the board from "activist shareholders", particularly when there has been a fall out between the executive and the board. When such claims are unfounded, the Companies Act allows the court to dismiss the application and to make a costs order against the shareholder.

Share valuation and settlement of share-related claims

It is usual in share disputes for the executive and the company to agree a mechanism for valuing shares.

If there is agreement on the value of the shares, the court will usually uphold this in the case of an unfair prejudicial petition. Otherwise the court will usually order that an expert is to determine the value of the shares. The court can specify what the expert should and should not take into consideration.

Generally, the threat of a section 994 petition is used by the executive as an additional weapon to maximise his overall exit package.

CHAPTER **9**

Assessing the severance package

Overview

When assessing the executive's termination package, the company will need to assess the likely compensation which would be awarded to the executive if he is successful in his claims, whether these are for wrongful dismissal, breach of contract, unfair dismissal and/or discrimination. Additional factors for consideration by the board include:

- the merits of the executive's alleged claims and any other potential claims;
- the evidence the executive has in supporting his claims;
- the burden of proof, having regard to the nature of the claims;
- the executive's employability and the buoyancy of the labour market;
- the financial resources available to the parties;
- the likely costs of instigating and defending any legal proceedings;
- the management time in dealing with the executive's claims;
- any reputational issues for the company;
- proximity to the expiry of relevant time limits for the executive to bring claims.

Formalities under the Companies Act 2006

With effect from 1 October 2007, termination payments are regulated by sections 215 to 222 CA 2006. Under section 215(1), "payment for loss of office" means a payment (or provision of benefits) made to a director or past director:

- as compensation for loss of office as director of the company;
- as compensation for loss of any other office or employment with the company in connection with the management of the affairs of the company or any of its subsidiaries while a director or in connection with ceasing to be a director;
- as consideration for or in connection with the director's retirement from office or

any other office or employment with the company or its subsidiaries in connection with the management of their affairs

Under the old section 317 of the Companies Act 1985, it had been asserted that a payment for loss of *employment* could be distinguished from a payment for loss of *office*, in that the former did not require shareholder approval. However, the provisions in the 2006 Act make it clear that, unless an exception applies, a payment to a director on termination of employment requires shareholder approval. In particular, payments for loss of office under sections 217 (payment by company: requirement of members' approval), 218 (payment in connection with transfer of undertaking) and 219 (payment in connection with share transfer) all require shareholders approval, unless the company is not a UK-registered company, or is a wholly-owned subsidiary of another body corporate.

The company may not make a payment for loss of office to a director of the company (or holding company) unless the payment has been approved by a resolution of the members of the company (section 217(1) and (2) CA 2006). The shareholders must receive a memorandum detailing the proposed payment before the meeting at which they will vote. There is no need for approval if the payment is less than £200 (section 221(1) CA 2006).

If a payment is made unlawfully, it is held by the recipient on trust for the company making the payment, and any director who authorised the payment is jointly and severally liable to indemnify the company that made the payment for any loss resulting from it.

In most cases, the company should be able to rely on the exemptions in section 220(1). Approval is not required under sections 217, 218 or 219 for a payment made in *good faith*:

- in discharge of an *existing* legal obligation not entered into in connection with the event giving rise to the payment;
- by way of damages for breach of such an obligation;
- by way of settlement or compromise of any claim arising in connection with the termination of a person's office or employment; or
- by way of pension in respect of past services.

The company must therefore examine closely any "loss of office" payment to a departing director before agreeing to make such a payment in a compromise agreement. Payments in lieu of notice or other payments under the director's service agreement or damages for breach of contract should not require shareholder approval, as they constitute payments in discharge of an *existing* legal obligation. However, the company would still have to demonstrate that factors such as mitigation of loss and accelerated receipt have been taken into account in determining the amount of damages. The "good faith" requirement could also potentially affect contractually agreed entitlements such as a "golden parachute" payment or "change of control" payment to a director, where they appear excessive.

Corporate governance rules for listed companies

The Combined Code encourages remuneration committees to carefully consider compensation terms contained in a director's service agreement in the event of termination. In summary, the board should aim to avoid rewarding directors for poor performance and take a robust line on reducing compensation, to reflect the departing director's obligations to mitigate loss. Further, notice or contract periods should be set at one year or less.

The ABI and NAPF also recommend in their best practice statement dated December 2003 that boards of listed companies consider phasing termination payments over the notice period and to take into account mitigation, avoid liquidated damages (golden parachute) payments, reduce notice periods for poor performance, avoid compensation for failure and avoid "change of control" protection clauses unless exceptional circumstances apply. The revised statement on 18 February 2008 contains eight principles on aligning management and shareholder interests (see Appendix J).

Structuring the financial package

Salary

All salary up to the executive's termination date should be subject to tax and NIC in the final pay slip.

Holiday pay

All accrued but untaken statutory holidays in the relevant holiday year as at the termination date should be included in the termination package. Tax and NIC must be deducted from the holiday pay.

Notice pay

Where there is an express or discretionary PILON clause in the service agreement or staff handbook, or a customary practice of making such payments, such sums will have to be subject to tax and NIC. Some employers take a commercial risk and offer the executive a tax-free sum on the basis that the payment was not made pursuant to any

PILON clause but represents a settlement of a dispute, but this approach is vulnerable to challenge by HMRC and should be avoided if possible.

Bonus

Most scheme rules would provide that the executive has no right to a bonus if at the time the payment is due the executive has (or has been given) notice for termination of employment or no longer employed by the company. If a bonus is payable, tax and NIC needs to be deducted and should be made via the final payroll.

If the bonus scheme is purely discretionary, the company has to exercise its discretion in a way which is not irrational or capricious. Recent cases suggest that the courts are increasingly vigilant against sharp practice particularly when the employer behaves in such a way to deprive the employee of a bonus (*Takacs v Barclays Services Jersey Ltd* [2006] IRLR 877). In the *Takacs* case, the High Court held that the implied term of "trust and confidence" implied into all contracts of employment includes an implied term of "co-operation" and an implied "anti-avoidance term", with the result that it is unlawful for an employer to make it difficult or impossible for an employee to become entitled to benefits provided for by his contract – in this case, the bonus was conditional upon the employee reaching a particular sales target.

In relation to sign-on bonuses, particularly those which are staggered over a period of time, when the executive's employment is prematurely terminated, it is important to check the forfeiture rules. Usually, the executive will lose the right to any future payments if their employment has been terminated for "cause" as defined in the service agreement.

Company car and other equipment

Where the executive has use of a company car, there is the option of permitting the executive to retain or purchase the vehicle as part of the severance package. It is important to ensure that the executive agrees to arrange for separate insurance cover on termination, otherwise the company may be vicariously liable in the event of an accident.

If the executive wishes to retain a home computer or their work mobile phone, the company should ensure that retention of such items is conditional upon the deletion of all confidential and proprietary information belonging to the company, or that the company has the right to inspect those items before ownership is transferred to the executive. The executive should be required to comply with the terms of any licences for software on the computer and to arrange the transfer of the mobile phone number and contract to his own name by the termination date.

Where the executive is purchasing any company property at trade value, tax on the benefit of the balance between the trade and market value is payable. This should be included on Form P11D by the company.

If the executive refuses to return company property to the company on termination, this is a potential offence under the Theft Act 1968 (as amended).

Shares/share options/share incentive plans

In relation to shares, reference should be made to the articles of association, shareholders' agreement and/or share incentive plan as to whether there is any obligation on the executive to transfer his shares back to the company or whether they should be sold to other shareholders, and the mechanism for valuing those shares on termination. If the executive has share options which have matured but not yet been exercised, it is important to check if such options will automatically lapse or remain exercisable for a certain period of time.

It is not unusual to see an exclusion clause that prevents damages being recovered on a contractual basis for loss of entitlements under the share or share option scheme where termination takes place in breach of contract. In *Micklefield v SAC Technology Ltd* [1990] IRLR 218, the court held that such contractual exclusions are valid. It should however be noted that a "*Micklefield* clause" will not be effective against an unfair dismissal claim or other statutory claim, since these can only be waived by way of a compromise agreement, so the contractual exclusion is not effective.

Where there is no "*Micklefield* clause", the scheme might contain "good leaver" provisions or "bad leaver" provisions, as discussed earlier. These should be checked as the value of the share options in a breach of contract claim can easily exceed the value of the executive claims for wrongful and unfair dismissal.

Where the share incentive scheme is expressed as discretionary and based on performance criteria, the company needs to ensure that the exercise of its discretion is not open to legal challenge. In *McCarthy v McCarthy & Stone Plc* [2006] EWHC 1851 (Ch), Mr McCarthy, an executive director, was granted options over a number of shares in the company. The rules of the scheme provided that the company's remuneration committee "shall at its absolute discretion determine whether the options will be exercisable having considered the extent to which the Performance Condition was satisfied" at the termination date. Although the performance condition, which related to an increase in the company's earnings per share, was met, the company initially refused to allow Mr McCarthy to exercise the options completely but subsequently allowed him to exercise his option over 75 per cent of the shares granted to him. The remuneration committee based its decision on a number of grounds, including the fact that Mr McCarthy had allied himself with the interests of a competing business, that he had been responsible for a press announcement suggesting that the company's shares were over-valued, and circulated an email to staff implying that their interests would be better served by joining the competing business of which he was to become a director. Further, the remuneration committee gave no reasons how it arrived at the 75 per cent figure. The High Court held that it was not open to the remuneration committee to take into account conduct which had nothing to do with the performance condition. Since that condition had been met, the company had to allow Mr McCarthy to exercise 100 per cent of his option.

If the scheme is administered by trustees or by some other third party, then the share option provisions will need to be carefully analysed on termination of employment. Bear in mind that the company cannot properly commit to treating the options in a particular way which is outside its power or which fetters with the trustees powers under the scheme. In such situations, it is safer to agree with the executive that the company will use reasonable endeavours to procure the outcome or will recommend a particular outcome to the trustees/administrators of the scheme.

Ex-gratia payments

This is an area where the executive or those advising him would be pushing hard to maximise the exit package, particularly considering the £30,000 tax-free threshold. It is important to ensure that any ex-gratia payment is not treated as pensionable salary.

Also, it is not unusual for some proportion of the ex-gratia payment to be withheld pending compliance with, for example, post-termination restrictions or an obligation to return company property. Payment in instalments can sometimes be combined with a contractual obligation on the executive to mitigate his losses by seeking alternative employment and a provision that, should they be successful in their search, then further payments to them will cease, or be reduced accordingly.

Writing off loans is a taxable benefit and can complicate tax arrangements. As such, it is probably simpler to increase the compensation to the executive by such an amount as will, after the deduction of tax, equal the outstanding amount. The executive would then remain obliged to repay the loan to the company from his final payslip.

Insurance-related benefits

Continuation of insurance policies or other benefits post termination of employment may add value to a departing executive, especially where a payment in lieu of notice has been made. The company should always obtain prior clearance with the insurer, otherwise it may have to bear the cost of any claim directly. Extension beyond the policy's next renewal date is likely to attract payment of a further premium. Also, most permanent health insurers will not offer continued cover after employment (except where a claim is already in motion, and a continuation policy may be agreed). Another option is to offer the executive the possibility of purchasing a continuation policy at his own expense. Such continuation policies are often on better terms than purchasing a stand-alone insurance policy, particularly with regard to coverage of pre-existing medical conditions.

Outplacement assistance schemes

Under section 310 of the Income Tax (Employment and Pensions) Act 2003 (ITEPA 2003), no liability to income tax arises in respect of the provision of services to a person in connection with the cessation of the person's employment, or the payment or reimbursement of fees or travelling expenses for such provision. The main purpose of the provision of the services must be to enable the person to adjust to the cessation of the employment and/or or to find other gainful employment (including self-employment). The outplacement service can include: (a) giving advice and guidance; (b) imparting or improving skills; or (c) providing or making available the use of office equipment or similar facilities. The executive must have been employed in full-time employment for a period of at least two years. The company must ensure that such outplacement assistance is available generally to employees or former employees.

Directors and officers liability insurance

Under section 233 CA 2006, it is possible for the company to indemnify its directors in respect of liabilities which they incur in the performance of their duties and to reimburse directors for the legal costs incurred by them in defending claims against them by purchasing directors' and officers' liability insurance for the benefit of the director. Further, section 235 CA 2006 allows the indemnification of directors of companies acting as trustees of occupational pension schemes.

In addition, section 239 CA 2006 allows the company's shareholders to ratify a director's conduct amounting to negligence, default, breach of duty or breach of trust in relation to the company. Significantly, votes of the director in breach and any connected persons are to be disregarded, the effect of which is to increase protection for minority shareholders. The ratification is to be by ordinary resolution unless the company's articles require a higher majority.

Any relevant indemnity must comply with the strict requirements of CA 2006. For example, the company may not indemnify a director for criminal fines or penalties imposed by regulatory bodies (section 234(3) CA 2006). The 2006 Act contains detailed rules requiring copies of qualifying indemnities to be kept and these must be available for inspection for a year after they have expired or terminated (section 237(4) CA 2006). The existence of a qualifying indemnity must also be disclosed in the director's annual report (section 236 CA 2006).

In the context of a compromise agreement the company should ensure that any insurance cover post termination of employment is expressed as subject to the terms of the policy, approval of the insurer and limited to a period of time only e.g. covering acts or omissions occurring before the executive's termination date, or only for such period as existing directors will continue to get the benefit of such insurance. If the company is not proposing to renew the policy on its expiry, the executive may require the company to retain "run off" cover, i.e. permitting the executive to notify claims for an extended period following non-renewal.

Legal fees

Under HMRC's Extra Statutory Concession A81 (http://www.hmrc.gov.uk/manuals/eimanual/EIM13740.htm), legal costs incurred where a dispute is settled without recourse to the courts are tax-free where the costs are paid direct to the employee's solicitor in full or partial discharge of the solicitor's bill of costs in connection with the termination, and are payable under a specific term of a settlement agreement. Invoices should be addressed to the employee but marked payable by the employer. Further, no charge will be applied where the dispute goes to court and a payment of costs is made by the employer directly to the employee in accordance with a court order (whether this is made following judgment or compromise of an action). The concession only applies to legal costs and not to professional costs (e.g. accountancy fees) or fees over and above the employer's liability or agreed contribution.

Tax issues

Section 401 ITEPA 2003 states that payments and other benefits which are received directly or indirectly in consideration or in consequence of, or otherwise in connection with: (a) the termination of a person's employment; (b) a change in the duties of a person's employment; or (c) a change in the earnings from a person's employment, are deemed as "employment income" and taxable. However, under section 403 ITEPA 2003, tax is only payable if and to the extent that the payments and benefits exceeds the £30,000 threshold. Section 403 therefore provide partial exemption to what is otherwise chargeable under section 401.

Payments made on termination of an employee's service fall into one of the categories for tax purposes:

- employment income and employment benefits are taxable in full (section 6 ITEPA 2003);
- payments which are not employment income or employment benefits are tax free (section 403 ITEPA 2003) unless they exceed £30,000 (section 401 ITEPA 2003).

The following payments fall within section 6 ITEPA 2003 and are subject to National Insurance Contributions (NICs), whether they are paid before or after termination of employment. The payment must derive from employment, but need not necessarily be a reward for past services or remuneration and can be made voluntarily. Examples of such payments include:

- wages;
- award for unlawful deduction of wages;
- sick pay (section 221 ITEPA 2003);
- contractual bonus or commission payments;
- retention bonus e.g. to ensure that key employees stay for a specified period to complete a project following a redundancy exercise;
- tips (*Calvert v Wainwright* 27 TC 475);
- notice pay given under an express payment in lieu of notice clause, discretionary payment in lieu of notice clause (*Thorn EMI Electronics Ltd v Coldicott (Inspector of Taxes)* [1999] STC 803) or paid by the company in recognition of notice period (HMRC Tax Bulletin February 2003);
- golden hello payments (*Shilton v Wilmshurst* [1991] STC 88);
- garden leave payments;
- consideration for restrictive covenants (sections 225 and 226 ITEPA 2003) (*RCI Europe v Kate Woods (HMIT)* (unreported) ChD, 2003 decided under the old section 313 ICTA 1988);
- ex-gratia payment under an unapproved retirement benefits scheme (section 224 ITEPA 2003);
- exercise of share options during or after termination of employment;
- payment on a "change of control" (golden parachute) or contractual golden handshake;
- payment for a variation of contractual rights.

Sums paid for a variation of duties are likely to be caught by section 6 ITEPA 2003, unless there is a fundamental change of duties or there is termination followed by re-engagement on new terms, in which case HMRC may accept that the variation falls under section 403 ITEPA 2003. Where a variation of rights payment attracts income tax, NIC is likely to be payable also.

The following payments fall within section 403 ITEPA 2003 when they are paid on or after termination of employment and are tax-free if they do not exceed £30,000. A section 401 termination payment is generally not subject to NIC and they include:

- statutory redundancy payment;
- non-statutory redundancy payment (i.e. contractual redundancy scheme – see SP1/94);
- non-contractual golden handshake payment;

- protective award (section 188 TULRCA 1992, regulation 15 TUPE 2006; *Mimtec Limited v CIR Sp.* C [2001] SSCD 101 – note however that NIC remains payable under regulation 2(b) Social Security (Contributions) (Employment Protection) Regulations 1977);
- damages for wrongful dismissal, e.g. non-payment of notice pay and/or for sums due under a discretionary PILON clause (*Cerberus Software v Rowley* [2001] ICR 376): note however that breach of an express PILON clause may be claimed as a contractual debt as opposed to damages);
- payments on account of damages (i.e. payment of liquidated damages on breach of contract or redundancy termination);
- non-contractual benefits in kind;
- compromises of disputed claims;
- unfair dismissal compensation.

Lump sum payment to employee's pension scheme

As part of the arrangements on termination of an employment, the company and executive may agree that that the company will make a contribution into a tax-exempt pension scheme, or makes a contribution into an approved personal pension scheme for the executive's benefit. Normally this will involve an adjustment to the overall termination payment.

HMRC state that these payments are not charged under section 401 ITEPA 2003 provided that RP CS SPSS (Nottingham) confirms that they do not breach any approval rules. Such payments should not be treated as using up any of the £30,000 threshold. So if the company makes a contribution of £30,000 satisfying the above conditions and there is also a payment within section 401 ITEPA 2003 of a further £30,000, there will be no charge at all under section 401 ITEPA 2003.

For further details, go to: http://www.hmrc.gov.uk/manuals/eimanual/EIM13660.htm.

The following payments are entirely free of income tax and NIC and not subject to the £30,000 limit under section 403 ITEPA 2003.

- Payment on account of total or partial disability (section 406 ITEPA 2003) (*Horner v Hasted (Inspector of Taxes)* [1995] STC 766): note that the definition of "disability" under the Disability Discrimination Act 1995 does not apply here.
- Payment on account of injury or death (section 406 ITEPA 2003).
- Injury to feelings awards in discrimination claims where there is no termination of employment involved. Note that where there is a dismissal which is discriminatory and an injury to feelings award is made, HMRC clearance should be sought as to whether the compensation (if it is more than £30,000) can be made free of tax.

When structuring a termination package, it should be borne in mind that HMRC can recover unpaid income tax and NIC from the company (Income Tax (Employment) Regulations 1993 (as amended); Social Security (Contributions) Regulations 1979) including interests and penalties (sections 86 and 96 Taxes Management Act 1970). The company should ensure that it has a tax indemnity from the employee in the event that it is pursued by HMRC for any unpaid income tax or NIC.

Grossing up

If the executive is only awarded his loss net of income tax and NIC but is required to pay tax under section 403 ITEPA 2003 because his damages exceed £30,000, the executive may end up paying tax twice. As such, it is not uncommon for those advising executives to negotiate an additional sum to "top up" the net settlement in order to make good the executive's tax liability.

So if the executive receives £36,000, £6,000 is taxable under section 403 ITEPA 2003. Assuming that the tax payable by the executive on the excess is at the higher rate of 40 per cent, the company in grossing up the figure should ensure that the executive receives £6,000 net (60 per cent worth) in his hands. Thus, the tax payable by the company is £4,000 (since £6,000 equates to 60 per cent and £4,000 equates to 40 per cent). It is wrong to assume that the tax is £2,400 i.e. 40 per cent of £6,000.

Payment structures

The tax-free benefit of £30,000 is an entitlement in respect of one particular employment. The executive can spread out a termination payment in excess of £30,000 over different years by carrying forward any unused relief until it has been fully exhausted. The attractiveness of this strategy will largely depend on how much the executive had already earned in the tax year when the severance payment was offered and his anticipated income for the subsequent tax years. For example, if the executive has been offered a termination payment of £45,000, he may wish to receive the first £30,000 in the current tax year (tax-free) and £15,000 in the next tax year so that he may, where appropriate, pay tax at a lower rate.

If any tax is payable on the termination payment and this is made after the issuance of the executive's P45 or his effective date of termination, the company only needs to deduct tax at basic rate (currently 22 per cent), not the higher tax rate (currently 40 per cent) if this applies to the executive at the time of his dismissal.

Structuring the non-financial package

Restrictive covenants

Where there are restrictive covenants in the service agreement or better still, more favourable restrictive covenants under the shareholders' agreement, particularly in terms of its duration, the executive should be required to acknowledge that these restrictions remain in full force on and after the termination date.

If these covenants are potentially unenforceable (either because they have been challenged by the executive as void for unreasonableness or because the service agreement and/or shareholders' agreement have been repudiated by the company) or there are no covenants to fall back on at all, the company should use the exit negotiation process as an opportunity to negotiate new post-termination restrictive covenants with the executive.

If new covenants are being introduced or there is a need to vary existing covenants then fresh consideration will be needed, even if the compromise agreement is by way of deed (*Mitchel v Reynolds* (1711) 1 PWms 181; *Gravely v Barnard* (1874) LR 18 Eq 518). Section 225 ITEPA 2003 requires consideration for such covenants to be subject to tax and NIC.

Bearing in mind that there is a cost to introducing new covenants, the company should be pragmatic about the scope of protection it is seeking. Where a client has already expressed that it has no interest in doing any business with the company following the executive's departure, imposing a non-dealing restriction will achieve very little commercially for the business. It may be more productive to use the opportunity to "tighten up" the covenants ensuring that they capture the company's key clients.

Whilst it is usual practice to ascribe nominal consideration for new covenants (e.g. a few thousand pounds) but this may potentially affect the enforcement of any injunctive relief should the executive subsequently breach his covenants because the courts may take the view that damages are an adequate remedy. The company therefore has to balance tax considerations and the effectiveness of enforcement in the event of a breach of such covenants carefully. If no separate consideration or inadequate consideration is given, HMRC may look towards the executive's settlement sum to satisfy the payment under section 225 ITEPA 2003.

Confidentiality

It is important to remind the executive of his continuing duty to maintain confidentiality in relation to information he has been privy to during his employment and office.

In addition, the executive should be required to keep the circumstances of the departure and terms of the severance confidential, save that he would be allowed to discuss such details with his immediate family, professional advisers (e.g. his lawyer and accountant) provided that such persons also comply with their duty of non-disclosure and pursuant to any other agreed authorised disclosure (e.g. an agreed employment reference).

Where the confidentiality obligations are expressed as bilateral, the company should ensure that persons who have been involved with the executive's exit are excluded from the obligation and that Human Resources has the flexibility to disclose the executive's terms of severance to a third party e.g. the executive's mortgagee, particularly where there is a claim for redundancy insurance cover, or to the Department for Work and Pensions where there is a claim for social benefits.

Non-disparagement or derogatory remarks

It is usual practice for the parties to agree not to disparage or damage each other's reputation when and after the executive leaves the business. Where the obligation is expressed as bilateral, the company should never promise something which it cannot deliver. At best, the company should agree to use reasonable endeavours to ensure that neither it nor its officers and employees shall make any derogatory or disparaging comments about the executive. Phrases such as "critical", "adverse" and "negative" should be avoided as they are subjective and open to interpretation. Where a derogatory statement has already been made by a member of staff, the company should be prepared to agree to publish an equivalent retraction of the offending statement as part of the terms of severance.

Agreed departure statements

One way of minimising the risks of breaching the non-disparaging obligation is to contractually agree an internal statement to members of staff and an external departure statement to clients, the press, and in the case of listed companies, to the London Stock Exchange. Typically, the statement will cite a neutral reason as why the executive is leaving the organisation, to avoid or end adverse speculation on the executive's exit.

Agreed references

In relation to prospective employers, agreeing a reference can not only promote an amicable departure but will also minimise the risks of a negligent reference claim. Reference requests should be addressed to a person holding a particular position, and not an individual who may leave the company in the future.

The usual practice is to offer a basic reference, confirming job title and dates of employment. If the executive is asked to prepare his own reference, the company should reject flowery language, opinions and embellishments. The golden rule is to always stick to a factual reference only.

Specific considerations apply when dealing with "approved persons" registered under the Financial Services Authority (FSA). If the executive is an "approved person", the company cannot fetter or dilute its obligations to provide information to the FSA, namely whether the executive is a "fit and proper" person. It is also important to reserve the right to qualify any references given if new information comes to light that affects any earlier references given or to refuse to provide the reference which had been agreed between the parties.

CHAPTER **10**

Exit management strategies

Amicable exit versus acrimonious exit

Careful consideration of the most appropriate strategy will be required in the proposed exit of an executive. The strategy will very much depend on the circumstances and/or reason for the executive's termination. The more acrimonious the proposed departure is likely to be, the higher the risks of litigation. The most risky method for employers is to "dismiss first, worry later", due to the risks of litigation. The safest method is to establish a legitimate or fair reason to dismiss, and act fairly prior to any dismissal. Between these two options is a middle option which involves a combination of the two and engaging in "without prejudice" negotiations with the executive.

High risk – "fire now worry later"

Where the executive has one year's continuous service, he is protected from unfair dismissal. The executive is also protected from wrongful dismissal, breach of contract and discrimination which are not dependent on his length of service with the company. If the executive is dismissed summarily in the absence of gross misconduct, he would be potentially able to claim compensation for his notice pay, bonus, share options and compensation for unfair dismissal. Where the executive has less than one year of continuous service or there is evidence that the executive has already secured alternative employment which is of equivalent (or better) salary and benefits, some employers may be more inclined to go for this option as the financial exposure to any claims may be limited in scope. Where the executive is highly employable and the labour market is buoyant, employers would also go for this option and in doing so put the onus on the executive to mitigate his losses. This option is particularly attractive if there is an urgent need to remove the executive from the business altogether. However, to preserve the enforceability of any post-termination covenants, the executive should be offered his notice pay so that there is no repudiation of the contract at common law. Where the executive is entitled to a long notice period, it is likely that even if there is a potential unfair dismissal claim, compensation would be negligible. Bonus and share option claims may however remain significant unless such losses are also closed off in the executive's termination package.

Low risk – "playing by the book"

Until the statutory dismissal procedures have been repealed by Parliament, the company has to comply with the three-step procedure before dismissing an executive for a reason related to their conduct, capability, redundancy, on expiry of a fixed-term contract or where the termination is for "some other substantial reason".

In conduct cases, it may be necessary to suspend the executive pending further investigations. Where no further investigation or suspension is necessary after the disciplinary meeting, the company can only proceed to termination where the allegation amounts to gross misconduct or where the executive has a prior disciplinary record which justifies his dismissal (e.g. a final written warning). Where summary dismissal is not justified but there remains a commercial need to remove the executive from the workplace and the company's clients, placing the executive on garden leave should be considered, provided that dismissal with notice is reasonable and lawful. Where dismissal is appropriate, steps should be taken to facilitate the executive's removal from the premises in the manner which is least disruptive to the business, particularly if the employee is required to vacate his desk immediately in the presence of other employees. Typically, the executive's access to his computer should be "frozen" whilst he attends the disciplinary meeting so that the risks of the executive accessing his emails and confidential information immediately after the termination meeting are closed off. Such an exercise will clearly require careful co-ordination with the company's IT department prior to the dismissal meeting. A letter confirming the employee's dismissal should then be sent to the employee also setting out his right of appeal.

In capability cases (e.g. ill-health or persistent poor performance), the executive should be asked if he wishes to be accompanied at the dismissal meeting, bearing in mind the sensitivities of the issues. It is not unusual in such situations for the executive to refuse to attend the disciplinary meeting, on grounds of work-related stress. It is not unusual for executives who have been placed in such a predicament to go on sick leave, exhaust their sick pay entitlement, look for another job and then resign, in order to avoid the stigma of a dismissal. Sometimes, the executive will raise a grievance, which then adds another layer of complication to the exit process. When faced with "stress cases", it is prudent to adjourn the meeting and reschedule at the next earliest opportunity bearing in mind that that the statutory procedures only require the company to invite the executive to a step 2 meeting twice, after which it is deemed to have complied with its statutory obligations. If the executive refuses to attend, he should be invited to submit written representations as an alternative. It is also advisable to be flexible with dates, venues and the executive's right of accompaniment. as this can reap dividends should an issue arise subsequently as to whether the company acted fairly prior to the executive's dismissal. Where a grievance has been raised, this can be heard at the same time as the disciplinary meeting so that the exit process is not frustrated by the executive.

In individual redundancy cases, the company must write to the executive and advise him that he is at "at risk of redundancy", that consultation will follow and what the executive would be entitled to if made redundant at the end of the consultation process. It is important to remember that notifying a person that his job is at risk of redundancy does not constitute consultation, but this is not to say that it is not possible to combine an "at risk" meeting with a redundancy consultation meeting. However, it is prudent to separate the two, as often news of the redundancy can be particularly unsettling, which may impact on the meaningfulness of any consultation meeting. Also, in individual redundancy cases, there is no minimum period by which employers have to consult. This flexibility means that provided that consultation is meaningful, it can last for as short as a week and as long as four weeks. The usual practice is to have at least two redundancy consultation meetings. In collective redundancy cases, the employer must consult with trade union representatives or employee representatives for at least 30 days (20-99 affected employees) or 90 days (100 or more affected employees) before the first dismissal. In practice, employers have to work backwards when managing large scale redundancies to ensure that sufficient time has been factored into the process in order to achieve the desired results particularly in the case of a phased exit of the workforce. As it is not legally possible to contract out liability for a protected award arising from a failure to consult, some employers offer their employees 30 or 90 days' pay for the protected period so that they can effect the collective redundancies immediately without necessarily having to exhaust the protected period. In the case of voluntary redundancies, where going through the full consultation period would clearly be futile, compromise agreements should be entered into to minimise risks of claims. Alternatively, the executive should be required to sign a letter confirming acceptance of his voluntary redundancy and agreed terms of severance.

The company should bear in mind that although an executive with less than two years of continuous service has no right to claim a redundancy payment, the executive is protected from unfair dismissal or unfair redundancy provided that they have been continuously employed for one year.

In the case of the expiry of a fixed-term contract and a decision has been taken not to renew it, the executive should be advised in writing shortly before his fixed-term contract expires:

- of the purpose for which he was originally employed (e.g. to cover someone on maternity leave or to assist with a certain task or purpose);

- the date on which the fixed term is due to expire;
- whether his predecessor, if any, is or is not returning to work; and
- whether there will be any other vacancies within the organisation after the fixed-term has expired.

Particular problems arise in relation to the employment of temporary employees to cover those on extended maternity leave (12 months), as on the termination of a 12-month fixed-term contract, such employees would have the right not to be unfairly dismissed. It is advisable therefore to employ two different employees on a six-month fixed-term contract.

In retirement cases, the statutory retirement procedure set out in Chapter 8 should be followed to the letter, otherwise there is a risk that the reason for dismissal will not be deemed as retirement. Provided that the statutory procedure is adhered to, there is no requirement to provide reasons if the executive's employment is not extended. It is also difficult for the executive to claim age discrimination where another executive's employment has been extended but not his own. Further, if the executive's employment is extended for six months or less, there is no longer any requirement to go through the statutory retirement procedure on the expiry of the extended period of employment.

Medium risk – "calling the bluff"

A medium-risk option is to instigate the legal procedure part-way and then negotiate with the executive on a "without prejudice" basis. "Without prejudice" means that the parties cannot use the content of the discussions as evidence in court. This option opens up channels for negotiation without the parties being too guarded about their respective positions. It gives the employer the opportunity to ascertain the financial boundaries of settling the employee's termination of employment. Conversely, it gives the executive the chance of a more dignified exit, by agreeing the basis and terms of his termination. This method has the benefit of making the company appear strong and throwing the risk of an imminent dismissal on the executive. The disadvantages for the company are the costs of the management time that must be invested in the process and the continuing obligation to pay the executive.

A variation of this option is to instigate the legal procedure, dismiss (with or without notice) and then negotiate on a "without prejudice" basis. This method may be appropriate in cases where the procedure is protracted (e.g. ill-health or poor performance cases) or where evidence acquired by the employer part-way through the procedure shows that the executive's claim is unlikely to succeed. Typically, a "without prejudice" offer would comprise an enhanced termination package open for acceptance by a specified deadline and subject to the executive signing a compromise agreement. The deadline for acceptance is usually before the legal procedure is fully exhausted. Once the legal procedure has been exhausted, and provided that the company has acted fairly, there will no longer be any basis to offer any enhanced termination package.

Litigation in this area of the employment relationship often centres on whether the executive voluntarily resigned or was dismissed by his employer. Where a person chooses to resign rather than to be the subject of disciplinary proceedings that will be held to be a resignation as the outcome of the disciplinary hearing would not be known (*Staffordshire County Council v Donovan* [1981] IRLR 108). There are, however, risks in inviting the executive to resign on "favourable terms" during a disciplinary hearing, as such a proposal has been held to breach the implied term of trust and confidence (*Billington v Michael Hunter & Sons Ltd* [2003] All ER(D) 83). In *Charles Sandhu v Jan de Rijk Transport Ltd* [2007] EWCA Civ 430, the employee was invited to a meeting about which he knew nothing. At the outset he was told that his employment was "going to end" because of alleged misconduct. The employee did as best he could in negotiating a favourable termination package and then signed a resignation letter. He subsequently claimed that he had been unfairly dismissed. The Employment Tribunal and EAT both held that the employee left because of the favourable terms he negotiated – the enforced resignation became a termination by mutual consent, as he had negotiated satisfactory financial terms of severance (*Crowley v Ashland (UK) Chemicals Ltd* EAT 31/79; *Sheffield v Oxford Controls Ltd* [1979] IRLR 133). The Court of Appeal disagreed and held that the employee had been dismissed, because he was not negotiating his exit freely, he had had no warning that the purpose of the meeting was to dismiss him, he had had no advice, and no time to reflect. The employee was doing his best on his own to salvage what he could from the inevitable fact that he was going to be dismissed. Further, the terms of severance were "pretty small beer". To minimise the commercial risks, it is important for the company to act fairly during the exit negotiation process, document what has been discussed, even if these discussions are on a "without prejudice" basis, and wrap things up with a compromise agreement.

CHECKLIST "Without prejudice" discussions

- Written or oral communications, which are made for the purpose of a genuine attempt to compromise a dispute between the parties, may generally not be admitted in evidence in court (*Cutts v Head* [1984] Ch 290) or in an Employment Tribunal (*Independent Research Services v Catterall* [1993] ICR 1, EAT) because they are deemed to be privileged, or "without prejudice", information. This legal principle is to encourage parties to settle a dispute without recourse to litigation and to avoid the fear that anything which had been said in settlement negotiations may later be used against them if settlement is unsuccessful.

- To acquire without prejudice privileged protection, there must be an extant dispute which is capable of being settled. Litigation need not be commenced so long as it was contemplated or might reasonably be contemplated if the parties could not agree on a compromise (*Framlington Group Plc & AXA Famlington Group Limited v Ian Barneston* [2007] EWCA Civ 502). For example, it has been held that exchanges as far removed as 21 months before the start of litigation can attract without-prejudice privilege in the same way as exchanges after the start of litigation (*Bradford & Bingley v Rashid* [2006] 1 WLR 2066, HL).
- Even where oral or written discussions are described as "without prejudice", there are certain circumstances where they may still become disclosable before a court or Employment Tribunal, for example:
  - where there is no genuine dispute to settle (*Re Daintrey* (1893) 2 QB 116);
  - there is no valid agreement that the discussions will be treated as "without prejudice" (*BNP Paribas v Mezzotero* [2004] IRLR 508);
  - the "without prejudice" status is being used as a cloak for perjury or blackmail (*Unilever plc v Procter & Gamble Co* [2000] 1 WLR 2436);
  - the "without prejudice" status is being used to cover up "unambiguous impropriety" (*Berry Trade Ltd v Moussavi & Others* [2003] EWCA Civ 715; *Savings & Investment Bank Ltd (In Liquidation) v Fincken* [2004] 1 WLR 667) e.g. discriminatory treatment (*BNP Paribas v Mezzotero* [2004] IRLR 508);
  - where it is necessary to rely on its contents to prove that terms were agreed (*Prudential Assurance Company Ltd v Prudential Insurance Company of America* [2003] EWCA Civ 327);
  - where the contents have been expressed as "without prejudice save as to costs" and disclosure is needed in a costs application (*Calderbank v Calderbank* [1976] Fam 93); or
  - where it is necessary to rely on the contents to prove mitigation of loss or to explain to the court why there has been a delay in taking certain procedural steps.
- Before engaging in any "without prejudice" discussions, it is advisable to explain to the executive what it means and ascertain whether he wishes to carry on with such discussions. Consider adjourning the meeting so that the executive can go away and think about the consequences of accepting such a proposal and to seek independent legal advice.
- A grievance alone does not mean that there is an extant dispute given that grievance procedures are well recognised in the workplace and provide a mechanism whereby an employee who is aggrieved about a particular matter can raise it through appropriate internal channels. Discussions to resolve a grievance (particularly at the early stages) may therefore not attract "without prejudice" protection.

- There are some risks for employers in simply calling an executive into a meeting and offering them a lump-sum payment to leave. Also, employers should assess the risks of making a "without prejudice" offer while simultaneously continuing with any disciplinary, dismissal or grievance procedures.
- Without-prejudice status can only be waived with the consent of both parties.
- If a settlement offer is agreed, a compromise agreement should be entered into to ensure that finality is brought to an extant dispute. Otherwise, the Employment Tribunal or court may allow the executive to rely on any "without prejudice" discussions in order to enable the executive to prove facts relevant to his claims.

CHAPTER **11**

Managing the notice period

Dealing with the outgoing senior executive

Notice periods are often tricky for both the company and the executive. Whilst a parting of the ways between employers and employees is an accepted fact of life, it can nonetheless be a sensitive situation, for a number of reasons. The executive may have acquired specialist industry knowledge and skills as a result of the company's investment in him over the years, so the last thing the company hopes to see is the fruits of their labour ending up in a competitor's hands. Alternatively, the executive may be leaving the business because of poor working relationships. Where a key figure is leaving, this can also damage team morale and unsettle established client relationships. Whatever might be the reason(s) for the executive's departure, such times often pose a threat and cause disruption to the employer's business.

Depending on the company's business needs, a decision needs to be made by the board as to whether the executive should be required to work out his notice period, placed on garden leave, paid in lieu of notice, or a combination of the three. It can sometimes be useful to initiate a "cards on the table" conversation with the executive. By flushing out the intentions of the executive early, this can help the company to decide on an appropriate exit strategy. If there is a good working relationship between the person charged with initiating the conversation with the executive, this can help to ensure that the reasons for the executive's departure are understood and in turn avoid an acrimonious exit.

Working out the notice period

It is widely accepted that employees are unlikely to be a source of future generosity to the employer when notice for termination has been given. If the executive is asked to serve his full notice, he might view the period as a "sentence" and even become hostile towards the company and the remaining directors. In these situations, it is most likely that the executive's main focus will be on his new job or business rather than ensuring the long-term success of the company's business. On the other hand, the company may wish to reap some benefits out of its obligation to honour the executive's notice pay, perhaps relying on the executive's continuing duty of fidelity to the company during the notice period. The reality is that the notice period is often a tricky phase in the employment relationship so it is not unusual for the parties to fall out over acts and omissions between them. In particular, if the executive needs to start his new employment quickly or escape the grasps of their post termination restrictions, it is not unusual for the executive to allege constructive dismissal or repudiation of his contract by the company as he rides out his notice period. Whilst requiring the executive to work out his notice period has its pros and cons, the scales should be weighed very carefully indeed.

Garden leave

The company may prefer to cut ties with the executive as soon as possible, by placing him on garden leave. Garden leave is appropriate in the following circumstances:

- where there are no post-termination restraints;
- where there are perceived risks of the executive interfering with the company's business relationships;
- where there are concerns with potential misuse of confidential information or acrimony with the board; and
- where cashflow makes a lump sum payment in lieu of notice by the company undesirable.

Garden leave provisions are extremely handy as they allow the company to immediately isolate the executive from the workplace, its clients and the industry for the duration of the notice period whilst a succession plan is put in place. The executive is usually required to remain available for work at the company's behest. Typically, a "garden leave" letter should confirm that notice for termination of employment has been given and that the executive is required to be on garden leave for the stipulated period. The letter should also spell out the terms of the garden leave, in particular what the executive can and cannot do whilst he is on garden leave. These restrictions should include contact with the company's clients, employees or business contacts, and spell out the steps the director is to take if contacted by such persons. It is useful to remind the executive of his duty of fidelity to the company during the garden leave period. It is not unusual to require the executive to surrender work-related equipment (e.g. mobile phones, laptops, access to computer systems and emails, keys) although the executive should continue to have access to other non-work related contractual benefits.

Placing an executive on garden leave without any contractual right to do so will generally be a repudiatory breach of contract, the effect of which is to discharge the executive from his post-termination restrictive covenants. Where there is no contractual right to place the executive on garden leave, there is still the possibility of negotiating for such a provision using the executive's notice period, any potential bonus payments (given that these are not usually payable when notice for termination has been given), and any other ex-gratia payments as "trade offs". Another option is to negotiate a reduction in the duration of any post termination restraints if the executive agrees to spend some or all of notice period on garden leave.

Payment in lieu of notice

Where there is a contractual right to make a payment in lieu of notice, the company will be allowed to bring the executive's employment to an end instantly without being in breach of contract. Any restrictive covenants will continue to have effect in so far as they are enforceable. This option is appropriate where:

- the executive's departure is not acrimonious;
- there are no risks of competition with the company's business;
- a successor is in place; or
- the executive's position is redundant.

Succession planning

When notice for termination has been given, one of the first priorities for the company is to put in place a succession plan. The executive should be instructed to prepare, or where appropriate, comply with a handover plan. One of the first tasks is to agree on what should be said to team members and to the company's clients and when news of the executive's departure should be made and by whom. It does not always pay to keep the news secret as this can harm established client relationships. Honesty and transparency can often help to make the exit process more smoothly. Very often, clients do not appreciate being told about a departure at the eleventh hour where there has been a strong working relationship with the departing executive. Where there are client teams already in place, the handover process will be less cumbersome. Where there are no client teams, the executive should be required to involve team members in ongoing and new projects and to gradually minimise his direct client contact. Clearly, the timing of the handover is crucial. The company can use the notice period to its advantage especially where the executive has expressed a desire to be released from his notice period. A quid pro quo is to require that the executive co-operates with the transition and succession plan if he wants the company to reduce his notice period.

Preparatory steps to compete

Previously, the courts have permitted preliminary steps that fell short of actual competitive activities. For example, the executive would be allowed to identify business premises, negotiate a lease and buy an off-the-shelf company (*Balston v Headline Filters* [1990] FSR 385; *Framlington Group v Anderson* [1995] 1 BCLC 475; *Coleman v Oakes* [2001] 2 BCLC 749). Such acts are no longer likely to be permissible in the light of the recent case of *Shepherds Investments Ltd v Walters* [2006] EWHC 836 (Ch).

In *Shepherds*, three employees who owed fiduciary duties to the company began discussing the creation of a new investment fund to compete in the traded life policy market whilst they were in employment. These discussions resulted in a draft business plan including significant improvements to the "*Shepherds* model". The employees also developed possible links with banks and auditors for future transactions and prepared financial predictions for the first few years of trading. Much of the groundwork for the future business was in place by the time some but not all the three employees handed in their resignation. The High Court held that as the employees' preparatory steps crossed the line between legitimate entrepreneurial activities and illegitimate competition, they had breached both their fiduciary and contractual duties. Whether the employee's act is legitimate or otherwise is for determination by the courts. The issue is whether an irrevocable intention had been formed by the performance of a particular act by the employee.

In *Helmet Integrated Systems Ltd v Tunnard* [2007] IRLR 126 the Court of Appeal held that a salesman did not breach his contractual duties when he failed to inform his employer that he was taking preparatory steps to develop a product which he intended, following his resignation, to market in competition with his employer. The Court's decision was influenced by the fact that the employee was not a director or senior manager but a middle-ranking senior salesman. Had he been a director, or had his role in the company involved designing rather than selling helmets, his duties might have been interpreted differently. In *PennWell Publishing Ltd v Isles & Others* [2007] EWHC 1570, QB, the High Court followed the principles in *Helmet*, but held that the executive director had gone too far and was in breach of his express and implied duties when he failed to prevent a former colleague from diverting business away from the employer to a new company. Where information is used by the executive as an illegitimate springboard to compete with the ex-employer, such information must involve confidential information otherwise injunctive relief may not be available to the company. If no confidential information is involved, the company should consider if the executive has infringed its database rights. In *Crowson Fabrics Limited v Rida & Ors* [2007] All ER (d) 338, the High Court held that two former employees had infringed the company's database rights even though information used by them to create a rival business was not confidential information.

CHECKLIST

- When notice for termination is given, consideration should be given as to whether the executive should be required to work out his notice period, be placed on garden leave or paid in lieu of his notice period.
- A succession plan needs to be put in place quickly as part of the exit strategy.
- The legitimate interests that are capable of protection by way of restrictive covenants include the company's confidential information, customer connections and workforce stability. In relation to customers and staff, this is particularly the case where the executive has acquired personal influence over customers or other employees because of his employment.
- The duties owed to the company by the executive during employment and during the notice period are more onerous if he is a statutory director.
- Where the executive is not subject to any post termination restraints, consideration should be given as to whether the executive owes fiduciary duties (whether as a statutory director or senior executive) and/or whether there has been a misuse of confidential information belonging to the company.
- The executive's implied obligation of good faith and fidelity covers a wide range of matters. Generally, the following types of conduct will amount to a breach of the executive's implied obligation to the company:
  - competing during employment;
  - copying or memorising trade secrets or other confidential information;
  - accepting business offers from customers;
  - recruiting or inciting other employees to leave;
  - diverting business opportunities;
  - misusing confidential information;
  - failing to reveal the competitive intentions of other employees;
  - intentionally giving false answers to straight questions.
- Where the executive is also a statutory director, the following types of conduct will amount to a breach his fiduciary duty to the company:
  - making a secret profit or accepting bribes, gifts and any related business opportunities for himself;
  - allowing his own interest to conflict with those of the company;
  - failing to disclose his own misconduct or breaches of duty by other employees;
  - failing to resign after he has formed a irrevocable intention to compete with the company.
- The following "preparatory steps" are likely to breach the duty of fidelity or fiduciary duty:
  - identifying suitable premises for the new business and negotiating a lease and signing it;

- purchasing an off-the-shelf company;
- negotiating and agreeing terms of employment with a competing business;
- encouraging or failing to thwart the recruitment of employees by a competitor;
- preparing a company for incorporation;
- contacting investment banks for support several months prior to the commencement of trading;
- contacting lawyers with details of the proposals.

CHAPTER **12**

Housekeeping rules on termination of employment

What goes in the letter of termination?

An executive with one year of service is entitled to receive a written reason for dismissal within 14 days, if one is requested (section 92(1) ERA 1996). Typically, the termination letter should state the reason for dismissal, the executive's termination date, entitlement to salary, accrued holidays and benefits as at the termination date, his obligations on termination of employment (e.g. return of company property) and after termination of employment (e.g. duty of confidentiality and post-termination restraints). The executive should also be offered the right of an appeal against his dismissal. In providing a reason for dismissal, the company minimises the risks of the executive arguing that his dismissal was for a discriminatory reason.

Delivering up company property

Ensure that all company property (e.g. keys, passes, credit cards, mobile phones, Blackberries, business cards, company car etc.) have been duly returned by the executive. It may be useful to have a checklist to make sure that nothing is forgotten. In any event, all company property should be returned by the executive before the company parts with any termination payment monies. One way of managing this process is through an exit interview.

Notifying company announcement office

If the company is a public listed company, it is required under paragraph 9.611R of the UK Listing Authority Listing Rules to notify the Regulatory Information Service ("RIS") without delay, and no later than by the end of the business day, about any board changes, including a decision to terminate an executive's directorship. This is to minimise the risk of a leak of potentially price-sensitive information to the public and stock exchange. Due to the strict time limits, it may be desirable to obtain a letter of resignation from the executive director which is without prejudice to his legal and statutory rights under the service agreement. The official resignation is then followed with settlement negotiations.

Notifying FSA

If the company is a self-regulating organisation under FSMA 2000, it must notify the Financial Services Authority of a change of personnel.

Notifying trustees of pension scheme

Remove the executive as a trustee of the company pension scheme.

Filing forms at Companies House

Ensure that the executive signs Form 288B if he is required to resign from the board; alternatively whether there is provision for a power of attorney to do so on his behalf. If the executive is required to transfer his shares, the relevant stock transfer forms need to be executed. These forms should be filed with Companies House promptly.

Obtaining HMRC clearance for termination packages exceeding £30,000

Notify HMRC by 6 July following the year in which the termination occurred if the executive's settlement (comprising of cash and non-cash benefits, or just non-cash benefits) exceeds £30,000 (Income Tax (Employment) (Amendment No.2) Regulations 1999 (SI 1999/2155). If the executive's settlement was not more than £30,000 but there is subsequently a change in the package which exceeds the £30,000 threshold, the company must file a report to HMRC (providing the executive with a copy) within 92 days of the end of the year in which the change occurred (regulation 92 of the Income Tax (Pay As You Earn) Regulations 2003 (SI 2003/2682)).

Internal and external departure statements

Where applicable, an internal statement (usually agreed between the company and outgoing executive, and annexed to the compromise agreement) should be circulated to members of the relevant department. It is important to ensure that any statements made to a third party, whether internally or externally (e.g. employment references), are consistent with what was mutually agreed. Where there is no agreed public statement, informal communications with staff members and third parties must not be defamatory.

CHECKLIST On housekeeping rules on termination

- Ensure that your termination letter captures not only the financial aspects of the executive's departure but also the non-financial aspects such as return of company property, and post-termination obligations such as confidentiality and competiton.
- Facilitate the prompt return of company property. This ideally should be immediately before the executive goes on garden leave, or before any termination payment is made to the executive.
- Secure Form 288B and stock transfer forms from the executive as appropriate.
- Ensure that all relevant third parties are notified of the executive's termination, e.g. FSA, RIS, trustees of the pension scheme, HMRC and Companies House.
- To minimise claims for breach of contract and defamation, agree the contents of any internal and external departure statements and the timing of when such statements will be made to existing staff and the company's clients, suppliers and contacts.

CHAPTER **13**

Using compromise agreements effectively

The statutory requirements

Depending on the exit strategy and risks of litigation in relation to the executive's termination, a compromise agreement may be necessary to close off any alleged, pending or potential claims against the company. The purpose of a compromise agreement is to settle all claims which the executive has or may have against the company in consideration of a settlement payment (see Appendix G).

Under section 203 ERA 1996, a statutory compromise agreement must:

- be in writing;
- relate to the particular complaint (i.e. the subject of the dispute);
- state that the employee must have received independent legal advice from a qualified lawyer as to the effect of the employee's ability to pursue their rights before an Employment Tribunal (*Lambert v Croydon College* [1999] IRLR 346). "Qualified lawyers" may include officers, official employees and members of an independent trade union, voluntary workers at advice centres (Schedule 1 Employment Rights (Dispute Resolution) Act 1998 incorporating section 203(3A) ERA 1996) and a Fellow of the Institute of Legal Executives employed by a solicitors' practice, provided that such a Fellow is supervised by a solicitor holding a practising certificate issued by the Law Society of England and Wales (Compromise Agreements) (Description of Person) Order 2004 (SI 2004/754).

The adviser must be covered by professional indemnity insurance in respect of any advice given and identified in the agreement; and the compromise agreement must confirm that the above conditions are satisfied.

Waiver of claims by the executive

Section 203 requires the compromise agreement to relate to "the particular complaint" only. This means that specific claims which have been raised by the parties can be the subject of a valid compromise agreement. In other words, if any claims have not been raised, they will not be compromised. As the settlement agreement in most cases would be aimed at achieving a "clean break" between the parties, it is important to ensure that any actual claims which the employee has with the company at the time of his proposed exit are clearly identified, and that any potential claims which the employee may have, whether arising at the time of the signing the compromise agreement or sometime in the future, are also identified.

From a drafting perspective, it is important to ensure that the executive's warranty to settle all claims within the operating provisions is wide enough to capture their present and future belief and that this extends to all or any actual, potential, known or unknown claims (*BCCI v Ali* [2002] AC 251; *Royal National Orthopaedic Hospital Trust v Howard* [2002] IRLR 849) in relation to the executive's employment and termination thereof. It is also important to ensure that the statutory claims are clearly identified by a generic description or by reference to the relevant statutory provisions (*Hinton v University of East London* [2005] EWCA Civ 532; *Hilton UK Hotels Ltd v McNaughton* [2005], EAT/0059/04). In *Palihakkara v British Telecommunications plc* [2006] UKEAT/0185/06/DM & UKEAT/0186/06/DM, the employee was able to pursue race discrimination claims against her former employer despite the existence of a compromise agreement because the agreement only precluded her from pursuing claims related to the termination of her employment. In any event, the agreement was invalid as it had not satisfied specific statutory requirements.

Any actual or potential dispute under the shareholders' agreement (e.g. in relation to the executive's entitlement to shares, transfers, valuation, forfeitures etc.) should be closed off within the compromise agreement also. The more claims are flushed out within the agreement, the more likely it is that they will be compromised under the agreement

Release of claims by the executive

If the language of the agreement is categorised as a "release", then there is a duty of disclosure on the company (e.g. claims which the executive has against the company which he is unaware of). However, if the agreement is categorised as a "compromise", there is no such duty. Whether there is a free-standing "release" or a "compromise" depends upon the substance rather than the form of the agreement. A "compromise" is a release of claims for a valuable consideration. In *Bell v Lever Brothers* [1932] AC 161, the court held that neither party to an employment contract or a contract of compromise had a duty to disclose their own breaches of contract. In *BCCI International SA (In Compulsory Liquidation) v Ali & Ors (No.1)* [1999] IRLR 226, ChD), the High Court held that it was not realistic to infer that at the time of the signing of the agreement, BCCI had deliberately concealed the breach of the trust and confidence claim, as it did not exist at law.

Not all statutory rights can be compromised by the company. It is not possible to exclude the following statutory claims.

Protective awards

A protective award (up to 90 days' pay) arising from the failure to consult in a collective redundancy under section 188 TULRCA 1992 cannot be contracted out (section 288(2C) TULRCA 1992). Most employers will therefore include 90 days' pay in the employee's termination package, if they do not wish to engage in any collective consultation at all.

Personal injury claims

The usual practice is to extinguish any personal injury claims in connection with a discriminatory act (*Sheriff v Klyne Tugs (Lowestoft) Limited* 1999 IRLR 481). Claims arising from industrial injury are usually not part of the compromise agreement but can be compromised if they have already arisen. The company should notify its employer's liability insurers before settling such claims, to avoid invalidating their policy. In relation to claims which have not arisen, bear in mind that under the Unfair Contract Terms Act 1977, any clause excluding liability for personal injury or death arising from negligence is void. The usual practice is to extract a warranty from the employee that he/she is not aware of any such claims against the company, particularly if the employee is refusing to agree to compromise the personal injury claim.

Pension claims

Section 91 Pensions Act 1995 contains restrictions on contracting out of an employee's accrued pension rights. This provision is complex, and pension advice should always be sought. It is again usual practice to carve out any pension claims from the waiver clause. However, if there is a dispute about pension contributions by the employer, there is technically no reason why this cannot become the subject of the compromise agreement as it does not relate to accrued pension rights.

In the case of *A F Blakemore & Son Limited v Machin* 2007 EWHC 963, a pension dispute claim between the employee and the employer was effectively compromised, however, the High Court held that there was no reason why the employee should be barred from bringing a claim against the trustees of the pension scheme. It is therefore important to ensure that if any pension claims are to be extinguished, the waiver clause extends not only to the employer but also to the trustees.

TUPE claims

Regulation 18 TUPE 2006 contains restrictions on contracting out also, except where contractual variations are permitted under the legislation (e.g. post transfer for an ETO reason or in insolvency cases) or where the usual safeguards under section 203 ERA 1996 regulating compromise agreements or a COT3 ACAS settlement are met. Note however that claims between the transferor and transferee in relation to the transferor's failure to provide "employee liability information" cannot be compromised under section 203 which applies to employers and employees only, not between sellers and buyers or outsourcers and outsourcees.

The legal consideration

This may take the form of financial or non-financial compensation. If the executive is being asked to waive his rights in relation to any *future* claims which he may have in addition to actual claims which he has, some thought should also be given to providing legal consideration in relation to such a waiver. A ball park settlement figure to close off all claims is acceptable practice.

Waiver of claims against the executive

Although a compromise agreement is concerned with the executive waiving claims against the company, in practice the company may sometimes be asked to waive any claims it has or may have against the executive as part of the settlement. This is a matter of negotiation between the parties. Any provision that purports to exempt a director of the company from any liability that would otherwise attach to him in connection with any negligence, default, breach of duty or breach of trust in relation to the company is void (section 232(1) CA 2006). The usual practice is for the executive to require the company to continue to extend the benefit of any directors' and officers' liability insurance after the termination date.

Securing warranties from the executive

It is common practice to require the executive to provide a number of warranties to the company in consideration of the severance payment he would be receiving under the compromise agreement. Typically, the executive would be asked to warrant that he has not done anything which would entitle the company to summarily terminate his employment with no compensation payable.

In the recent case of *Sean Mervyn Collidge v Freeport Plc* 2007 EWHC 1216, QB, the chief executive of Freeport Plc agreed to resign, in return for which he would receive a termination sum of £445,000 under the terms of a compromise agreement.

Clause 7 of the compromise agreement stated as follows:

"You warrant as a strict condition of this agreement that as at the date hereof:-

a) you have not failed to disclose any personal injuries of which you are aware (or of which you ought reasonably to be aware) in relation to which you reasonably believe you could claim against the Company or any Company in the Group; and
b) there are no circumstances of which you are aware or of which you ought to be aware which would constitute a repudiatory breach on your part of your contract of employment which would entitle or have entitled the Company to terminate your employment without notice; and
c) [no proceedings issued by Mr Collidge]
d) You have not at the date of this agreement obtained employment ….."

Before payment was made, the company discovered, amongst other things, that Mr Collidge had dishonestly obtained expenses on a number of occasions involving hotels, flights, cigar purchases and meals. The company believed that Mr Collidge's conduct amounted to a repudiation of his contract and entitled it to dismiss him summarily.

Mr Collidge issued proceedings for payment under the compromise agreement. The High Court was not persuaded that the word "condition" in clause 7 had to be construed in the strict contract law sense such that the company would have to accept the repudiation bringing the whole agreement to an end. Even if it were construed in the strict sense, it was open to the company to keep the agreement alive and sue Mr Collidge for damages by way of a counterclaim. Looking at the intention of the parties, clause 7 simply meant that if certain facts warranted by Mr Collidge were not true and were such as would have entitled the employer to dismiss him summarily for gross misconduct, the company was under no obligation to pay the compensation under the terms of any compromise agreement. The waiver of claims against the company arising from the termination of employment remained intact, even though Mr Collidge was no longer receiving financial consideration for his waiver.

It should however be noted that it is certainly not the case that breach of *any* type of warranty would entitle the company to withhold the termination payment or to recoup all the sums which have already been paid to the executive. The employer in the *Collidge* case was able to withhold the termination payment because the employee could have been summarily dismissed had the employer known about his gross misconduct at the time the compromise agreement was signed by the parties. If it was a breach of a different type of warranty (e.g. the executive had lied about the offer of alternative employment), then the termination sum should arguably be reduced rather than completely extinguished (see Recoupment and penalty clauses, below).

Misrepresentation by the executive

If the company has been enticed to enter into the compromise agreement through fraudulent misrepresentation by the executive, the company may be able to set aside (or rescind) the compromise agreement altogether, or recover compensation for consequential loss in lieu of rescission.

In *Crystal Palace FC (2000) Limited v Dowie* [2007] EWHC 1392, QB, Iain Dowie was employed as the manager of Crystal Palace until 30 June 2008. One of the terms of his contract was that if he left the club early and took a post at another football club, he would have to pay Crystal Palace £1 million in compensation. In May 2006, Mr Dowie decided to leave the club and advised Crystal Palace that he wanted to work geographically closer to his family in Bolton. He later signed a compromise agreement whereby the club waived its right to the £1 million against him. Over a week later, Mr Dowie was unveiled as the new manager at Charlton Athletic, just 10 miles away from his ex-employer. Crystal Palace served Mr Dowie with a High Court claim for £1 million in damages on the basis that he had deliberately lied about his reasons for wanting to leave Crystal Palace and had enticed it to agree to forfeit the £1 million in compensation. The High Court held that Crystal Palace had been induced to enter a compromise agreement by Mr Dowie's fraudulent misrepresentations as to his future employment intentions. The Court declined to order the rescission of the compromise agreement as a remedy. Rescission would have revived Mr Dowie's contract of employment (which neither party wanted). Furthermore, the position of third parties (i.e. Mr Dowie's successor and his new employer) would be affected by an order for rescission. Mr Dowie was ordered to pay compensation to his ex-employer and their legal costs exceeding £360,000.

Execution of the agreement

To avoid losing the tax benefits, this should be done as near as possible to the termination date or, if possible, after the termination date. Whilst it is generally acceptable to negotiate the executive's terms of departure and get the documentation in readiness, it is not advisable to pre-sign the agreement and then date it afterwards. Doing so can affect both the company and the executive's tax liability in the event that the compromise agreement and the circumstances upon which it was entered into is later scrutinised by HMRC.

Recoupment of sums paid and penalty clauses

Given that achieving finality is the primary aim of a compromise agreement, it is not uncommon for employers to require employees to repay compensation which they have received under a compromise agreement in the event that they continue with their existing claims or issue new claims in breach of the compromise agreement. Whether such a repayment provision is enforceable very much depends on whether the courts deem it a penalty clause (which is unenforceable) or a liquidated damages clause (which is enforceable).

In CMC *Group Plc v Michael Zhang* [2006] EWCA Civ 408, the Court of Appeal had to consider if a repayment clause in a settlement agreement was a penalty. Mr Zhang was a real time internet trader. He placed a trade instruction with CMC's online trading service. He alleged that his instruction appeared not to have been executed by CMC. As a result, he had lost money. CMC agreed to settle the dispute for US$40,000 in full and final settlement of all past, present and future claims arising out of or in connection with the subject matter of his complaint. Mr Zhang further agreed to cease making threats of violence to any officer or employee of CMC or their families, harassing employees of CMC and making derogatory or unfavourable communications about or in connection with CMC. The settlement agreement stated that any breach of the settlement rendered Mr Zhang liable to CMC for a sum equal to the settlement sum together with a claim for reimbursement of legal costs and a claim for damages in relation to their loss of business. Mr Zhang subsequently went to CMC's premises, and got in touch with its staff and allegedly made a thorough nuisance of himself. CMC then issued proceedings for the recovery of the settlement sum.

The Court of Appeal unanimously held that the repayment clause was a penalty. The settlement sum had no direct relevance to the harassment claim. It could not have been said to be an attempt to valuate any loss or damage that arose from Mr Zhang's breach by continued harassment. Further, although the terms of settlement provided for a payment to be made to Mr Zhang on a specified basis and for a repayment of that sum if that basis of payment fell away, there was no total failure of consideration from Mr Zhang on the facts.

There are a number of ways to get round the penalty clause trap through appropriate drafting. One option is to quantify the value of the executive's existing claims first and then top it up with an additional sum to reflect any other potential claims that the executive may have which they are also agreeing to waive. Any "claw back" provisions should be limited to the value of those potential claims and not the entirety of the settlement sum. Another option is to ensure that the claw back sum is drafted in such a way so as to allow the company to set off any additional compensation subsequently awarded by a tribunal or court against the settlement sum. The third option is to retain the right to recoup any additional compensation subsequently awarded to the executive. Through careful drafting, this will demonstrate to the court that the company's repayment clause was not simply a deterrent which took no account of the materiality of the executive's breach of the settlement sum, but is a genuine estimate of the executive's losses.

Where the executive is in breach of other aspects of the compromise agreement, for example, breaches of confidentiality or non-disparagement, other forms of enforcement such as injunctive relief, defamation and malicious falsehood are alternative remedies to consider apart from financial recoupment.

CHECKLIST For compromise agreements

- Parties to the agreement – always check who needs to be protected. Do you need to protect any associated group companies, trustees of a pension scheme or transferee in a TUPE situation? If a third party needs to be protected but is not a party to the compromise agreement, use the Contracts (Rights of Third Parties) Act 1999 to confer the benefit on them.
- Recitals – use scene setters as this demonstrates the underlying basis and scope of the compromise agreement.
- Waiver clauses – ensure that all actual and potential claims are identified and effectively compromised. Where the executive refuses to waive all claims against the company (e.g. for personal injury), secure warranties from the executive that he is not aware of any such claims as at the termination date.
- Reason for termination – bear in mind the effect of the reason for termination on any employment benefits (e.g. bonuses and share options) and the risks of any employment reference which you have agreed to give to a prospective employer.
- Compensation and set-offs – ensure that any ex-gratia compensation is not pensionable. Remember to recoup any outstanding loans, excess holidays taken etc. against the termination payment.
- Tax – when in doubt as to whether a termination payment or scheme attracts tax and NIC liability, always obtain prior clearance from HMRC. The executive's indemnity is as good as his word and creditworthiness!
- Payment structures – consider whether to make a lump sum payment or periodic payments, bearing in mind the tax advantages in spreading payments over different fiscal years.
- Expenses – it is important to impose a deadline for any expenses claims and ensure that only claims which comply with the company's policy will be made.

- Pensions – check if the company's pension scheme is approved or unapproved. Any top-up payments need to comply with HMRC rules and limits.
- Agreed departure statements and references – these do not add to the exit costs and help to avoid victimisation claims, post termination disputes and satellite litigation.
- Execution – beware of the commercial risks of signing the agreement too early, both on the tax and enforcement fronts. Contracts entered into by deed (e.g. service agreements and deed of covenants) can only be discharged by deed so the compromise agreement needs to be in the form of a deed also. Note that under section 44 of the Companies Act 2006, if the company does not have a company secretary, then the deed needs to be witnessed by an external party.

CHAPTER 14

Dealing with competition on and after termination of employment

Information gathering

The saying "there is no smoke without fire" cannot be further from the truth when it comes to competition in the employment field. Employers can become suspicious of their employees due to hearsay, unusual behaviour by the departing employee, information from informants, and sometimes, out of paranoia.

Before making any allegations that the executive is in breach of contract or the terms of the compromise agreement, it is important for the company to embark on a fact-finding mission. Investment in this process will reap dividends and avoid expense and potential embarrassment with members of staff, clients and suppliers of the company and the media. The following questions should be considered:

- What is the role of the executive in the company?
- Is the executive a statutory director under the CA 2006?
- What are the contractual obligations owed by the executive?
- What has the executive done which could be said to amount to, or which could potentially amount to, a breach of those obligations?
- Have competitive activities been carried out during employment or at the executive's own time?
- How did the executive's employment end?
- What sort of threat does the competitive activity pose to the company?
- Who are the executive's key client contacts?
- What revenue did the executive generate directly and indirectly for the company?
- What is the likelihood of the executive poaching the company's business?
- Are customers or clients involved, or will they become involved?
- Has the executive notified customers and suppliers of their intention to compete?
- Has the executive sought to interfere with the dealings between customers and suppliers and the company?

- Has there been a wave of resignations?
- Has the executive enticed away or is he likely to entice away other employees as part of a team move? If so, does this significantly impact on the company's business?
- Where would the executive be operating from?
- Has the executive misused or removed confidential information?
- Has the executive been asked to return company property on termination of their employment?

Whilst it is tempting to react to suspicion, it would be more constructive to obtain some evidence of improper behaviour before confronting the executive with the threat of litigation. Potential sources of information include computer records such as emails (especially deleted emails), downloads, CD ROMs, USB memory sticks or cards, disks, information held on the ex-employee's laptop or home computer, electronic devices such as Blackberries and mobile phones, itemised mobile phone bills, photocopying records, security videos, records of unusual attendance at the company's premises, and unusual levels of expenses claims.

To retain the element of surprise, it is advisable not to discuss the situation with members of staff who are particularly close with the executive. This will reduce the risk of "tipping off" and of evidence being destroyed by the executive and/or any other accomplices within the company. Very often, clients and suppliers may not wish to become embroiled in the company's internal dispute either, so a commercial decision needs to be made as to whether external parties should be approached about the company's investigatory process. Where the customer or supplier has alerted the company to the executive's competitive activities, it is sensible to ask the customer whether they are willing to confirm any information in writing, in the event that subsequent court proceedings become necessary. Where there is some email evidence of the executive diverting business opportunities away or stealing confidential information, it may be prudent to instruct external forensic IT consultants to survey the extent of the executive's wrongdoing.

Whilst covert monitoring of the executive's electronic communications such as emails, telephone calls, voicemails etc. may be tempting, the company needs to be aware of the Human Rights Act 1998, Data Protection Act 1998 and Telecommunications (Lawful Business Practice) (Interception of Communications) Regulations 2000 (SI 2000/2699). Generally, employees should have been made aware that their communications at work may be monitored for business-related reasons, to avoid breaches of their right to privacy.

Effective use of letters before action against the former executive and poacher (new employer)

The first port of call is to write to the executive about the breach of their contractual obligations and/or the new employer for inducing the executive to breach their contract. The sole purpose of the letter is to avoid court proceedings and should therefore have the effect of causing the executive to "own up" to any wrongdoing and/or undertake to comply with his contractual obligations going forward. Typically, the letter before action (see Appendix E) would have the following aims:

- Set out a summary of the executive's employment with the company, including position held, key contractual terms and benefits, how and when the employment came to an end.
- Set out the alleged breaches/anticipated breaches by the executive – the aim is to cast the executive in a bad light as this can encourage the court and the executive's legal adviser to find in your favour.
- Create the impression that you know more than you actually do – warn the executive that investigations into unlawful competition are continuing, to heighten their sense of worry and guilt.
- Require the executive to immediately deliver up property belonging to the company, delete any other such information from their personal electronic and analogue records and provide written confirmation to the company that all property has been returned.
- Require the executive to preserve all relevant documents particularly where these items are held by a third party e.g. the executive's new employer.
- Require the executive to provide a written statement disclosing his activities in so far as such activities are in breach of his obligations to the company.
- Require undertakings from the executive that he will comply with the restrictive covenants in the future.
- Set a short deadline for the executive to comply with the company's requests.
- Warn the executive that non-compliance will result in an immediate application to the court, the costs of which will be borne by him.
- Advise the executive to seek legal advice immediately.
- Mark the letter "Private & Confidential Addressee Only" and send it by special delivery or courier.
- Consider using a process server if the executive is evasive.

It should be noted that the provision of "contractual undertakings" by the executive following a letter before action, whilst helpful to the company, is not as powerful as "court undertakings". Breach of a court undertaking is contempt of court, for which the executive could be imprisoned, and is therefore a very potent deterrent. On the other hand, the company can have the benefit of a contractual undertaking without having to provide a cross-undertaking as to damages, which otherwise applies in court undertakings.

Injunction proceedings

Unlawful competition can be restrained where the executive has breached enforceable restrictive covenants, misused confidential information or done an unlawful act during their employment. The remedy is typically an application for injunctive relief. The main types of injunction include:

- garden leave injunctions to prevent the executive from commencing with his new employer prior to the expiry of the notice period;
- injunctions to enforce restrictive covenants;
- delivery-up injunctions or search orders, to require the return of confidential and proprietary information;
- springboard and similar injunctions to prevent the commencement or continuation of competition.

In addition, these injunctions will often be combined with claims for damages or an account of profits for breaches in relation to which the company has already sustained financial losses.

The court application must be based upon evidence in the form of witness statements (or affidavits for a search order). In a garden leave or covenants case, the company will need to provide evidence for the assertion that the covenants or garden leave clauses are enforceable. In confidential information cases, it is usual to have private witness statements and exhibits and where appropriate, a partially private hearing.

The initial application (interim injunctive hearing) must be brought speedily and will normally not be fully argued. Unless the company's case is plainly unarguable, or the balance of convenience falls in favour of the executive, the court will seek to grant interim injunctions (temporary restraints pending a full trial) and list the case for a speedy trial (usually within a couple of months of the initial hearing). If interim injunctions are granted to the company, the executive is protected by a cross-undertaking in damages if at trial it is apparent that the company should not have been entitled to injunctive relief at all.

As it is very costly and often not possible to bring a case to trial in a matter of weeks, such cases often settle soon after the initial injunction hearing. An alternative to resolving disputes of this nature is mediation, which is increasing popular because it is confidential, less adversarial, more cost effective and allows for more creative solutions, compared to the traditional remedies awarded by the courts. Due to time constraints in relation to the enforcement of restrictive covenants, weighing up mediation as against an application for interim relief in the courts remains a challenge for employers.

PART 3

APPENDICES OF SPECIMEN DOCUMENTS

Appendix A
Conditional offer letter

[COMPANY LETTERHEAD]

Private & Confidential

[Executive]

[Address]

Dear [Executive]

Offer of employment with ABC Limited ("the Company")

Further to your meeting with [XXX] on [date], I am pleased to confirm that the Board wishes to make you a formal offer of employment with the Company in the position of [XXX], subject to the terms of the enclosed Service Agreement.

You will be employed by the Company but may be required to work for other Group Companies. "Group" or "Group Company" means the Company or any subsidiary undertaking or holding company for the time being of the Company, or any subsidiary undertaking of such holding company (as defined in Sections 474(1), 1159 and 1162 of the Companies Act 2006).

CONDITIONAL FORMALITIES

This offer of employment is subject to the following conditions:

(*delete as appropriate)

REFERENCES

In accordance with the Company's policy, this offer of employment is conditional on our receiving satisfactory reports from the pre-employment screening process we undertake upon receipt of your written acceptance. The screening undertaken includes address verification, residency and credit checks, qualification, verification, professional body/institute membership affiliation, employment history confirmation, taking up references and company directorships.

The pre-employment screening process will be undertaken by Human Resources.

The Company reserves the right to withdraw this offer of employment should references or any aspect of the pre-employment screening reports be unsatisfactory. If your employment has commenced, then the Company will by notice to you on becoming aware of this, notify you that this condition of your employment is not satisfied and that your employment has automatically terminated. Every effort will be made to obtain references as quickly as possible.

RESTRICTIONS ON WORKING

In accordance with the Immigration, Asylum and Nationality Act 2006, all offers of employment are conditional upon receipt of satisfactory evidence that you are entitled to work lawfully in the UK. You are therefore required to submit your passport and any other supporting documentation to Human Resources prior to the commencement of your employment.

QUALIFICATIONS/REGULATORY APPROVAL

This offer is subject to you possessing the relevant qualifications as set out in the job application form and you producing original evidence of your qualifications.

It is a condition of this offer of employment that if you are required to be approved by the Financial Services Authority (FSA) in order to perform your duties, you must hold and retain "approved person" status in accordance with the FSA Handbook and at all times comply with the sections of the Company's Compliance Manual which are relevant to you.

DRIVING LICENCE

It is an essential condition of your employment that you possess and continue to hold a valid driving licence If you receive any criminal convictions for any motoring offences or lose your driving licence through a conviction, this must be reported to the Company.

MEDICAL EXAMINATION

This offer of employment is also subject to a satisfactory medical report carried out on you by either our Company doctors as [address] or [insert alternative medical practitioner]. Please contact either of these before the commencement of your employment and arrange an appointment as soon as possible. The Company's equal opportunities policy is committed to providing fair employment opportunities to people with disability.

ACCEPTANCE

This offer of employment expires on [insert date]. Any extension to this date will be subject to the written agreement of the Company. To confirm your acceptance of our offer, please could you sign the duplicate copy of this letter, confirming your start date, and return it to me as soon as possible.

May I take this opportunity of welcoming you to the Company and trust that your career with us will be both enjoyable and successful.

Yours sincerely

....

Director

I accept the conditions stated and will commence employment on........................

....

Executive Date

Appendix B

Service agreement

THIS AGREEMENT is made on [ ]

BETWEEN:-

1. *[Name of Company]* (registered in England under Company No.) whose registered office is at ***[Address]*** ("the Company"); and

2. *[Name of Executive]* of ***[Address]*** ("the Executive").

WHEREBY it is agreed that the Company shall employ the Executive upon and subject to the following terms and conditions:

IT IS AGREED as follows:-

1. INTERPRETATION

1.1 In this Agreement the following words and expressions shall have the following meanings unless the context otherwise requires:

[**"AIM"** means the AIM market of the London Stock Exchange;]

[**"AIM Rules"** means the rules of the London Stock Exchange which govern the admission of securities to trading on and the regulation of AIM;]

"Board" means the board of directors of the Company [or any Group Company] including any duly appointed committee or sub-committee thereof;

"Confidential Information" means any information which the Executive knows or ought reasonably to know concerns the business of the Company [or any Group Company] or any of its or their suppliers, agents, distributors, customers or others and which shall have been acquired, received or made by the Executive during the Term (whether or not expressly designated "confidential" and whether or not in legible or tangible form) including (without limitation) Inventions and the matters set out in Schedule [.....];

"Executive Intellectual Property" means all Intellectual Property rights in any Inventions, works, processes, methods, data, products and/or materials created or devised by the Executive in the course of his employment by the Company (whether during normal working hours or whether using the premises, facilities or resources of the Company or any Group Company and irrespective of whether the same is recorded in material form);

[**"FSA"** means the Financial Services Authority;]

[**"Group"** means the Company and any Group Company from time to time;]

[**"Group Company"** means any company which is from time to time a holding company or a subsidiary (as those expressions are defined in Sections 474(1) and 1159 of the Companies Act 2006) of the Company, or a subsidiary of any such holding company and so that 'subsidiary" shall also include a subsidiary undertaking as defined in Section 1162 of the Companies Act 2006);]

"Intellectual Property" means all intellectual property rights throughout the world whether currently in existence or otherwise and whether vested or contingent, including copyright, moral rights, rights in the nature of copyright, trade secrets, patents, rights to inventions, discoveries and improvements, utility models, design rights, database rights, trade marks, service marks, logos, trading and business names, rights in internet domain names, know how, confidential information, unfair competition rights, rights in get-up, rights in goodwill, rights to sue for passing off, topography rights, Confidential Information, other intellectual property rights and rights in the nature of intellectual property (in each case whether registered or not and including both registrations and applications therefor) and all rights or forms of protection of a similar nature or having equivalent or similar effect in any part of the world;

"Invention" is as defined in Clause [13.1];

"Records" means notes, memoranda, tape recordings, films, photographs, plans, designs, drawings, computer data, software or any form of record (whether electronic or otherwise), material or document relating to any matter within the scope of the business, finances, management or administration of the Company [or any Group Company] or any of their respective clients, customers, shareholders, employees, officers, suppliers, distributors and agents or concerning any of its or their respective dealings, transactions or affairs; and

"Term" means the term of the employment as defined in sub-clause [2.1].

[**"UK Listing Authority"** means the FSA in its capacity as the competent authority, for the purposes of Part VI of the Financial Services and Markets Act 2000.]

1.2 Any reference in this Agreement to the employment of the Executive is a reference to the Executive's employment by the Company under this Agreement.

1.3 The headings in this Agreement (and any descriptive notes in brackets following references to statutes or to other documents) and any front or back sheet or cover and any index hereto are for convenience only and shall not affect the construction or interpretation of this Agreement.

1.4 Any reference in this Agreement to a person shall (unless the context otherwise requires) include a reference to a natural person and a body corporate and to any unincorporated body of persons including any firm, association, partnership, trust, society or charity.

1.5 Any reference in this Agreement to any "party" or to the "parties" are to the parties to this Agreement.

1.6 A reference to a particular law is a reference to it as it is in force for the time being taking account of any amendment, extension or re-enactment and includes any subordinate legislation for the time being in force made under it.

1.7 Save as herein expressly otherwise provided, expressions and words which are defined in the Companies Act 1985 including any statutory modification, amendment or re-enactment thereof being in force from time to time, and the Companies Act 2006 including any statutory modification, amendment or re-enactment thereof being in force from time to time, insofar as they apply to the Company and/or to any Group Company shall have the same meanings in this Agreement.

1.8 This Agreement shall be binding upon and enure for the benefit of the Company and its successors in title and assigns.

1.9 No right of any party to agree any amendment, variation, waiver, or settlement, under or arising from or in respect of this Agreement, or to terminate this Agreement, shall be subject to the consent of any person who has rights under this Agreement by virtue of the Contracts (Rights of Third Parties) Act 1999.

2. APPOINTMENT AND TERM

2.1 The Executive shall provide [his] services as [insert job position] or in such other capacity as the Company may from time to time require. [The Executive primary duties include but are not limited to: [detail duties].]

2.2 [indefinite term]

The term of the employment shall commence on [ ] and, subject to clause [15], shall continue until terminated by either party giving to the other not less than [ ] [month[s]] notice in writing (the "Term").

[OR]

[initial fixed term with notice thereafter]

The term of the employment shall commence on [ ] and, subject to clause [15], shall continue for a fixed period of [...] [month[s]/year[s]] until [ ] and thereafter unless or until terminated by either party giving to the other at anytime not less than [ ] month[s] notice in writing to expire on [ ] or at any time thereafter (the "Term").

[OR]

[Pure fixed term]

The term of the employment shall commence on [ ] and, and shall continue, subject to the remaining terms of this Agreement, until it terminates on [ ] without the need for notice (the "Term").

[OR]

[Fixed term subject to notice within the fixed term]

The term of the employment shall commence on [ ] and, shall continue, subject to the remaining terms of this Agreement, until it terminates on [DATE] without the need for notice unless previously terminated by either party giving the other not less than [] months notice in writing.

2.3 The Executive's period of continuous employment for statutory purposes shall be deemed to have commenced on ***[insert date of first employment]***. [No employment with a previous employer **shall** counts towards the Executive's period of continuous employment with the Company.]

2.4 The first [ ] months of employment shall be a probationary period and the employment may be terminated during this period at any time on [ ] week's prior notice. The Company may, at its absolute discretion, extend this period. During the probationary period the Executive's performance and suitability will be monitored. [At the end of the probationary period, the Executive will be informed in writing if [he] has successfully completed [his] probationary period].

2.5 The Executive represents and warrants to the Company that [he] is entitled to enter into this Agreement and to carry out its terms and that by doing so [he] will not be in breach of any obligation (contractual or otherwise) to any third party which would entitle that third party to damages or any other remedy, or which may in any way restrict or prohibit [him] from entering into this Agreement or from performing [his] duties under this Agreement. [The Executive undertakes to indemnify the Company against any claims, costs, damages, liabilities or expenses which the Company may incur as a result of any breach].

2.6 The Executive warrants that he is entitled to work in the United Kingdom without any additional approvals and will notify the Company immediately if he ceases to be so entitled during his employment.

2.7 The Executive warrants that [he] holds [PROFESSIONAL QUALIFICATION] and shall continue at all times during the employment to be so qualified. The Employee shall immediately notify the Company if [he] ceases to hold [PROFESSIONAL QUALIFICATION] during employment.

3. OBLIGATIONS DURING EMPLOYMENT

3.1 The Executive shall during the Term (unless prevented by sickness or injury):

3.1.1 devote the whole of [his] time, attention, skill and ingenuity during working hours to [his] duties under this Agreement;

3.1.2 faithfully and using [his] best endeavours carry out all work consistent with [his] position which may be required of [him];

3.1.3 faithfully and diligently perform such duties and exercise such powers consistent with [his] position as may from time to time be assigned to or vested in [him] by the Board;

3.1.4 comply with all reasonable and lawful requests made by the Board;

3.1.5 use [his] best endeavours to promote the success of the Company and protect and extend the business, reputation, welfare and the interests of the Company [or any Group Company];

3.1.6 comply with all the Company's rules, regulations, policies and procedures from time to time in force;

3.1.7 give to the Board or such persons as it shall nominate at all times promptly (in writing if so requested) all such information and explanations as are known to the Executive regarding the affairs of the Company [or any Group Company] as the Board may require;

3.1.8 report to the Board any matters of concern that come to the Executive's attention, it being the duty of the Executive to report any acts of misconduct, dishonesty, breach of Company rules or breach of any of the rules of any relevant regulatory bodies committed, contemplated or discussed by any other member of staff or other third party. The Company shall keep confidential whatever is reported save as required by law or a court or authority of competent jurisdiction. Failure to act in accordance with this provision is a disciplinary matter which may lead to summary dismissal;

3.1.9 work at the Company's offices at [] or at any of the Company [or any Group Company] offices in the United Kingdom or overseas as directed from time to time. [If the Company requires the Executive to relocate, the Company shall in accordance with the Company's relocation policy from time to time pay the Executive's reasonable costs];

3.1.10 travel on Company [or any Group Company] business in the United Kingdom or overseas as the Company [or any Group Company] may from time to time require which may include travelling outside normal business hours, at weekends and on bank or public holidays[; and]

3.1.11 [do such things as are necessary to ensure compliance by [himself] and [the Company [or any Group Company] with the [Combined Code on Corporate

Governance of the UK Listing Authority (as amended from time to time)] **OR** [AIM Rules(as amended from time to time)];]

3.1.12 [comply with all requirements, recommendations or regulations, as amended from time to time, of the UK Listing Authority (including the Model Code for transactions in securities by directors and certain senior executives of listed companies, a copy of which is available from [POSITION], the FSA and all regulatory authorities relevant to the Company [or any Group Company] and any code of practice issued by the Company (as amended from time to time) relating to dealing in the securities of the Company [or any Group Company];]

3.1.13 [not do anything that would cause [him] to be disqualified from acting as a director;]

3.2 Notwithstanding the foregoing or any other provision of this Agreement:

3.2.1 the Company may during the Term, without further fees or remuneration, make the Executive's services available to any other person within or outside the Group at such locations and for such periods and on such terms as the Company and the Executive shall reasonably agree and the Executive shall enter into any agreement with such other person as the Company may reasonably require to give full effect to such arrangement; and

3.2.2 the Company may at any time during the Term appoint another person or persons to act jointly with the Executive in discharging [his] duties.

3.3 The Company reserves the right to suspend all or any of the Executive's duties and powers on such terms as it considers expedient (including a term that the Executive shall not attend at the Company or any Group Company's premises and/or that the Executive shall not contact or have dealings with any customer, client, supplier or employee of the Company [or any Group Company]) or to require the Executive to carry out the duties of another position [of equivalent status] either in addition to or instead of [his] duties as [***Job Title***]. The Company shall be under no obligation to assign any duties to the Executive and shall be entitled to exclude [him] from its premises. The Executive shall remain bound by [his] obligations of good faith, fidelity and loyalty to the Company during such suspension.

3.4 [The Company reserves the right to assign its rights and obligations under this Agreement to any Group Company and thereafter any reference to the Company in this Agreement shall be a reference to any such Group Company.]

4. INTERESTS IN OTHER BUSINESSES

4.1 During the Term the Executive shall not (unless the Board shall in its absolute discretion so consent in writing) carry on or be concerned, engaged or interested in or assume responsibilities or duties for, whether directly or indirectly in relation to, any person whether corporate or not (other than any of the businesses of the Group) save that notwithstanding this clause the Executive may:

4.1.1 be interested as a holder directly or through nominees for investment purposes only in any securities in any person which are for the time being admitted to trading on a recognised stock exchange, provided that none of the holdings of such securities in which the Executive shall be so interested shall at any time exceed [three] per cent in aggregate of the nominal value of the securities concerned for the time being in issue; and

4.1.2 to the extent that and only for so long as the Board shall in its absolute discretion so consent in writing, be concerned or take an interest in or assume responsibilities or duties in any person, provided always that:-

4.1.2.1 the business or activity of such person does not conflict nor compete with and is not likely to conflict or compete with any business of the Company [or any Group Company]; and

4.1.2.2 the Executive's concern and interest in and responsibilities and duties towards such person do not and are unlikely to interfere with the proper performance of the Executive's duties under this Agreement.

4.1.3 Subject to any regulations issued by the Company, the Executive shall not be entitled to receive or obtain directly or indirectly any inducement, discount, rebate or commission in respect of any sale or purchase of goods effected or other business transacted (whether or not by him) by or on behalf of the Company [or any Group Company] and if [he] (or any firm or company in which [he] is interested) shall obtain any such discount, rebate or commission [he] shall account to the Company [or the relevant Group Company] for the amount received by [him] [(or a due proportion of the amount received by such company or firm having regard to the extent of [his] interest therein).]

5. HOURS OF WORK

[The Executive shall work such hours as are necessary or appropriate from time to time to carry out [his] duties properly and effectively, with no allowance or additional payment for overtime [for a weekly minimum of [40] hours] [from [9.00 am] to [5.00 pm] Monday to Friday]. [In particular the Executive agrees whenever necessary to work longer than 48 hours per week. The Executive may withdraw [his] consent to working in excess of 48 hours per week on [three months] written notice to the Company.]

OR

[For the purposes of the Working Time Regulations 1998, the Executive confirms that [he] is an Executive with autonomous decision making powers and that the duration of [his] working time cannot be measured or pre-determined and that [he] is therefore not prohibited from working longer than 48 hours per week].

6. **REMUNERATION AND BENEFITS**

6.1 The Company shall pay the Executive during the Term a salary of £[***amount***] per year (inclusive of any director's fees payable by the Company [or any Group Company]) less deductions for tax and National Insurance Contributions ("Base Salary") which shall accrue from day to day and shall be payable by 12 equal monthly instalments in arrears, on or about the [] day of each calendar month by credit transfer direct to the Executive's bank account.

6.2 The Executive's salary shall be subject to a review (but not necessarily an increase) which shall take place annually [usually in [***insert month***]]. The Executive's salary may be increased with effect from any such review date at the absolute discretion of the Board. [There will be no salary review or increase if notice is served by either party].

6.3 The Executive agrees and hereby authorises the Company to deduct from any wages (as defined in Part II of the Employment Rights Act 1996) due to the Executive any sums due from the Executive to the Company [or any Group Company].

[6.4 The Executive shall also be entitled to such additional remuneration and/or benefits as are set out in the attached Schedule[s] [ ].]

7. **[DISCRETIONARY BONUS]**

7.1 The [Company or Board] may in its absolute discretion pay the Executive a bonus of such amount, at such intervals and subject to such conditions as the [Company or Board] may in its absolute discretion determine [from time to time or taking into account specific performance targets,] [to be notified to the Executive or as agreed between the Executive and [the Company or Board] from time to time].

7.2 Any bonus payment to the Executive shall be purely discretionary and shall not form part of the Executive contractual remuneration under this agreement. If the Company makes a bonus payment to the Executive [in respect of a particular financial year of the Company (being the period from [DATE] to [DATE])], it shall not be obliged to make subsequent bonus payments [in respect of subsequent financial years of the Company].

7.3 [The Company may alter the terms of any bonus or withdraw it altogether at any time without prior notice.]

7.4 The Executive shall in any event have no right to a bonus or a time-apportioned bonus if:

7.4.1 [he] has not been employed throughout the whole of the relevant financial year of the Company; or

7.4.2 [his] employment terminates for any reason or he is under notice of termination (whether given by the Executive or the Company) at or prior to the date when a bonus might otherwise have been payable].

7.5 Any bonus payable in accordance with clause [7.1] shall not be pensionable.

8. EXPENSES

Subject to any Company policies, the Company shall reimburse the Executive for all reasonable travelling, accommodation, entertainment and other out-of-pocket expenses wholly and necessarily incurred by the Executive during the Term in the proper performance of [his] duties under this Agreement upon production of receipts or such appropriate evidence of payment as the Company may require.

9. HOLIDAYS

9.1 The Executive shall, in addition to public and bank holidays, be entitled to [] working days paid holiday in each calendar year or such proportionate number of days as shall correspond to the actual period that the Executive may have worked for the Company during the calendar year, to be taken at such times as shall have been approved by [***insert name***] or another duly authorised person.

9.2 The Company's holiday year is from [***insert date***] to [***insert date***].

9.3 [A day's holiday pay shall be calculated based on 1/260 of salary[1]].

9.4 The Executive shall not be entitled to carry forward any annual holiday entitlement untaken by [him] for any reason during the calendar year in which it accrued without the prior written consent of [***insert name***] or another duly authorised person. [Any carried forward holiday must be taken within the first [] month[s] of the next holiday year].

9.5 Upon the termination of the Executive's employment the Executive's entitlement to accrued holiday pay shall be calculated on a pro rata basis in respect of each completed month of service in the calendar year in which [his] employment terminates provided that where:-

9.5.1 the Executive shall have taken more holiday than [his] accrued entitlement the Company is hereby authorised (for the purposes of Part II of the Employment Rights Act 1996) to make an appropriate deduction from the Executive's final salary payment (and so that to the extent that any sums due to the Executive from the Company are insufficient to cover the excess, the Executive shall pay the balance immediately upon request); and

[1] This figure will need to be reduced for part-time employees.

9.5.2 the Executive's employment is terminated summarily for cause [he] shall not be entitled to receive any pay in lieu of accrued holiday in excess of his statutory entitlement as at the termination date.

9.6 [The Company, at its absolute discretion, may request the Executive to take any outstanding holiday entitlement during any period of notice, and should the Executive fail to do so, the Executive shall then lose any entitlement to holiday pay in lieu.]

9.7 The Company shall be entitled to withhold any entitlement to holiday pay in lieu if the Executive fails to give the Company proper notice of termination or if the Executive leaves before such notice has expired. In such a case the Executive's holiday pay in lieu shall be reduced by the number of days notice not worked. In any case where the Company agrees to waive the requirement for the Executive to work out his notice, this sub-clause shall not apply.

9.8 [During any continuous period of absence of [one month or more] unrelated to holiday taken under this clause, the Executive shall accrue statutory holiday during this absence under the Working Time Regulations and not contractual holiday as set out at clause [9.1]].

10. SICKNESS AND INJURY

10.1 If at any time during the Term the Executive is absent from work due to sickness or injury [he] shall promptly forward to the Company, if required, evidence of such sickness or injury in a form satisfactory to the Board.

10.2 Provided the Executive complies with sub-clause [10.1] and the Company's sickness absence procedures (as set down from time to time) the Company shall pay the Executive's salary under sub-clause [6.1] (inclusive of any statutory sick pay) for the first [] days in aggregate of absence due to sickness or injury in any rolling 12 month period but shall not be required to pay the Executive any salary and/or other remuneration for any further periods of such absence in any calendar year, although the Company may at its discretion do so.

10.3 If any incapacity is caused by any alleged action or wrong of a third party and the Executive decides to claim damages in respect thereof, the Executive shall use all reasonable endeavours to recover damages for loss of earnings over the period for which salary has been paid or shall be paid to the Executive by the Company under this clause and shall account to the Company for any such damages recovered (less any costs borne by the Executive in achieving such recovery) in an amount not exceeding the actual salary paid or payable by the Company under this clause in respect of such period.

10.4 At such time as the Company may reasonably request and at the expense of the Company the Executive agrees to undergo a medical and/or psychological examination by a doctor or doctors of the Company's choice and permit unconditional disclosure of the results of such medical examination to the Company pursuant to the Access to Medical Reports Act 1988, including copies of any documents referred to in any such reports. The Company shall keep the results of such medical examination confidential save insofar as it is necessary to disclose the results for the purpose of obtaining or maintaining any policy of insurance required by the Company or save as required by law.

11. CONFIDENTIALITY

11.1 The Executive shall not (other than in the proper performance of [his] duties or with the prior written consent of the Company or unless ordered by a court or other authority of competent jurisdiction) at any time either during the Term or afterwards disclose or communicate to any person or use for [his] own benefit or the benefit of any person other than the Company [or any Group Company] or through any failure to exercise all due care and diligence cause, enable, authorise, assist or permit any unauthorised use or disclosure of any Confidential Information, or attempt or purport to do any of the foregoing.

11.2 All Records embodying or relating to any Intellectual Property or Confidential Information shall be and remain the exclusive property of the Company [or the relevant Group Company].

11.3 The provisions of this clause shall not apply to any Confidential Information which:-

11.3.1 is in or enters the public domain other than by breach of this Agreement by the Executive; or

11.3.2 is obtained from any third party who is lawfully authorised to disclose such information.

11.4 The Executive shall at all times both during the Term and afterwards use best endeavours to prevent the unauthorised use, publication or disclosure of any Confidential Information and shall inform the Company of any actual, suspected or threatened use, publication or disclosure of any Confidential Information in contravention of this Agreement as soon as the same becomes known to the Executive and shall unconditionally render such assistance to restrain such farther use or disclosure as the Company may request.

12. RECORDS

12.1 During the Term the Executive shall not (otherwise than for the exclusive benefit of the Company [or any Group Company] and on the basis that it is the intention of the parties hereto that the Records and any copies or reproductions thereof shall be and remain the exclusive property of the Company [or the relevant Group Company]):-

12.1.1 make, copy or reproduce in any form any Records in whole or in part;

12.1.2 use or permit any Records to be used by or for the benefit of any other person; or

12.1.3 attempt or purport to do any of the foregoing or cause, enable, permit, authorise or assist any other person to do any of the foregoing.

12.2 During the Term the Executive shall observe and comply with all security measures introduced by or on behalf of the Company [or any Group Company] from time to time to safeguard and protect the Records from theft or unauthorised access by any person or from loss or damage caused by computer bugs or viruses or otherwise howsoever.

12.3 The Executive shall at any time during the Term on request by the Company and in any event immediately upon termination of this Agreement howsoever caused, at the Company's discretion:-

12.3.1 deliver up to the Company [or any Group Company]; and/or

12.3.2 destroy, erase or delete from any data storage medium, including without limitation, from any computer hard disk or drive and any floppy disk in the Executive's possession, power, custody or control

all Records and/or Confidential Information which the Executive has made, copied, or reproduced in any form, and all other documents, papers, materials or property belonging or relating to the Company [or any Group Company] in the Executive's possession, power, custody or control [and the Executive shall within [] days thereafter serve a written statement signed by [him] on the Company certifying that [] has complied with this sub-clause [12.3].]

13. INTELLECTUAL PROPERTY

13.1 The Executive shall immediately notify the Company in writing of the general nature of any discovery, invention, idea, development, process, innovation or improvement made created, devised or discovered wholly or partially by [him] during the Term (irrespective of whether it was so made or discovered during normal working hours or using the premises, facilities or resources of the Company [or any Group Company] and irrespective of whether it is recorded in material form and irrespective of whether or not the Executive considers that by virtue of Section 39 of the Patents Act 1977 or any similar provision of applicable law not capable of exclusion rights thereto fail to vest in the Company [or any Group Company]) and which in any way relates or may be related to any product, service, work, method or process of the Company [or any Group Company] or to any Confidential Information and/or which is capable of being used in the business of the Company [and/or any Group Company] ("Invention").

13.2 As between the Company [or any Group Company] on the one hand and the Executive on the other hand the entitlement to any Invention shall be determined in accordance with the provisions of the Patents Act 1977.

13.3 The Executive shall promptly provide to the Company [or any Group Company] full written disclosure of any Invention and if and whenever required by the Company [or any Group Company] so to do (whether or not during the Term) shall at the reasonable expense of the Company [or any Group Company] but without additional payment to the Executive (except to the extent provided in Section 40 of the Patents Act 1977 or any similar provisions of applicable law) apply or join with the Company [or any Group Company] or any other person(s) in applying for letters patent or other equivalent protection (except only to the extent that by virtue of Section 39 of the Patents Act 1977 or any similar provision of applicable law not capable of exclusion such rights fail to vest in the Company [or any Group Company]) in the United Kingdom and in any other part of the world for such Invention and unconditionally do such things and execute such documents as the Company [or any Group Company] may reasonably request.

13.4 It is agreed that (subject only to sub-clause [13.2]) the Company [or any Group Company] shall be solely and exclusively entitled to the entire and unencumbered legal and beneficial interest throughout the world in all Inventions and all other Executive Intellectual Property and all materials embodying any of the foregoing (together "the Specified Rights"). To the extent that (notwithstanding the foregoing) any Specified Right does not vest automatically in the Company or any Group Company, the Executive shall hold it on trust for the Company.

13.5 The Executive undertakes at the reasonable expense of the Company [or any Group Company] [(but without additional payment to the Executive except to the extent provided in Section 40 of the Patents Act 1977 or any similar provisions of applicable law)] immediately and unconditionally to execute all documents and do all things as the Company [or any Group Company] shall require for the purpose of confirming to and assuring in the name of the Company [or any Group Company] any Specified Right and/or maintaining or protecting any Specified Right and/or registering any Specified Right in the name of the Company [or any Group Company], including (without limitation) waiving any statutory moral right therein.

13.6 The Executive undertakes immediately to inform the Company [or any Group Company] of the creation or coming into existence of any Executive Intellectual Property.

13.7 The Executive waives all his present and future moral rights in or to any copyright forming part of any Executive Intellectual Property in favour of the Company [or any Group Company] and for the avoidance of doubt such waiver shall extend to the licensees and successors in title of the Company or [or any Group Company].

13.8 The Executive shall at all times during the Term inform the Company of any actual, suspected or threatened infringement of any Intellectual Property of the Company [or any Group Company] as soon as the same becomes known to the Executive and shall at the reasonable cost and expense of the Company unconditionally render such assistance as the Company may request to restrain such further infringement, to enforce such Intellectual Property against third parties, to apply for the registration of any such Intellectual Property and to defend any claim made against any Company [and/or Group Company] of infringement of third party Intellectual Property.

13.9 Subject only to his rights under the Patents Act 1977 and except as otherwise provided by law, the Executive accepts and agrees that no further compensation other than that provided for in this Agreement shall or may become due to him in respect of his compliance with this Clause [13].

13.10 The Executive hereby irrevocably appoints the Company to be his attorney to execute all documents and do all things for the purpose of giving the Company [and/or any Group Company] the benefit of this Clause [13].

13.11 The Executive shall not without the prior written consent of the Company register any Executive Intellectual Property or any Invention or attempt to do so.

13.12 The Executive acknowledges that, because of the nature of his duties and the particular responsibilities arising from the nature of his duties, he has a special obligation to further the interests of the Company [and each Group Company].

13.13 All rights and obligations under this Clause [13] in respect of any Executive Intellectual Property shall continue in full force and effect after the termination of the Executive's employment and shall be binding upon [his] personal representatives.

14. RESTRICTIVE COVENANTS

14.1 In relation to the restrictions set out in this sub-clause[14.1]:

14.1.1 **"Business"** means any businesses of the Company [and any Group Company] at the Termination Date and with which the Executive was involved to a material degree in the [12] months immediately preceding the Termination Date;

14.1.2 **"Customer"** means any person, who at any time in the period of [12] months immediately preceding the Termination Date, was a customer or client of or who had regular dealings with the Company [or any Group Company] and with whom or which the Executive had material contact during the Term;

14.1.3 **"Employee"** means any person who, at the Termination Date, was employed or engaged by the Company [or an Group Company]:

14.1.3.1 [at a senior or key level] [at a level at least equal to the Executive's level and who was a person with whom [he] had material contact during [ ]; or

14.1.3.2 [in a position which reported directly to the Executive either at the Termination Date or at any time in the [12] months immediately preceding that date;]

[and who could cause material loss or damage to the Company [or any Group Company] if he was to be employed in any business competing or seeking to complete with any Business];

14.1.4 **"Prospective Customer"** means any person, firm or company who, at the Termination Date, the Company [or any Group Company] were in discussions or negotiations with for the purposes of them becoming a customer and with whom the Executive had material contact or dealings during such discussions or negotiations.

14.1.5 **"Supplier"** means any person who was a supplier of the Company [or any Group Company] at any time in the period of [12] months immediately preceding the Termination Date and with which the Executive had material contact during the Term;

14.1.6 **"Termination Date"** means the date of termination of the Executive's employment.

14.2 The Executive will not, for a period of [six] months after the Termination Date, canvass, approach or solicit or cause to be canvassed, approached or solicited for orders (in respect of any services provided or goods sold by any Business) or seek to entice away from the Company [or any Group Company] any business or trade of a Customer or Prospective Customer with the intention of supplying goods or services to that Customer or Prospective Customer so as to compete or seek to compete with any Business.

14.3 The Executive will not, for a period of [six] months after the Termination Date, supply goods, or services to, or otherwise have business dealings with, any Customer or Prospective Customer in the course of any business or entity which is, or seeks to be, in competition with any Business.

14.4 The Executive will not for a period of [six] months after the Termination Date, for [himself] or on behalf of any business or entity which is in competition with any Business, employ or offer employment to an Employee, or in any way try to entice an Employee away from the Company [or any Group Company].

14.5 The Executive will not, for a period of [six] months after the Termination Date, be engaged in or concerned in any capacity in any business or entity which is or seeks to be in competition with any Business. [As at the date of this Agreement such entities include, without limitation:

14.5.1 [ ];]

14.6 The Executive will not, for period of [six] months after the Termination Date contact or interfere or have dealings with any Supplier, for himself or on behalf of any business or entity which is in competition with any Business nor do any act or omission which results directly or indirectly, in the Supplier;

14.6.1 ceasing to supply or substantially reducing such supplies or services to the Company [or any Group Company]; or

14.6.2 changing substantially the basis or terms on which it is prepared to enter into contracts, do business or supply such products or services with the Company; or

14.6.3 changing substantially the basis or terms on which it is prepared to enter into contract, do business or supply products or services with the Company [or any Group Company].

14.7 Nothing in this clause shall prevent the Executive from being engaged in or by, or participating in, any business or entity to the extent that any of his activities for such business or entity shall relate solely to matters of a type with which the Executive was not materially concerned in the [12] months immediately preceding the Termination Date.

14.8 The restrictions set out in this clause apply whether the Executive is acting for [his] own benefit or on behalf of any person and whether [he] acts directly or indirectly.

14.9 The Executive hereby agrees that [he] shall at the cost of the Company enter into a direct agreement or undertaking with any Group Company whereby [he] shall accept restrictions and provisions corresponding to the restrictions and provisions in sub-clauses [14.1 to 14.6] above (or such of them as may be appropriate in the circumstances) in relation to such activities and such area and for such period not exceeding that specified in these sub-clauses as such Group Company may reasonably require for the protection of its legitimate business interests.]

14.10 The Executive agrees that in the event of receiving from any person an offer of employment either during the Term or during the continuance in force of any of the restrictions set out above [he] shall forthwith provide to such person making such offer of employment, a full and accurate copy of this clause.

14.11 [Any period spent by the Executive on "Garden Leave" in accordance with clause [16] below shall be deducted from the period of restriction referred to in sub-clauses [14.1 to 14.6] above.]]

14.12 Each of the obligations contained in sub-clauses [14.1 to 14.6] above constitutes an entirely separate and independent restriction on the Executive notwithstanding that it may be contained in the same sub-clause, paragraph, sentence or phrase. If these obligations or any part of them are found to be held invalid or unenforceable or void but would not be if some part of the obligation were deleted, modified or varied then the provision shall apply with such deletion, modification or variation as is necessary to make it valid and effective.

15. TERMINATION OF DIRECTORSHIP & EMPLOYMENT

15.1 [The employment of the Executive under this Agreement shall terminate automatically in the event of his ceasing to be a director of the Company and in that event, the Executive shall have no claim for damages against the Company unless he shall so cease (i) by reason of his not being re-elected as a director of the Company at the AGM of the Company held next after the commencement of his employment, (ii) by reason of his not being elected as a director of the Company at any AGM of the Company at which he is to retire by rotation; or (iii) by virtue of a resolution passed by the members of the Company in a general meeting to remove him as a director] **OR** [If during his employment under this Agreement the Executive shall cease to be a director of the Company (otherwise than by reason of his death, resignation or disqualification pursuant to the Articles of Association of the Company or by statute or court order), his employment shall continue and the terms of this Agreement (other than those relating to the holding of the office of director [and remuneration and benefits]) shall continue in full force and effect and the Executive shall have no claims against the Company in respect of his cessation of office.]

Subject to sub-clauses [15.2, 15.3, 15.4] and [16] the Executive's employment may be terminated by either party giving not less than [] months' notice in writing to the other party.[2] The Company may at its absolute discretion elect to terminate the Executive's employment with immediate effect by paying the Executive's Base Salary only in lieu of notice (excluding any benefits or emolument referable to the employment of the Executive under this

[2] This will need amending if employment is for a fixed term.

Agreement). Furthermore, the Company may in its absolute discretion pay the payment in lieu of notice in equal monthly instalments in arrears on the dates on which the Executive's Base Salary would normally have been paid and if the Company elects to make such payment by instalments, the Executive's entitlement shall cease immediately on the date on which the Executive accepts an offer of alternative employment or engagement and the Executive shall as soon as reasonably practicable notify the Company in writing of any such acceptance. For the avoidance of doubt, the right of the Company to make a payment in lieu of notice, whether as a lump sum or by way of instalments does not give rise to any right of the Executive to receive such a payment or payments.

15.2 Without prejudice to the Executive's right to statutory minimum notice under section 86 ERA 1996, the employment of the Executive may be terminated by the Company with immediate effect without payment in lieu of the notice period under clause 15.1 for any of the following non-exhaustive list of reasons:-

15.2.1 commits any serious breach or non observance of any of his duties hereunder or otherwise as an Executive of the Company [or any Group Company]; or

15.2.2 commits, (after warning) any persistent or continued breach or non-observance of any of his duties hereunder or otherwise as an Executive of the Company [or any Group Company]; or

15.2.3 is guilty of any negligence, gross misconduct or dishonesty in connection with or affecting the business or affairs of the Company [or any Group Company] for which the Executive is required to perform duties; or

15.2.4 is guilty of conduct which in the reasonable opinion of the Board brings or is likely to bring the Executive, the Company [or any Group Company] into disrepute; or

15.2.5 is convicted of an arrestable offence other than a road traffic offence for which a non-custodial penalty is imposed; or

15.2.6 becomes bankrupt or makes any arrangement or composition with [his] creditors generally or has an interim order made against [him] pursuant to section 252 of the Insolvency Act 1986; or

15.2.7 causes any agreement entered into by the Company [or any Group Company] relating to the provision of the Executive's services to be terminated without notice by any other party to such agreement; or

15.2.8 in the reasonable opinion of the Company becomes incapable by reason of mental disorder of discharging [his] duties; or

15.2.9 is or becomes prohibited by an applicable law or regulation from being a director of the Company [or any Group Company] or from performing any of his duties, is removed from office pursuant to the Company's articles of association (unless the removal is caused by sickness or injury other than mental disorder) or (except at the request of the Company) the Executive resigns as a director; or

15.2.10 is guilty of any breach or non observance of any code of conduct, rule or regulation referred to in sub-clause [3.1] or fails or ceases to be registered with or authorised by (where such registration or authorisation is, in the opinion of the Board, required for the performance of [his] duties) any regulatory body in the United Kingdom or elsewhere; or

15.2.11 or in any other circumstances where the Company may legally terminate the directorship of the Executive.

15.3 The employment of the Executive shall terminate upon the Executive attaining the age of [65].[3]

15.4 If the Executive is absent from work due to sickness or injury or other incapacity for periods in excess of [] weeks in aggregate in any consecutive period of 52 weeks the Company may terminate [his] employment by giving [him] not less than [ ] months' notice in writing expiring at any time or the statutory minimum notice in accordance with section 86(1) Employment Rights Act 1996, whichever is the lesser.][4]

15.5 Upon termination of the Executive's employment for whatever reason:

15.5.1 the Executive shall not take away, conceal or destroy but shall immediately deliver up to the Company all Records and Confidential Information in accordance with sub-clause [12.3];

15.5.2 the Executive shall not at any time thereafter make any untrue or misleading oral or written statement concerning the business or affairs of the Company [or any Group Company] nor represent [himself] nor permit [himself] to be held out as being in any way connected with or interested in the business or affairs of the Company [or any Group Company] (except as a former employee for the purpose of communications with prospective employers or complying with any applicable statutory requirements); and

15.5.3 the Executive shall immediately repay all outstanding debts or loans due to the Company [or any Group Company] and the Company is hereby authorised to deduct from any wages (as defined in Part II of the Employment Rights Act 1996) of the Executive a sum equal to any such debts or loans together with any interest thereon as appropriate; and

[3] The Company must still comply with the retirement procedures set down in the Employment Equality (Age Discrimination) Regulations 2006 SI 2006/1031.

[4] A fair procedure must be followed and the Company should be aware of any potential disability.

15.5.4 the Executive shall upon request by the Company immediately resign from [his] office as a director of the Company and from all other offices and appointments held by the Executive in or on behalf of the Company [or any Group Company] in each case without compensation for loss of office.

15.6 Any rights or obligations of the Executive, the Company [or any Group Company] under this Agreement which are expressed to continue or are capable of continuing after the date of termination of [his] employment shall continue in full force and effect notwithstanding the termination of the Executive's employment.

16. GARDEN LEAVE

16.1 The Company shall be entitled, during the period of any notice given pursuant to clause [15], or if the Executive purports to terminate [his] employment in breach of contract, or, if the Company so decides, at any time during [his] employment or in order to investigate a reasonable belief that the Executive is guilty of gross misconduct, and without limiting the Company's right to suspend any of the Executive's duties and powers under sub-clause [3.3], to require the Executive to cease to attend at the premises of the Company [or any Group Company] or to undertake any work during all or any part of the period of notice ("Garden Leave").

16.2 During such period or periods of Garden Leave the Executive shall nevertheless remain available to perform any such duties and/or to exercise any such powers, authorities and discretions (if any) if and when called upon to do so by the Company and remain bound (subject to this sub-clause) by the remaining provisions of this Agreement which shall continue to remain in fall force and effect.

16.3 The Executive shall not be entitled to any payment in damages or be entitled to make bring or base any claim or counterclaim whatsoever upon or as a result of the exercise by the Company of its rights under this clause.

16.4 The Executive shall continue to receive [his] salary and other benefits (if any) should the Company exercise its rights under this clause. The Executive, in turn, shall remain bound by [his] obligations of good faith, fidelity and loyalty to the Company such that the Executive shall not compete against the Company, solicit customers or clients of the Company to transfer their business to the Executive or any third party, or otherwise make any secret profit, or solicit members of staff to leave the Company's employment, or breach [his] obligations not to reveal to any third party Confidential Information.

16.5 During any period of Garden Leave, the Executive shall:

16.5.1 not, without the prior written consent of [POSITION], attend [his] place of work or any other premises of the Company [or any Group Company];

16.5.2 not, without the prior written consent of [POSITION], contact or deal with (or attempt to contact or deal with) any officer, employee, consultant, client, customer, supplier, agent, distributor, shareholder, adviser or other business contact of the Company [or any Group Company];

16.5.3 (except during any periods taken as holiday in the usual way) ensure that [POSITION] knows where [he] will be and how [he] can be contacted during each working day [and shall comply with any written requests to contact a specified employee of the Company at specified intervals];

16.5.4 upon request by the Company immediately resign from [his] office as a director of the Company and from all other offices and appointments held by the Executive in or on behalf of the Company [or any Group Company] in each case without compensation for loss of office; and

16.5.5 deliver up to the Company [or any Group Company]; and/or destroy, erase or delete from any data storage medium, including without limitation, from any computer hard disk or drive and any floppy disk in the Executive's possession, power, custody or control all Records and/or Confidential Information which the Executive has made, copied, or reproduced in any form, and all other documents, papers, materials or property belonging or relating to the Company [or any Group Company] in the Executive's possession, power, custody or control.

17. CORPORATE CHANGE

[Notwithstanding any other provision of this Agreement, at any time after the occurrence of a change of control of the Company, the Executive shall have the right to elect, by written notice delivered to the Company within [30] days of such change of control, to treat such change of control as a termination of the Executive's employment by the Company without cause. Upon such election by the Executive, the Employment shall be deemed to be terminated and notwithstanding sub-clause [15.1], the Executive shall be paid a sum equal to [ ] months only of his normal salary due under sub-clause [6.1] in lieu of any notice by the Company in respect of such change of control. For the purposes of this sub-clause "control" means holding directly or indirectly shares which carry 50% or more of the voting rights of the Company.]

[OR]

[If the employment of the Executive is terminated by reason of the liquidation of the Company for the purpose of reconstruction or amalgamation or as part of any arrangement for the amalgamation or reconstruction of the Company not involving liquidation and the Executive is offered employment with any concern or undertaking resulting from this reconstruction or amalgamation on terms and conditions which taken as a whole are not less favourable than the terms of this Agreement then the Executive shall have no claim against the Company in respect of such termination]

18. **DISMISSAL, DISCIPLINARY AND GRIEVANCE PROCEDURES**

Copies of these procedures have been provided to the Executive with this Agreement. These procedures do not have contractual affect.

19. **USE OF ELECTRONIC COMMUNICATIONS**

19.1 The Executive shall have access to the Company's email, internet and telephone systems, mobile telephone and other forms of electronic communication for the better performance of [his] duties provided that the Executive shall not send any emails of a defamatory or abusive nature or which constitute sexual, racial or any other form of harassment and he shall be prohibited from downloading any sexually explicit, pornographic or other offensive material and the Executive indemnifies the Company during and after the Term against all liability arising from the Executive's breach of this sub-clause.

19.2 The Company reserves the right to monitor all electronic communications sent and received by the Executive and to monitor the Executive's internet access, including, as appropriate, the right to open attachments to business and if appropriate other emails and any files or other material downloaded from the internet during and outside office hours and whether for personal or company use.

19.3 This clause is without prejudice to the Executive's obligations under Clause [20] (Data Protection).

20. **DATA PROTECTION**

20.1 For the purposes of complying with the Data Protection Act 1998 the Executive agrees to provide the Company [or any Group Company] with any personal data and sensitive personal data relating to [him] that either may request and [he] further consents to the holding and processing (in manual, electronic or any other form) of such data by the Company [or any Group Company] and/or any agent or third party nominated by the Company and bound by a duty of confidentiality, for the purpose of:

20.1.1 employee related administration;

20.1.2 processing [his] file and management of its business;

20.1.3 compliance with applicable procedures, laws and regulations;

20.1.4 providing data to external suppliers for the provision and administration of [his] remuneration and any benefits and any benefits; and/or

20.1.5 to evaluate the efficiency of the Company [and any Group Company's] business systems.

21. NOTICES

21.1 Notices to be given to either party under this Agreement shall be given in writing by hand or by post addressed, in the case of the Company, to its registered office for the time being marked for the attention of the [Chief Executive] or, in the case of the Executive, to [his] last known address.

21.2 Any such notice sent by post shall be deemed (in the absence of evidence of earlier receipt) to have been received 2 days after posting (6 days if sent by air mail) and in proving the time such notice was sent it shall be sufficient to show that the envelope containing it was properly addressed, stamped and posted and any such notice delivered personally shall be deemed to have been given at the time of such delivery.

22. FORMER SERVICE AGREEMENTS

This Agreement supersedes all previous agreements and arrangements whether written, oral or implied (if any) relating to the employment of the Executive (such agreements and arrangements (if any) shall be deemed to have been terminated by mutual consent as and with effect from the commencement of the Term) and this Agreement sets out the entire agreement of the parties in relation to the Executive's employment.

23. POWER OF ATTORNEY

23.1 The Executive hereby irrevocably and by way of security grants to the Company [(with power for the Company to grant a separate power to any Group Company on behalf of the Executive)] power of attorney on behalf of the Executive to sign all such documents, execute all such deeds and do or refrain from doing all such things as the Company exercising the power or such concurrent power may in its entire unfettered discretion consider appropriate convenient or necessary in any part of the world for the purposes of fulfilling the Executive's obligations under this Agreement. The Executive shall grant such separate powers of attorney in such form or forms as the Company [(or the relevant Group Company)] may reasonably require for such purposes, and the power granted by this clause shall empower the attorney to grant such further powers in the name and on behalf of the Executive.

23.2 Notwithstanding the foregoing and merely as a matter between the Company [(or the relevant Group Company)] and the Executive, the powers granted by the Executive under this clause shall not be used except with the consent of the Executive or following the failure of the Executive to sign or execute the relevant document or to do or refrain from doing the relevant act forthwith upon request made to the Executive in writing, and no party dealing with the power of attorney shall be concerned as to whether the procedure of this clause shall have been followed.

24. MISCELLANEOUS

24.1 The Executive acknowledges that any breach by him of any of the terms of clauses [11, 13 and 14] of this Agreement may inflict irreparable damage to the Confidential Information and/or Intellectual Property referred to in those clauses and entitle the Company [or any Group Company] to an injunction as well as to damages, costs and other relief.

24.2 The failure to exercise or delay in exercising a right or remedy under this Agreement shall not constitute a waiver or right or remedy or a waiver of any other rights or remedies and no single or partial exercise of any right or remedy under this Agreement shall prevent any further exercise of the right or remedy or the exercise of any other right or remedy.

In the event of any clause or sub-clause or parts thereof contained in this Agreement being held invalid or unenforceable by any judicial, arbitral, regulatory or other authority of competent jurisdiction all other clauses or sub-clauses or parts thereof contained in this Agreement shall remain in full force and effect to the fullest extent permitted by law and (subject as aforesaid) shall not be affected thereby.

25. RIGHTS OF THIRD PARTIES

The Contract (Rights of Third Parties) Act 1999 shall not apply to this Agreement save for clauses 3, 4, 11, 12, 13, 14, 15, 16, 20, 23 and 24 which apply for the benefit of the Group Company.

26. GOVERNING LAW AND JURISDICTION

This Agreement shall be governed by and construed in all respects in accordance with English law and each of the parties hereto submit to the exclusive jurisdiction of the Courts of England and Wales.

IN WITNESS whereof this Agreement has been executed and delivered as a Deed on the date first above written.

SIGNED as a **DEED** by)
[ ])
acting by:-)

Director

Director/Secretary

SIGNED as a **DEED** by)
The said **[*Full Name of Executive*]**)
in the presence of:-)

Witness Signature:

Witness Name:

Witness Address:

Witness Occupation:

SCHEDULE [1] – BENEFITS

1. LIFE ASSURANCE

1.1 [After successful completion of any probationary period, the Executive shall be entitled to participate in the Company's life assurance scheme which shall pay to the Executive dependents a sum equal to [SPECIFY] times the Executive salary if the Executive dies during employment. Participation is subject to:

1.1.1 the terms of the Company's life assurance scheme, as amended from time to time;

1.1.2 the rules or the insurance policy of the relevant insurance provider, as amended from time to time; and

1.1.3 the Executive satisfying the normal underwriting requirements of the relevant insurance provider and the premium being at a rate which the Company considers reasonable.

Full details of the scheme are available from [POSITION]

1.2 If the insurance provider refuses for any reason to provide life assurance benefit to the Executive the Company shall not be liable to provide to the Executive any replacement benefit of the same or similar kind or to pay any compensation in lieu of such benefit.

1.3 The Company in its sole and absolute discretion reserves the right to discontinue, vary or amend its life assurance scheme (including the level of the Executive cover) at any time on reasonable notice to the Executive.

2. PRIVATE MEDICAL INSURANCE

2.1 [After successful completion of any probationary period] the Executive [and [his] spouse or civil partner and any children under the age of 18] shall be entitled to participate in the Company's private medical insurance scheme subject to:

2.1.1 the terms of that scheme, as amended from time to time;

2.1.2 the rules or insurance policy of the relevant insurance provider, as amended from time to time; and

2.1.3 the Executive [and his spouse or civil partner and any children under the age of 18] satisfying the normal underwriting requirements of the relevant insurance provider and the premium being at a rate which the Company considers reasonable.

Full details of the Company's private medical insurance scheme are available from [POSITION]

2.2 If the insurance provider refuses for any reason to provide private medical insurance benefit to the Executive [or his spouse or civil partner and any children under the age of 18] the Company shall not be liable to provide any replacement benefit of the same or similar kind or to pay any compensation in lieu of such benefit.

2.3 The Company in its sole and absolute discretion reserves the right to discontinue, vary or amend the scheme (including the level of the Executive's cover) at any time on reasonable notice to the Executive.

3. PERMANENT HEALTH INSURANCE

3.1 [After successful completion of any probationary period] the Executive shall be entitled to participate in the Company's permanent health insurance scheme at the Company's expense, subject to:

3.1.1 the terms of the Company's scheme, as amended from time to time;

3.1.2 the rules or insurance policy of the relevant insurance provider, as amended from time to time; and

3.1.3 the Executive satisfying the normal underwriting requirements of the relevant insurance provider and the premium being at a rate which the Company considers reasonable.

Full details of the scheme are available from [POSITION].

3.2 The Company shall only be obliged to make payments to the Executive under the scheme [if it has received payment from the insurance provider for that purpose OR if the Executive is not receiving benefits from the insurance provider directly].

3.3 The Company in its sole and absolute discretion reserves the right to discontinue, vary or amend the scheme (including the level of the Executive's cover) at any time on reasonable notice to the Executive.

3.4 If the insurance provider refuses for any reason to provide permanent health insurance benefit to the Executive, the Company shall not be liable to provide to the Executive any replacement benefit of the same or similar kind or to pay any compensation in lieu of such benefit.

3.5 If the Executive is receiving benefits under the Company's permanent health insurance scheme:

3.5.1 [[he] shall resign as a director of the Company [or any Group Company] if so requested by the Company; and]

3.5.2 the Company shall be entitled to appoint a successor to the Executive to perform all or any of the duties required of the Executive.

4. CAR

4.1 [Provided that the Executive holds a current full driving licence,] the Company shall supply the Executive with a car of such make, model and value as is determined by the Company for [his] sole business [and private] use. [The Company may at its discretion permit the personal use of the car by the Employee or his spouse or civil partner, but permission for such personal use may be withdrawn at any time.]

4.2 The Company shall be responsible for payment of all reasonable standing and running costs of the car including insurance, tax, MOT, maintenance and repair and shall [bear the cost of fuel incurred during business [and private] mileage OR reimburse the Executive for the cost of fuel properly incurred during business [and private] mileage [at an agreed rate OR at a rate specified in the Company's car policy from time to time]].

4.3 The Company shall replace the car at such times as are specified in the Company's car policy from time to time.

4.4 The Executive shall:

4.4.1 take good care of the car and ensure that the provisions of [the Company's car policy as amended from time to time and] any policy of insurance relating to the car are observed;

4.4.2 [pay all expenses directly connected with the Executive's [and his spouse's] private use of the car];

4.4.3 be responsible for the payment of any congestion charge and any fines for non-payment;

4.4.4 be responsible for payment of all fines incurred for traffic offences and parking fines;

4.4.5 notify the Company of any accidents involving the car (whether or not these take place while the Executive is on business);

4.4.6 immediately inform the Company if [he] is convicted of a driving offence or disqualified from driving; and

4.4.7 return the car, its keys and all documents relating to it to [the Company's registered office] or such other place as the Company may reasonably stipulate immediately upon the termination of employment howsoever arising or upon the Executive becoming no longer legally entitled to drive.

OR

5. CAR ALLOWANCE

5.1 [Provided that the Executive holds a current driving licence,] the Executive shall receive a car allowance for use of the Executive's own car of £[AMOUNT] per annum which shall be payable together with and in the same manner as the salary in accordance with [clause 6] of the Agreement. The car allowance shall not be treated as part of the basic salary for any purpose and shall not be pensionable.

5.2 The Company shall reimburse the Executive in respect of fuel costs for business miles [at the Company's business mileage rate OR at HM Revenue and Customs approved rates] [and reasonable private mileage].

5.3 The Executive shall immediately inform the Company if [he] is disqualified from driving and shall cease to be entitled to receive the car allowance [or reimbursement of fuel expenses].

6. PENSION BENEFITS

[occupational scheme]

6.1 The Executive may participate in [the Company's occupational pension scheme from time to time] OR [name scheme] subject to the rules of the scheme as amended from time to time. Full details of the scheme are available from [POSITION].

6.2 The Executive shall pay such contributions to the Company's occupational pension scheme as may be required by the rules of the scheme as amended from time to time. The contributions shall be made by way of deduction from the Executive's salary.

6.3 [The Company shall procure that any scheme which is set up to replace its occupational pension scheme will provide benefits which, taken as a whole, shall be no less favourable to the Executive than the benefits to which [he] would have been entitled had he continued to be a member of its original occupational pension scheme[5]]

[5] Use with extreme caution as this commitment is potentially very onerous.

6.4 A contracting-out certificate is [not] in force in relation to the Executive's employment.

OR

[group personal pension scheme]

6.1 During each year of employment, the Company shall contribute an amount equal to [the amount of the contributions paid by the Executive subject to a maximum of] [[NUMBER] per cent] of the Executive's salary to its group personal pension scheme from time to time. The Company's contributions to such scheme shall be payable in equal monthly instalments in arrears. Full details of the scheme are available from [POSITION].

6.2 There is no contracting-out certificate in force in relation to the Executive's employment.

OR

[personal pension scheme]

6.1 During each year of the Appointment, the Company shall contribute an amount equal to [the amount of the contributions paid by the Executive subject to a maximum of] [[NUMBER] per cent] of the Executive's salary to the Executive's personal pension scheme (i.e., such registered pension scheme for the benefit of the Executive as the Executive may notify to the Company in writing from time to time). The Company's contributions to such scheme shall be payable in equal monthly instalments in arrears.

6.2 There is no contracting-out certificate in force in relation to the Executive's employment.

OR

[stakeholder pension scheme]

6.1 The Executive shall be entitled to become a member of the Company's designated stakeholder pension scheme (i.e., the stakeholder pension scheme from time to time designated by the Company for its employees). Full details of the scheme are available from [POSITION].

6.2 [During each year of employment, the Company shall contribute an amount equal to [the amount of the contributions paid by the Executive subject to a maximum of] [NUMBER]% of the Executive's salary to the stakeholder pension scheme. The Company's contributions to such scheme shall be payable in equal monthly instalments in arrears.][6]

6.3 There is no contracting-out certificate in force in relation to the Executive's employment.

[6] Note that there is no legal requirement for employer contributions to a stakeholder pension scheme (but that all employees must be eligible to join the stakeholder scheme if there are at least five employees and no other pension provision).

SCHEDULE [2] – CONFIDENTIAL INFORMATION

The following is a non-exhaustive list of matters which in relation to the Company [or any Group Company] are considered by the Company [or any Group Company] to be confidential and the Executive hereby agrees such matters are confidential:

1. all trade secrets of the Company [or any Group Company];
2. any and all information relating to prices, discounts, mark-ups, marketing, future business strategy, tenders and any price-sensitive information of the Company [or any Group Company];
3. any and all customer lists, supplier lists, details of contracts with or requirements of customers and suppliers, and any details relating to information on the Company [or any Group Company] database;
4. any and all details about the Company [or any Group Company] products, publications,
   processes, technologies, inventions, analysis or research;
5. any and all information relating to any computer software (both source code and object code) and other Intellectual Property of the Company [or any Group Company];
6. any and all technical data, know-how, information or operations manuals of the Company [or any Group Company]; and/or
7. any and all information in respect of which the Company [or any Group Company] is bound by an express or implied obligation of confidence to any third party.

It is important to note that the information contained within this document is current at the time of publication. For more information, contact: jyew@wedlakebell.com

Appendix C

Letter of appointment for non-executive director

[COMPANY LETTERHEAD]

[Name]

[Address]

Dear [Name]

This letter contains the terms which we have discussed and agreed for your appointment as non-executive director of [Company Name] ("the Company"). Although they are not specifically mentioned you will of course be subject to the normal duties and responsibilities of a director that are imposed at law. Please speak to me if you have any questions about this letter. It is agreed that this appointment is as an office holder only.

1. APPOINTMENT

(a) The Board is pleased to confirm that your appointment as a non-executive director will take effect from [Date] and will continue (subject to paragraphs [1.1.1] to [1.1.3] below) until terminated by either party giving to the other not less than [ ] month's notice in writing. The Company reserves the right, in its sole discretion, to pay your Fees (as set out in paragraph [3] below) in lieu of any period of notice. However, the Company may terminate your appointment immediately (and without entitlement to notice, pay in lieu of notice or compensation) if:-

1.a.1. you are not reappointed as a director at the Company's next Annual General Meeting (or at any subsequent Annual General Meeting at which you are required to retire by rotation), are removed as a director by a resolution passed at a General Meeting or you cease to be a director by reason of your office being vacated pursuant to any provisions of the Company's Articles of Association; or

1.a.2. you are guilty of any dishonesty or other misconduct or commit any serious or persistent breach of any of your obligations to the Company or any Group Company (whether under this agreement or otherwise) or refuse or neglect to comply with any lawful order or direction given to you by the Board; or

1.a.3. you are or become incapacitated from efficiently performing your duties for 90 working days in any 12 month period, or you become of unsound mind.

(b) [Subject to Board approval, you will be elected to act as Chairman of the Board.]

(c) If your appointment is terminated for any reason you shall immediately resign as a director of the Company without compensation for loss of office.

2. DUTIES

(a) Non-executive directors have the same general legal responsibilities to the Company as any other director. Your duties include, but are not limited to:

- Acting within your powers;
- Exercising independent judgment;
- Promoting the success of the Company;
- Exercising reasonable skill, care and diligence;
- Avoiding conflicts of interest;
- Not accepting benefits from third parties; and
- Declaring any interest in any proposed or existing transaction or arrangement with the Company.

(b) The Board as a whole is collectively responsible for the success of the Company. The Board:-

- Provides entrepreneurial leadership of the Company within a framework of prudent and effective controls which enables risk to be assessed and managed.
- Sets the Company's strategic aims, ensures that the necessary financial and human resources are in place for the Company to meet its objectives and reviews management performance; and
- Sets the Company's values and standards and ensures that its obligations to its shareholders and others are understood and met.

All directors must take decisions objectively in the interests of the Company.

In addition to these requirements of all directors, the role of the non-executive director has the following key elements:-

- **Strategy**. Non-executive directors should constructively challenge and help develop proposals on strategy;

- Performance. Non-executive directors should scrutinise the performance of management in meeting agreed goals and objectives and monitor the reporting of performance;
- Risk. Non-executive directors should satisfy themselves on the integrity of financial information and that financial controls and systems of risk management are robust and defensible; and
- People. Non-executive directors are responsible for determining appropriate levels of remuneration of executive directors and have a prime role in appointing, and where necessary removing, executive directors and in succession planning.

[As Chairman, you will also be required to:-

- Uphold the highest standards of integrity and probity;
- Set the agenda, style and tone of board discussions to promote effective decision-making and constructive debate;
- Promote effective relationships and open communication, both inside and outside the boardroom, between non-executive directors and the executive team;
- Build an effective and complementary board, initiating change and planning succession in board appointments, subject to board and shareholders' approval;
- Ensure a clear structure for and the effective running of board committees;
- Ensure an effective implementation of board decisions;
- Establish a close relationship of trust with the chief executive, providing support and advice while respecting executive responsibility; and
- Provide coherent leadership of the company, including representing the company and understanding the views of shareholders.]

(c) Overall the Board anticipates a time commitment of approximately [number] day[s] per month. This will include attendances at monthly Board meetings, the Annual General Meeting and any Extraordinary General Meetings of the shareholders of the Company, one annual Board away day and at least one site visit. In addition you will be expected to devote appropriate preparation time ahead of each meeting. In addition you may be expected to serve on and attend meetings of each of the Company's audit, nominations and remuneration committees and such other committees as the Board may from time to time require and to exercise such functions as may be specifically delegated to you by the Board from time to time. In the event that you are also asked to serve on one or more of the committees of the Board this will be covered in a separate letter setting out the terms of reference of the relevant committee(s), any specific responsibilities and any additional fees which may be involved.

(d) By accepting your appointment as a non-executive director you are confirming that you are able to devote sufficient time to meet the expectations of your role.

(e) As a non-executive director you will be expected to work with and through the Board and you are not expected to undertake or assume executive duties or responsibilities.

(f) You are required to comply with the Company's Articles of Association, any relevant internal guidelines and codes (including without limitation the Company's code on share dealings) and any general laws, regulations and requirements applicable to companies in force from time to time [including without limitation the AIM Rules, the Model Code, the City Code on Takeovers and Mergers, the Combined Code and the Disclosure and Transparency Rules].

3. FEES, EXPENSES AND INSURANCE

(a) Whilst you perform your duties as non-executive director, the Company will pay you an annual director's fee of £[amount] payable in monthly instalments in arrears subject to appropriate deductions for PAYE tax and Class 1 National Insurance Contributions. This will be reviewed at the absolute discretion of the Board. In addition you will be fully reimbursed for all out of pocket expenses which you may incur in the proper performance of your duties in accordance with the Company's normal procedures. However, you shall not participate in any Group share bonus or pension schemes or other benefit in kind arrangements of the Group nor will you be entitled to any compensation for loss of office. The Company shall however, maintain indemnity insurance for its directors, details of which will be available from the Company Secretary.

4. INDEPENDENT PROFESSIONAL ADVICE

(a) The Board recognises that, in discharging your responsibilities as a director, you may from time to time judge it necessary to take independent professional advice. The Company will bear or reimburse the cost of any such advice provided that:-

4.a.1. you have discussed the matter with the Board before seeking the advice;

4.a.2. you obtain a full estimate of the cost of such advice before obtaining it.

5. CROSS-DIRECTORSHIPS

If you are a member of the Remuneration Committee you must not hold any cross-directorships with any executive director except with the prior approval of the Board.

6. **DISCLOSURE**

You should advise the Company as soon as possible of any interests of both you and/or any person connected with you and the Company need to be aware in order to avoid any unintentional conflict of interest and in order to comply with the statutory requirements. If you have any questions regarding this disclosure, please speak to the Company Secretary.

7. **OUTSIDE INTERESTS AND CONFLICTS OF INTEREST**

(a) By accepting this appointment you confirm that, apart from those already disclosed in writing to the Board, you have no outside business or other interests which constitute actual or potential conflicts of interest with the business of the Company or any Group Company. In the event that you become aware of any actual or potential conflict of interest in the future you must disclose this to the Board as soon as it becomes apparent.

(b) During your appointment you may not, without the prior written consent of the Board, accept a directorship of a company which is, or provide your services to anyone who is, a competitor of the Company or any Group Company. The Board's consent will not be given if such involvement would, in the opinion of the Board, conflict with or be likely to interfere with this appointment.

8. **CONFIDENTIALITY AND PRICE SENSITIVE INFORMATION**

(a) As a director you owe fiduciary duties to the Company and the Group Companies which include, amongst others, a duty of confidentiality and an obligation not to bring the Company or any Group Company into disrepute. You must also observe the requirements under both legislation and regulation concerning the disclosure of price sensitive information. You should avoid making any statements which might risk breaching these requirements without prior clearance from the Board.

(b) You agree that you will not, either during your appointment or after it has ended, except in the proper performance of your duties or as required by law, misuse or directly or indirectly disclose any trade secrets or confidential information of the Company or any Group Company which may come to your knowledge during the course of your appointment.

9. **REVIEW PROCESS**

The performance of individual directors and the whole Board and its committees is evaluated annually. If, in the interim, there are any matters which cause you concern about your role you should discuss them with the Board as soon as is appropriate.

10. **POWER OF ATTORNEY**

(a) You hereby irrevocably and by way of security grant to the Company (with power for the Company to grant a separate power to any Associated Company on your behalf) power of attorney on your behalf to sign all such documents, execute all such deeds and do or refrain from doing all such things as the Company exercising the power or such concurrent power may in its entire unfettered discretion consider appropriate convenient or necessary in any part of the world for the purposes of fulfilling your obligations under this appointment. You shall grant such separate powers of attorney in such form or forms as the Company (or the relevant Associated Company) may reasonably require for such purposes, and the power granted by this Clause shall empower the attorney to grant such further powers in your name and on your behalf.

(b) Notwithstanding the foregoing and merely as a matter between the Company (or the relevant Associated Company) and you, the powers granted by you under this Clause shall not be used except with your consent or following your failure to sign or execute the relevant document or to do or refrain from doing the relevant act forthwith upon request made to you in writing, and no party dealing with the power of attorney shall be concerned as to whether the procedure of this Clause shall have been followed.

11. **GENERAL**

(a) You are appointed as an officer of the Company only and confirm that you are not an employee of the Company.

(b) In this agreement "Group Company" means and includes any holding company of the Company and any subsidiary of the Company or of any such holding company (as such expressions are defined in Sections 474(1), 1159 and 1162 of the Companies Act 2006).

(c) The terms set out in this letter constitute the entire and only agreement and understanding concerning your appointment as a non-executive director of the Company and supersedes any previous agreement or understanding in that regard between you and the Company or any Group Company.

Please indicate your acceptance of these terms by signing the enclosed copy and returning it to me.

Yours sincerely

....

[DIRECTOR]

For and on behalf of [Company Name]

I agree to the terms and conditions set out above relating to my appointment as non-executive director of the Company.

Signed: .... **Dated:** ....

Appendix D

Letter placing the executive on garden leave

Private & Confidential

[EXECUTIVE]

[ADDRESS]

BY HAND

[DATE]

Dear [EXECUTIVE]

RE: GARDEN LEAVE

Further to [your letter of resignation dated XXX] [the Company's decision to terminate your employment with [NOTICE PERIOD] notice as required under your Service Agreement dated [XXX], I am writing to confirm that your final day of employment with the Company will be [TERMINATION DATE] ("Termination Date").

As of the date of this letter you are no longer required to attend work unless specifically requested to do so and you should therefore refrain from attending the [offices] or contacting any of our customers, suppliers, employees, officers or representatives.

As you shall remain employed by the Company until the Termination Date, you must be available during normal working hours to deal with any work-related matters that may arise. You shall continue to receive your normal salary and contractual benefits up to your Termination Date.

During your notice period, you should not undertake any other business or profession without our prior written consent, or be or become an employee, officer or agent of any other firm, company or person.

I should also remind you that you remain bound, during your notice period and afterwards, by the following terms of your contract:

[SET OUT RESTRICTIVE COVENANTS AND CONFIDENTIALITY OBLIGATIONS].

[In accordance with the terms of your Service Agreement, you are required to resign immediately the office of [director **OR** company secretary] which you currently hold with the Company [and any associated companies].]

You should immediately return any property belonging to me in good condition [except [DETAIL ANY PROPERTY SUCH AS COMPANY CAR AND MOBILE TELEPHONE PROVIDED AS A CONTRACTUAL BENEFIT] which you may retain until [TERMINATION DATE]].

Yours sincerely

....

DIRECTOR

Appendix E

Letter before action to former executive (unlawful competition)

Private & Confidential

[EXECUTIVE]

[ADDRESS]

BY [SPECIAL DELIVERY][COURIER]

[DATE]

Dear [EXECUTIVE]

RE: TERMINATION OF EMPLOYMENT WITH ABC LIMITED ("the Company")

You were employed as an executive director of the Company since [DATE]. Your employment was terminated with [X] months notice on [DATE] at which time you were [placed on garden leave] [paid in lieu of notice]. Your last day of employment with the Company was [DATE].

Service Agreement

As an executive director of the company, you were entrusted with valuable confidential information and important client relationships. In return, you owed the Company fiduciary duties as well a duty of fidelity. In addition, under the terms of your Service Agreement (copy attached), you agreed to the following:-

[Set out contractual obligation during and after termination of employment]

Breach of contract

It has come to our attention that on [DATE], [set out details of the Executive's breach during the notice period and/or after the termination date].

In so doing, you have not only breached your fiduciary duty and duty of fidelity but also expressly breached the post termination restraints which you agreed to at the time you joined the Company. Having accepted these obligations and also reaped the benefits of your employment package, your recent conduct, which has fallen short of the standards and trust we had placed in you, has been particularly disappointing to the Board and our shareholders.

On the termination of your employment, you were obliged to return all property belonging to the Company. You were also reminded of your post termination restrictions in a letter to you dated [DATE].

Undertakings

To avoid formal legal action in the High Court, we require a formal acknowledgement of receipt of this letter and your immediate undertaking that you will:-

i) immediately return to [NAME OF COMPANY REPRESENTATIVE], any confidential information (including but not limited to client lists, business cards, client contact details) which belongs to the Company which is in your possession [and/or your new employer's possession or control] within 48 hours from the receipt of this letter;

ii) confirm that all additional copies of the items in (i) above will be irrevocably destroyed and not retained by you or a third party;

iii) provide to the Company full details of all the customers, clients and employees of the Company who you have solicited/contacted in breach of your contractual obligations and refrain in the interim from making any further contact with such persons;

iv) fully comply with the restrictions set out in clauses [XXX] of the Service Agreement from the date of the receipt of this letter.

Unless we receive the undertakings from you by 12 noon on [DATE], we will be issuing legal proceedings to protect our legitimate business interests. Such proceedings shall include a claim for injunctive relief, damages and legal costs. We strongly advise that you take legal advice without any delay.

In the interim, all of the Company's rights are expressly reserved.

Yours sincerely

....

Director

Appendix F

Letter before action to new employer (unlawful competition)

Private & Confidential
[EXECUTIVE'S NEW EMPLOYER]

[ADDRESS]

BY [SPECIAL DELIVERY][COURIER]

[DATE]

Dear Sirs

RE: [EXECUTIVE] and ABC Limited ("the Company")

[EXECUTIVE] was employed as an executive director of the Company from [DATE] to [DATE].

Service Agreement

As an executive director of the Company, [EXECUTIVE] was entrusted with valuable confidential information and important client relationships. He owed the Company fiduciary duties as well a duty of fidelity during his employment. In addition, under the terms of his Service Agreement (copy attached), [EXECUTIVE] agreed to the following:-

[Set out contractual obligation during and after termination of employment]

Economic tort of interference

It has recently come to our attention that [EXECUTIVE] has joined your company as [XXX]. [Set out details of what the Executive is doing for the new employer].

[EXECUTIVE] is fully aware of his contractual obligations post termination of his employment with the Company. As he agreed to these restraints at the time he joined our Company and has reaped the benefits of his employment package, his conduct has been particularly disappointing to us. We expect him to honour his legal obligations following his departure from the Company no more than you would expect the same standard of behaviour from your own members of staff on termination of their employment.

If you are unaware of the post termination restrictions to which [EXECUTIVE] continue to be bound to the Company, we have now brought them to your attention.

In seeking and accepting employment with your company, [EXECUTIVE] is acting in violation of his restrictive covenants. Further, in employing [EXECUTIVE], you are inducing [EXECUTIVE] to breach his contractual obligations to the Company, which is unlawful also.

To avoid formal legal action in the High Court, we require you to formally acknowledge receipt of this letter and provide us with the following undertakings:-

1. that [NEW EMPLOYER] will cease to employ [EXECUTIVE] forthwith and refrain from employing him during the restraint period i.e. [XX] months from [DATE]
2. that in so far as [EXECUTIVE] has provided you with any Confidential Information which belongs to the Company, such information (originals or copies, electronic or otherwise,) shall be returned by [NEW EMPLOYER] to us at our offices within 48 hours from the receipt of this letter;
3. that [NEW EMPLOYER] shall provide full details of all the Customers, Prospective Customers [and employees] of the Company with whom [EXECUTIVE] has solicited/contacted in breach of his contractual obligations; and
4. that [NEW EMPLOYER] shall immediately cease to have any business dealings with Customers and/or Prospective Customers [and employing former employees] of our Company in so far as doing so amounts to a breach of [EXECUTIVE'S] restrictions.

Unless we receive the information and undertakings from you by 12 noon on [DATE], we will be issuing legal proceedings to protect our legitimate business interests. Such proceedings may include a claim for injunctive relief, damages, account of profits and legal costs.

In the interim, all our legal rights are expressly reserved.

Yours faithfully

....

Director

Appendix G

Compromise agreement without prejudice/subject to contract

THIS AGREEMENT is made on [DATE]

BETWEEN:

1. [ABC Limited] (company registration number XXXXXXX) whose principal place of business is at [ADDRESS] ("the Company"); and
2. [NAME OF EXECUTIVE] of [ADDRESS] ("the Employee")

1. **PRELIMINARIES**

(a) The Employee commenced employment with the Company on [DATE] under the terms of a Service Agreement dated [XXXXXX] ("the Service Agreement");

(b) [INSERT BACKGROUND LEADING TO TERMINATION AND DETAILS OF ANY CLAMS ALLEGED]

(c) The Company denies that it is liable to the Employee in relation to any or all of the alleged claims.

(d) The Company, without admission of liability, and the Employee have agreed the terms set out in this Agreement by way of settlement of all common law and statutory claims that the Employee has made, has, or may have against the Company or any other company in the Group (as defined in Sections 474(1), 1159 and 1162 of the Companies Act 2006), whether such claims are known or unknown to the parties and whether they are or could be in the contemplation of the parties at the time of signing this Agreement or in the future, arising out of the Employee's employment and its termination up to and including the Termination Date as provided for in this Agreement.

2. **TERMINATION DATE**

The Employee's employment with the Company [ended on] [will end] on [DATE] ("the Termination Date") [by mutual agreement].

3. **SALARY TO TERMINATION DATE**

(a) The Employee [has received][shall receive] all salary for the period up to and including the Termination Date, less tax and employee National Insurance Contributions in the usual way.

(b) The Employee will also be paid the following sums less tax and employee National Insurance Contributions (and any other sums owed to the Company):

£[XXX] in respect of accrued but untaken holiday up to and including the Termination Date; and

£ [XXX] in lieu of notice.

4. **TERMINATION PAYMENT AND BENEFITS**

(a) Subject to the Employee's compliance with him obligations under this Agreement the Company will pay the Employee before [DATE] subject to receipt by the Company of this Agreement duly signed by the Employee together with the Adviser's certificate (Appendix A) the sum of £[XXX] [inclusive of statutory redundancy payment] as compensation for loss of office ("Termination Payment").

(b) The Company shall also continue to provide the Employee with the following benefits ("Termination Benefits") until [DATE] [such time as the Employee commences alternative employment]:

[INSERT DETAILS OF PERMANENT MEDICAL INSURANCE, LIFE ASSURANCE, DIRECTORS AND OFFICERS LIABILITY INSURANCE.]

(c) [The Termination Payment will be paid and made without deduction of tax and employee National Insurance Contributions on the basis that the payment is made on the termination of the Employee's employment and is less than £30,000.] **OR** [As the Termination Payment and Termination Benefits exceed £30,000, the sum falls to be taxed under section 403 of the Income Tax (Earnings and Pensions) Act 2003 and will be subject to the deduction by the Company of basic rate tax at 22%. The Employee shall be solely responsible for the payment of any further tax and employee's National Insurance contributions in respect of the payments and benefits referred to in this clause 4 in excess of PAYE deductions made by the Company.]

(d) The Employee warrants that he has not received a job offer from or has not accepted a job with another employer.

(e) The Employee's entitlement to any salary and benefits will cease with immediate effect on and from the Termination Date.

5. **TAX INDEMNITY**

The Employee undertakes to indemnify and keep indemnified and hold the Company and/or any other company in the Group harmless against all costs, fines, claims, expenses, proceedings, penalties and interest incurred by the Company and/or any other company in the Group which arise out of or in connection with any liability to pay (or deduct) tax or employee National Insurance Contributions in respect of the sum set out in Clause 4.1 above. Before meeting any liability to pay tax or employee National Insurance Contributions as described above, the Company agrees to give the Employee reasonable opportunity and at the Employee's own expense to make representations to H M Revenue & Customs in respect of any such liability.

6. **PENSION CONTRIBUTIONS**

Subject to the terms of this Agreement, the Company shall pay into the Employee's Money Purchase Pension Scheme ("the Pension Scheme") the sum of £[XXX] ("the Agreed Sum") by way of a contribution to the Pension Scheme to provide additional deferred benefits or an appropriate enhanced transfer value for the Employee provided that until the Inland Revenue has approved the additional benefits, the Agreed Sum shall be held in a joint interest bearing account (the Stakeholder Account) at [name of bank] by the [insert details] ("the Stakeholders"). If the Inland Revenue advises that the proposed additional benefits is exempt under ITEPA 2003, the Stakeholders shall release the Agreed Sum (and any interest accrued) from the Stakeholder Account for payment into the Employee's Pension Scheme. If the Inland Revenue advises that the proposed additional benefit is not fully exempt, then an approved sum less than the Agreed Sum shall be released from the Stakeholder Account for payment into the Pension Scheme and the excess over such sum shall be paid by the Company on receipt of the same from the Stakeholders as compensation for termination of employment (less any income tax deductions at Basic Rate).] OR [Subject to the terms of this Agreement, the Company shall pay to the trustees of the Employee's Final Salary Pension Scheme ("the Pension Scheme") the sum of £[ ] ("the Agreed Sum") by way of a contribution to the Pension Scheme to provide the additional deferred benefits:

a deferred pension payable at normal retirement date of £[ ];

a cash lump-sum benefit payable at normal retirement date of £[ ].

provided that until the Inland Revenue has approved the additional benefits, the Agreed Sum shall be held in a joint interest bearing account (the Stakeholder Account) at [name of bank] by [insert details] ("the Stakeholders"). If the Inland Revenue advises that the proposed additional benefits is exempt under ITEPA 2003, the Stakeholders shall release the Agreed Sum (and any interest accrued) from the Stakeholder Account for payment into the Employee's Pension Scheme. If the Inland Revenue advises that the proposed additional benefit is not fully exempt, then an approved sum less than the Agreed Sum shall be released from the Stakeholder Account for payment into the Pension Scheme and the excess over such sum shall be paid by the Company, on receipt of the same from the Stakeholders, as compensation for termination of employment (less any income tax deductions at Basic Rate).]

7. **[SHARE OPTIONS][TRANSFER OR PURCHASE OF SHARES]**

[The Company confirms that the reason for the Employee's dismissal for the purposes of Rule [ ] of the Company's Share Option Scheme is [redundancy] and that accordingly, the Company shall exercise its discretion to allow the Employee to exercise [his/her] share options subject to the rules of the Share Option Scheme as may be in force from time to time.] OR [The Employee shall execute a Stock Transfer Form and take any other action as may be necessary to transfer [ ] [ordinary/special] shares which he holds in the Company to [name of beneficiary] OR [The Company shall purchase and the Employee shall sell his [ ] [ordinary/special] shares in the Company for £[XXX]. The Employee shall execute a Stock Transfer Form and take any other action as may be necessary to transfer the above to the Company on or before the Termination Date.]

8. **COMPANY PROPERTY, CONFIDENTIAL INFORMATION & RESTRICTIVE COVENANTS**

(a) The Employee hereby confirms that he will on or before the Termination Date return to the Company's premises (or such other location as is mutually agreed and confirmed in writing), all property and Confidential Information belonging to the Company (including but not limited to the Company's marketing and business plans, lap top computer, documents, discs, credit cards, equipment, keys and passes), which is or has been in him possession or under him control. The documents and discs will include but not be limited to correspondence, files, e-mails, memos, reports, minutes, plans, records, surveys, software, diagrams, computer printouts, floppy discs, manuals, customer documentation and any other medium for storing information together with all copies, drafts, reproductions, notes, extracts or summaries (howsoever made) of the foregoing.

(b) The Employee agrees that he will on and after the Termination Date comply with the post termination restrictions pursuant to clauses [X] of the Service Agreement.

9. **OUTPLACEMENT ASSISTANCE**

Subject to the terms of this Agreement, the Company shall provide the Employee with outplacement assistance/counselling with [X Limited] after the Termination Date and shall [pay to X Limited/reimburse the Employee] up to a maximum of £[XXX] (plus VAT) provided that the outplacement service is utilised by the Employee within [12] months of the Termination Date and the Company receives a valid invoice from [X Limited]. This benefit is tax free subject to the conditions in s.310 of the Income Tax (Earnings and Pensions) Act 2003.

10. **STATEMENT**

(a) Subject to the remainder of this clause 7, the Company will not make or publish any statement to any person, firm, company or any other organisation concerning this Agreement or the circumstances surrounding the termination of the Employee's employment (except as may be required by law or a relevant authority or government agency. Equally, the Employee will not make or publish any statement to any person, firm, company or any other organisation concerning this Agreement or the circumstances surrounding him employment with the Company and its termination save the Employee's immediate family or Legal Adviser.

(b) Subject to the remainder of this clause 7, the Company agrees to use its reasonable endeavours to ensure that neither its employees or officers and/or *those officers and employees of the Company who are aware of the terms of this Agreement shall not* make or publish any statement about the Employee which is intended to or which might be expected to damage or lower him reputation (except as may be required by law or by a relevant authority or to its professional advisers). Equally, the Employee shall not make or publish any statement or do anything in relation to the Company or any other company in the Group or any of its or their officers, or employees which is intended to or which might be expected to damage or lower their respective reputations.

(c) The Company will provide any prospective employer of the Employee with a written reference in the terms set out at Appendix B, provided that any such request is made in writing to the Company's Human Resources Department. The Company undertakes that it will not make any oral and written statement or comment which is inconsistent with that reference

11. OBLIGATIONS

The Employee warrants that he has not prior to the date of this Agreement breached any of him obligations to the Company or any other company in the Group, whether under the terms of the Service Agreement or otherwise howsoever arising which would entitle the Company to summarily terminate him employment.

12. REPRESENTATION

The Employee undertakes that he will not after the Termination Date represent himself as an authorised agent, employee or officer of the Company or any other company in the Group.

13. CO-OPERATION CLAUSE

The Employee agrees to take all reasonable steps to make himself available to and co-operate with the Company in any internal investigation or administrative, regulatory, judicial or quasi-judicial proceedings. The Employee understands and agrees that the level of co-operation would include, but not be limited to, working with the Company and its legal advisers in responding to and/or defending any regulatory and/or legal process including providing information in relation to any such process, preparing witness statements and/or giving evidence on behalf of the Company. In the event the Company asks for the Employee's co-operation in accordance with this provision, the Company will reimburse the Employee for reasonable expenses incurred as consequence of complying with this obligation provided that such expenses are incurred with the prior approval of the Company.

14. SETTLEMENT

(a) This Agreement is made on the basis that the Employee accepts the terms set out in it in full and final settlement of all claims and rights of action against the Company (whether under statute, common law, or otherwise) in any jurisdiction in the world whether under English and/or European Community law including but not limited to [Employment Tribunal claim XXX and] the Employee's claims set out at 14.2.1 below which could be brought before any Employment Tribunal or Court of Law or otherwise. The Employee and the Company each acknowledge that it is their express intention on entering into this Agreement that it covers all claims whether known or unknown to one or other or either or both of them and whether or not the factual or legal basis for the claim is known or could have been known to one or other or either or both of them at the date of this Agreement or in the future.

(b) To give full effect to the provisions in Clause 14.1 above the Employee hereby:-

agrees, in particular, without limiting the general nature of Clause 14.1 above, to refrain from instituting or continuing any claims against the Company or proceedings before an Employment Tribunal and/or Court of Law for any or all of the following claims arising out of or in connection with the Termination:-

[wrongful dismissal;]

[unfair dismissal;]

[breach of contract including any claims for [bonuses][sick pay], [overtime pay] [time off in lieu];

[misrepresentation;]

[unlawful deduction of wages under section 13 of the Employment Rights Act 1996;]

[data subject request under the Data Protection Act 1998];

[unfair dismissal under section 94 105 of the Employment Rights Act 1996;]

[breach of the Statutory Dismissal Disciplinary and Grievances procedures under section 38 and Schedule 2 Employment Act 2002 and Regulations 11, 12 & 13 Employment Act 2002 (Dispute Resolution) Regs. 2004;]

[a statutory redundancy payment under section 162 of the Employment Rights Act 1996;]

[a protective award under section 189 of the Trade Union and Labour Relations (Consolidation) Act 1992 and Regulation 15(8) Transfer of Undertakings (Protection from Employment) Regulations 2006;]

[breach of Regulations 4 13 14 under the Working Time Regulations 1998 (as amended);]

[breach of Regulations 4 7 13 Transfer of Undertakings (Protection from Employment) Regulations 2006;]

[less favourable treatment under Regulations 5 and 7 of the Part-Time Workers (Prevention of Less Favourable Treatment) Regulations 2000;]

[less favourable treatment under Regulations 3 and 6 of the Fixed-Term Employees (Prevention of Less Favourable Treatment) Regulations 2002;]

[sex discrimination under sections 1 and 2 of the Sex Discrimination Act 1975;]

[race discrimination under section 1 of the Race Relations Act 1976;]

[disability discrimination under sections 3A, 3B, 4 and/or 4A of the Disability Discrimination Act 1995;]

[discrimination on grounds of religion or belief under Regulations 3 4 5 21 of the Employment Equality (Religion or Belief) Regulations 2003;]

[discrimination on grounds of sexual orientation under Regulations 3 4 5 21 of the Employment Equality (Sexual Orientation) Regulations 2003;]

[discrimination on grounds of gender reassignment under section 2A of the Sex Discrimination Act 1975;]

[harassment under Section 1 of the Protection from Harassment Act 1997;]

[discrimination on grounds of marital status under section 3 of the Sex Discrimination Act 1975;]

[harassment under section 1 of the Sex Discrimination Act 1975;]

[victimisation under section 4 of the Sex Discrimination Act 1975;]

[harassment section 3A of the Race Relations Act;]

[victimisation under section 2 of the Race Relations Act;]

[discrimination on grounds of age under Regulations 3 4, 5, 6, 24, Schedule 6, paragraph (11) and Schedule 7 Employment Equality (Age) Regulations 2006;]

[stress related injury and personal injury]

[insert any other claims]

confirms that he has received advice from a relevant independent adviser as defined in the Acts, being [NAME OF SOLICITOR] of [NAME OF LAW FIRM] ("the Adviser") concerning the terms and effect of this Agreement and in particular its effect on him ability to pursue him rights before an Employment Tribunal or any Court of Law and the effect of the warranties at Clauses 4.3, 8.1 and 10.1;

confirms that the Adviser has provided him with satisfactory evidence that there is in force a Contract of Insurance or an indemnity provided for members of a profession or professional body covering the risk of a claim by him in respect of loss arising in consequence of the advice;

agrees that the conditions regulating Compromise Agreements under Section 203(3) of the Employment Rights Act 1996, Section 77(4A) of the Sex Discrimination Act 1975, Section 72(4A) of the Race Relations Act 1976, Section 288(2B) of the Trade Union and Labour Relations (Consolidation) Act 1992, Schedule 3A Part 1 of the Disability Discrimination Act 1995, Regulation 35(3) of the Working Time Regulations 1998, Section 49(4) of the National Minimum Wage Act 1998, Regulation 41(4) of the Transnational Information and Consultation of Employees Regulations 1999, Regulation 9 of the Part-Time Workers (Prevention of Less Favourable Treatment) Regulations 2000, Regulation10 of the Fixed-term Employees (Prevention of Less Favourable Treatment) Regulations 2002, Schedule 4 of Part 1 of the Employment Equality (Sexual Orientation) Regulations 2003, and Schedule 4 of Part 1 of the Employment Equality (Religion or Belief) Regulations 2003, Regulation 19 of the Merchant Shipping (Working Time: Inland Waterways) Regulations 2003, Regulation 52(4) of the European Public Limited Liability Company Regulations 2004 and Regulation 40(4) of the Information and Consultation of Employees Regulations 2004, Schedule 5, Reg. 43 Employment Equality (Age) Regulations 2006 and Regulation 18 Transfer of Undertakings (Protection from Employment) Regulations 2006 are satisfied ("the Acts"); and

agrees to procure that the Adviser will sign and return the letter in the form of Appendix A to confirm the above.

(c) The Employee further agrees and warrants that the statutory, contractual and tortuous claims identified at Clause 14.2.1 above are the only statutory and/or contractual claims that he has made, has, or may have made against the Company and/or any other company in the Group or its or their directors, officers or employees arising out of him employment with the Company and its termination.

(d) The Employee further acknowledges that the Company enters into this Agreement in reliance upon the Employee's warranties at Clauses 4.3, 8.1 and 10.1 above and if the Employee brings any claims or proceedings, whether statutory or otherwise, in breach of this Agreement shall immediately pay to the Company by way of unliquidated damages an amount equal to the lesser of (i) the amount claimed by the Employee in the Proceedings (or the maximum amount of compensation which could be awarded in respect of those Proceedings) and (ii) the sums and benefits made to the Employee in Clause 4 above together with all costs, including legal costs, reasonably incurred by the Company in recovering such sums and interest thereon calculated at the judgment rate (currently 8% per annum) from time to time in force from the date such sums were paid to the Employee, or for him benefit, until the Company receives repayment in full.

15. LEGAL FEES

The Company agrees to pay up to a maximum of £[XXX] plus VAT on the Employee's behalf to [his/her] Adviser for obtaining advice on the termination of [his/her] employment and the terms of this Agreement. Any invoice should be in the Employee's name but expressed to be payable by the Company and sent under private and confidential cover to [insert details]. Payment will be made to the Adviser within [21] days of receipt by the Company of the Adviser's invoice.

16. ENTIRE AGREEMENT

The terms of this Agreement constitute the entire agreement and understanding between the Employee and the Company and it supersedes and replaces all prior negotiations, agreements, arrangements or understandings (whether implied or expressed, orally or in writing) concerning the subject matter hereof, all of which are hereby treated as terminated by mutual consent.

17. COUNTERPARTS

This Agreement may be executed in any number of Counterparts, each of which, when executed and delivered, shall be an original, and all counterparts together shall constitute one and the same instrument.

18. MISCELLANEOUS

(a) This Agreement is governed by English Law and the parties hereby submit to the exclusive jurisdiction of the English Courts.

(b) Headings are inserted for convenience only and will not affect the construction of this Agreement.

(c) Whilst this Agreement is marked "Without Prejudice/Subject to Contract" it will become a binding agreement between the Employee and the Company as soon as it is executed by both parties.

SIGNED AS A DEED BY THE COMPANY

....

[Director][Company Secretary] of [ABC LIMITED]

in the presence of [insert witness signature]

SIGNED AS A DEED BY THE EMPLOYEE

....

in the presence of [insert witness signature]

APPENDIX A

ADVISER'S CERTIFICATE TO BE WRITTEN ON HEADED NOTEPAPER OF ADVISER

Strictly Private & Confidential

[ABC Limited]

[ADDRESS]

Dear [XXX]

RE: [NAME OF EXECUTIVE]

I confirm that I am instructed by [EXECUTIVE] in relation to the Compromise Agreement entered into by him with [ABC LIMITED].

I hereby certify that:-

1. I am a qualified lawyer as defined in the Acts as referred to above.
2. I have given [EXECUTIVE] independent legal advice on the terms and effect of the Compromise Agreement and, in particular, its effect on him ability to pursue a claim before an Employment Tribunal or any Court of Law.
3. There is in force a Contract of Insurance or an Indemnity provided for members of a profession or professional body covering the risk of a claim by [EXECUTIVE] in respect of any loss arising in consequence of such advice (save for any uninsured deductible or excess).

Yours sincerely

[NAME OF LAW FIRM]

APPENDIX B

REFERENCE

Private & Confidential

[NAME OF PERSON REQUESTING REFERENCE]

[ADDRESS]

[DATE]

RE: [EXECUTIVE]

I confirm that [EXECUTIVE] was employed as [POSITION] with this organisation from [DATE] to [DATE]. At the time he was employed, [EXECUTIVE'S] remuneration package was as follows

[INSERT DETAILS OF SALARY AND BENEFITS].

[INSERT FACTUAL DETAILS OF RESPONSIBILITIES UNDERTAKEN BY THE EXECUTIVE].

This reference is given to the recipient only on the basis that no liability whatsoever is accepted for the contents. In particular, no warranty, representation or other guarantee is given that it is comprehensive as it is expressly limited to the contents set out above. It is entirely a mater for you whether to employ [EXECUTIVE] and it is for you to satisfy yourself that he is suitable for the post you are offering. No liability will be accepted by the Company for any loss that may be caused by your employment of [EXECUTIVE].

Yours sincerely

[XXX]

Human Resources

It is important to note that the information contained within this document is current at the time of publication. For more information, contact: jyew@wedlakebell.com

Appendix H

Compensation limits from 1 February 2008 to 31 January 2009

The Employment Rights (Increase of Limits) Order 2007

	Employment Rights Act 1996	Limit	Current maximum
Unfair dismissal – basic award limit on a week's pay	S.227(1)(a)	**£330**	**£9,900**
Unfair dismissal – compensatory award	s.124(1)		**£63,000**
Unfair dismissal additional award for failure to comply with a reinstatement/ re-engagement order – limit on a week's pay	s.227(1)(b)	**£330**	**£17,160** (all additional awards are for 26–52 weeks' pay)
Statutory redundancy pay – limit on a week's pay	s.227(1)(c)	**£330**	**£9,900**
Guarantee pay limit on a day's pay during short-time or temporary lay-off	s.31(1)	**£20.40**	**£102** (in respect of five days in any period of three months)
Breach of statutory right to be accompanied	s.11(3) Employment Relations Act 1999	**£330 × 2**	**£660**
Protective award – failure to consult in collective redundancy cases	s.188 Trade Union (Legal Relations) Act 1992	**Up to 90 days full pay**	No limit
Protection award – failure to consult in TUPE transfers	Reg. 15 Transfer of Undertaking (Protection of Employment) Regulations 2006	**Up to 13 weeks full pay**	No limit

Appendix I
Companies Act implementation timetable

The following parts will be introduced from 1 October 2007:
Part 9 (Exercise of members' rights);
Part 10 (A company's directors), other than provisions relating to directors' conflict of interest duties, directors' residential addresses and underage and natural directors;
Part 11 (Derivative claims and proceedings by members);
Part 13 (Resolutions and meetings), and, related to this, sections 485-488 of Part 16 (Audit);
Part 14 (Control of political donations and expenditure);
Section 417 of Part 15 (Contents of directors' report: business review);
Part 29 (Fraudulent trading);
Part 30 (Protection of members against unfair prejudice);
Part 32 (Company investigations: amendments).

The commencement provisions in respect of Part 9 will be drafted so as to enable nominee investment operators to send indirect investors' requests to companies from 1 October to entitle indirect investors to enjoy information rights from 31 December 2007.

The following parts will be introduced from 6 April 2008:
Part 12 (Company secretaries);
Part 15 (Accounts and reports), other than section 417;
Part 16 (Audit), other than sections 485-488;
Part 19 (Debentures);
Part 20 (Private and public companies);
Part 21 (Certification and transfer of securities);
Part 23 (Distributions);
Part 26 (Arrangements and reconstructions);
Part 27 (Mergers and divisions of public companies);
Part 42 (Statutory auditors).

The following parts will be introduced from 1 October 2008:
Part 1 (General introductory provisions);
Part 2 (Company formation);
Part 3 (A company's constitution);
Part 4 (A company's capacity and related matters);
Part 5 (A company's name);

Part 6 (A company's registered office);
Part 7 (Re-registration as a means of altering a company's status);
Part 8 (A company's members);
Part 10 (A company's directors) - provisions relating to directors' conflict of interest duties, directors' residential addresses and underage and natural directors
Part 17 (A company's share capital);
Part 18 (Acquisition by limited company of its own shares);
Part 24 (A company's annual return);
Part 25 (Company charges);
Part 31 (Dissolution and restoration to the register);
Part 33 (UK companies not formed under the Companies Acts);
Part 34 (Overseas companies);
Part 35 (The registrar of companies);
Part 41 (Business names).

Appendix J

Best practice on executive contracts and severance

In February 2008 the Association of British Insurers (ABI) and the National Association of Pension Funds (NAPF) published an update of the joint statement, which is reproduced in full below.

A Joint Statement by the Association of British Insurers and the National Association of Pension Funds

1. INTRODUCTION

1.1 Our two organisations, whose members are leading institutional investors in UK markets, are publishing an updated statement of best practice on contract and severance policy for directors.

1.2 This statement is aimed at assisting Boards and their Remuneration Committees with the design and application of contractual obligations for senior executives. Shareholders have an expectation that Boards will consider the risks of negotiating inappropriate executive contracts that can lead to situations where failure is rewarded.

1.3 Institutional shareholders believe executives of listed companies should be appropriately rewarded for the value they generate. However, they are also concerned to avoid situations where departing executives are rewarded for under-performance. For many years the ABI and NAPF have considered this to be a matter of good governance and it is clearly addressed in the FRC's Combined Code on Corporate Governance.

2. PRINCIPLES

2.1 The responsibility for setting directors' contracts lies primarily with the Remuneration Committee.

2.2 In line with the Combined Code, contracts should be set with reasonable notice periods.

2.3 Boards should ensure that executives show leadership by aligning their financial interests with those of the company.

2.4 The level of remuneration received by senior executives already factors in the risk associated with their role. Boards should ensure that contracts do not include any additional financial protection in the event of poor performance leading to termination.

2.5 The Remuneration Committee should carefully consider what commitments (including pension contributions and all other elements) their directors' terms of appointment would entail in the event of early termination.

2.6 Directors' contracts should ensure that severance payments arising from poor corporate performance should not extend beyond basic salary.

2.7 Companies should clearly disclose key elements of directors' contracts on their website and summarise them in the Remuneration Report.

2.8 Companies should fully disclose in their Remuneration Report the constituent parts of any severance payments and justify the total level and elements paid.

3. GUIDANCE

3.1 This Guidance is intended to emphasise certain aspects of the Combined Code and where appropriate provide guidance as to shareholders' expectations.

3.2 Contract policy including terminations and the approach to mitigation should be clearly explained in the Remuneration Report. Also, corporate objectives set for executives by the Board should be clear. The more transparent and understandable the objectives, the easier it is to determine how an executive has performed and therefore prevent payment for failure. Wherever possible, objectives against which performance will be measured should be made public.

Contract Terms

3.3 Remuneration Committees should ensure that the policy and objectives on directors' contracts are clearly stated in the Remuneration Report. Shareholders will take account of contracts and the way they are implemented in considering their vote on the Remuneration Report and the re-election of members of the Remuneration Committee.

3.4 When contracts are being negotiated, boards should consider and avoid the reputational risk of being obliged to make large payments to executives who have failed to perform. Contracts should be reviewed periodically and Remuneration Committees should consider whether the contract provisions are in line with their policy and this Statement.

Notice Periods

3.5 The Combined Code states that under normal circumstances directors should be retained on contracts of one year or less. However we believe that a one-year notice period should not be seen as a floor, and we would strongly encourage boards to consider contracts with shorter notice periods. Compensation for risks run by senior executives is already implicit in the absolute level of remuneration, which mitigates the need for substantial contractual protection.

3.6 If it is necessary to offer executives longer notice periods, for example for incoming executives at companies in difficulties, we would expect the length of the contract to be justified. In that case the termination provisions attached should be fully disclosed and the length of the contract should reduce on a rolling basis in line with the recommendations contained in this Guidance.

Severance Payments

3.7 Remuneration Committees should have the leeway to design a policy appropriate to the needs and objectives of the company, but they must also have a clear understanding of their responsibility to negotiate suitable contracts and be able to justify severance payments to shareholders.

3.8 From the outset, Boards should establish a clear policy to ensure any non-contractual payments are linked to performance. No director should be entitled to discretionary payments in the event of termination of their contract arising from poor corporate performance. Remuneration Committees should consider retaining their discretion to reclaim bonuses if performance achievements are subsequently found to have been significantly mis-stated.

3.9 Contracts should not provide additional compensation for severance as a result of change of control.

3.10 Remuneration Committees should ensure that full benefit of mitigation is obtained. This includes the legal obligation on the part of the outgoing senior executive to mitigate the loss incurred through severance by seeking other employment and reducing the need for compensation. Phased payments are generally appropriate for fulfilling compensation on early termination. The ABI and NAPF are not supportive of the liquidated damages approach which involves agreement at the outset on the amount that will be paid in the event of severance.

Pensions

3.11 Pension entitlement or contributions on severance can represent a large element of cost to shareholders. Remuneration Committees should identify, review and disclose in the Remuneration Report any arrangements that guarantee pensions with limited or no abatement on severance or early retirement. These pension arrangements are no longer regarded as acceptable, except where they are generally available to all employees. Where opportunities arise, existing contracts should be amended. Such conditions should not be included in new contracts.

Inspection Arrangements

3.12 Directors' contracts and any side letters relating to severance terms and pension arrangements should be readily available for shareholder inspection.

4. CONCLUSION

4.1 It is unacceptable that poor performance by senior executives, which detracts from the value of an enterprise and threatens the livelihood of employees, can result in excessive payments to departing directors. Boards have a responsibility to ensure that this does not occur.

18 February 2008

Enquiries

Please direct enquiries to

ABI
Marc Jobling – 020 7216 7541
Patrick Neave – 020 7216 7627

NAPF
David Paterson – 020 7808 1337

Index